7/2015

ATTACKING JUDGES

STANFORD STUDIES IN LAW AND POLITICS
Edited by Keith J. Bybee

ATTACKING JUDGES

How Campaign Advertising Influences
State Supreme Court Elections

Melinda Gann Hall

Stanford Law Books
An Imprint of Stanford University Press
Stanford, California

Stanford University Press
Stanford, California

Printed in the United States of America on acid-free, archival-quality paper

Library of Congress Cataloging-in-Publication Data

Hall, Melinda Gann.
  Attacking judges : how campaign advertising influences state supreme court elections / Melinda Gann Hall.
    p. cm. — (Stanford series in law and politics)
    Includes bibliographical references and index.
    ISBN 978-0-8047-8795-6 (cloth : alk. paper) —
    ISBN 978-0-8047-9308-7 (pbk. : alk. paper)
1. Judges—United States—Election. 2. Advertising, Political—Law and legislation—United States. 3. Courts of last resort—United States—States. 4. Political questions and judicial power—United States—States. I. Title.
    KF8776.H35 2014
    324.973—dc23
                                                              2014012610

ISBN 978-0-8047-9309-4 (electronic)

Typeset by Thompson Type in 10/14 Minion

To Rose Marie Corley Gann and James Earl Gann Sr.

Contents

Tables and Figures

Figures

Preface and Acknowledgments

IN ANY ACADEMIC ENDEAVOR, THERE ARE MANY WHO CONTRI-bute, both intellectually and personally, to a successful project. In this regard, I am indebted to numerous colleagues, friends, and family and wish to extend my sincere thanks for their generous support.

First, I thank my former student and regular collaborator Chris W. Bonneau. Over the past decade or so, Chris has been a frequent reminder of why I chose university teaching and research as a career. Many of my ideas about judicial elections have been shaped by conversations with Chris, and our collaborations have proven to be not only interesting and productive but also highly enjoyable. Particularly relevant to this project is the chapter on ballot roll-off, which began as a collaborative project with Chris to investigate the impact of *Republican Party of Minnesota* v. *White* on citizen participation in state supreme courts. Additionally, I drew on collaborative work with Chris and Matthew J. Streb in Chapter 2, which tests for differences in features of state supreme court elections between the pre-*White* and post-*White* periods. Finally, Chris generously shared his campaign spending data, which are used in the descriptions in Chapter 2 and the empirical analyses in Chapter 4 and Chapter 5.

Herbert M. Kritzer also has been an outstanding contributor to this project. Bert read Chapter 4 and Chapter 5 as they were being developed and made countless helpful suggestions for improving the manuscript. Bert also graciously included me in discussions with Chief Justice Tom Phillips and

Anthony Champagne about earlier races in Texas, which are described in Chapter 3. Overall, Bert has been a wonderful source of excellent advice, data of various sorts, good humor, and encouragement during this process.

For providing intriguing information about Texas Supreme Court elections in the 1980s and 1990s, I thank Anthony Champagne and Chief Justice Tom Phillips. I am grateful for their assistance and contributions to this work.

Many others in the fields of judicial politics and state politics have made a difference not only in this project but also in this line of inquiry. Particularly important is James L. Gibson. In this endeavor and over the span of my career, I have benefited immeasurably from conversations and encouragement from Jim. I am especially indebted to him for his intriguing insights into the practice of electing judges and for his wonderful collegiality expressed in countless ways, including in the ongoing intellectual debate about state judicial selection.

Also providing fascinating, challenging, and exciting ongoing conversations (and sometimes heated arguments) about state supreme courts, empirical research, and the practice of electing judges are Brandon L. Bartels, Damon Cann, Charles Gardner Geyh, Mark S. Hurwitz, and Matthew J. Streb. Matt was particularly helpful as a collaborator in the *White Noise* project, and some aspects of that analysis are replicated with additional data in Chapter 2. Mark also made a number of suggestions for improving this project and frequently is a source of interesting and enjoyable discussions about the study of law and courts.

At Michigan State University, I recognize and appreciate the outstanding work of Jonah Ralston, who served as my research assistant over the course of several years. Jonah did the lion's share of the work in organizing and merging the ads and elections data utilized throughout this volume. Without Jonah, this work would not have progressed so well. I also am grateful to Marty Jordan and Matthew Zalewski, who provided valuable assistance in the final editorial stages of this work. Finally, I appreciate the assistance of Paul Abramson, who generously shared data on elections to the U.S. House of Representatives.

At Stanford University Press, I thank Keith J. Bybee and Michelle Lipinski. Keith and Michelle have been very helpful and supportive, making this project a pleasure from start to finish. I also appreciate the hard work and careful attention of copyeditor Margaret Pinette, production manager Patricia Myers, and the entire production and artistic team on this project.

For sharing state supreme court advertising data with the public, I thank the Brennan Center for Justice at New York University. By posting CMAG storyboards and detailed information about the various ads, the Brennan Center made this work possible. Likewise, the Justice at Stake Campaign and National Institute on Money in State Politics, in collaboration with the Brennan Center for Justice, provided vital information about campaign advertising in their *New Politics of Judicial Elections* reports.

On a more personal note, I thank my terrific husband and love of my life Anthony R. Duce, who always is wonderfully supportive of every task I undertake. Tony is a constant source of ideas (especially reality checks), encouragement, love, and patience, as well as a very pleasant distraction. My work and life would be so much less without Tony, who always is the perfect partner in every way.

My brilliant and beautiful daughter Amber Hall Price, ever-gracious son-in-law Joe, and wildly entertaining, totally amazing grandchildren Henry and Fiona also greatly improve my life and make my work time much more pleasant.

Finally, I thank my parents, Rose Marie Corley Gann and James Earl Gann Sr., to whom this work is dedicated. Back in the early 1970s in south Louisiana, my parents could have responded with rejection and shame to a fifteen-year-old daughter's pregnancy, particularly given their own modest education and financial means. Instead, they provided unconditional love, helped tremendously with their granddaughter without complaint, and strongly encouraged me to continue to aspire and achieve. From my parents, I learned the value of devotion, responsibility, and plain hard work. Without their support, I would not have progressed from a high-school dropout and teenage single parent to a university distinguished professor with a happy and exciting life. They are the reason for this book and all of my other achievements.

As an important matter, I emphasize that although many contributed to this project, I am solely responsible for the arguments and analyses presented in the chapters. In no way do I represent the views of others, nor is anyone else responsible for any errors I may have made in this work.

In the following pages, I have endeavored to be as transparent as possible in the empirical choices made in the analyses, including measurement and alternative specification strategies. Chapter 4 and Chapter 5 provide extensive robustness checks on the central inferences, and Chapter 2 and Chapter 3 offer a valuable context for understanding these inferences. Overall, these analyses highlight many fascinating patterns in state supreme court elections while challenging some of the conventional wisdom about these races.

I very much hope that this work will inspire others to join in the scientific enterprise of seeking to understand state supreme courts and judicial elections. The opportunities to test significant hypotheses about campaigns and elections specifically, and judicial politics generally, are considerable in this line of inquiry. In many ways, studies of state judicial elections are in their nascent stages and much remains unexplored.

I also would like to emphasize that this book does not seek to present or constitute an argument for or against the practice of electing judges. Instead, this project adds to extant findings that collectively can be used to assess the benefits and pitfalls of any selection scheme. In this same vein, this study helps to shift the debate about judicial selection away from anecdotal evidence, unsubstantiated claims, and projected fears to more systematic evidence drawn from across the American states. Rigorous scientific studies should be a central element in any state's decisions about how to select and retain the state court bench and the cornerstone of any intelligent discussions of the practice of electing judges. At present, the nation falls considerably short of this goal.

ATTACKING JUDGES

1 Attacking Judges

*Another Dimension of Campaign Negativity
in American Politics*

O NE OF THE MOST NOTABLE AND WORRISOME TRENDS IN
contemporary American campaign politics is the rise of televised attack advertising. Going far beyond traditional measures to promote
candidates or draw distinctions among them, these nasty, below-the-belt
campaigns have raised concerns from some political scientists and other astute observers that such rancor may have deleterious consequences for representative democracy. Stated effectively by West (2010: 70), attack ads in contemporary democracy are thought by many to be "the electronic equivalent of
the plague."

Nowhere are these misgivings being expressed more vociferously than in
the context of state judiciaries by the nation's most distinguished court reform organizations and an almost singular voice in the legal community.[1]
Convinced that judges and courts "are being jeopardized by the corrosive effects of money in judicial election campaigns" and by "attack advertising calculated to persuade a majority of the electorate that incumbent judges should
be removed from office," the American Bar Association (2003: 102)[2] now is
advocating that the thirty-eight states currently using elections[3] to staff their
state court benches end the practice altogether.[4] Taking a somewhat more
moderate stance is retired U.S. Supreme Court Justice Sandra Day O'Connor,
who in an extraordinary level of political activism during a post-Court career,
is vigorously campaigning against contestable elections.[5] These high-profile
actors are merely the tip of the iceberg of the opposition to judicial elections

in their contemporary form among legal practitioners, legal scholars, and the interest groups who serve them.

Driving this movement to alter state judicial selection practices are two recent transformations in state supreme court election campaigns. First is the emergence of television campaign advertising on a nationwide scale beginning in 2002 (e.g., Brandenburg and Schotland 2008; Goldberg et al. 2005; Sample, Jones, and Weiss 2007). Although information about the scope and content of campaign advertising was not gathered in any systematic way before the Brennan Center for Justice and the University of Wisconsin Advertising Project began to capture and code televised advertising in state supreme court elections in 2000, these messages have become the norm in contested elections across the nation over the past decade and now play a central role in many judicial elections.[6]

Second are fundamental revisions in the rules of campaign engagement brought about by the U.S. Supreme Court's decision in *Republican Party of Minnesota v. White* (2002). In this landmark case, the Supreme Court invalidated "announce clauses" in state judicial codes of conduct that prevented candidates for judgeships from expressing their views on disputed legal or political issues. Although state supreme court elections have been competitive for decades (e.g., Dubois 1980; M. G. Hall 2001a, 2007a, 2011; Kritzer 2011, forthcoming) and in some states always have been "political" in tone (e.g., Dubois 1980; K. Hall 1984, 2005; M. G. Hall 2001a, 2007a, 2011; Kritzer 2011), judicial campaigns in other states prior to *White* were issue-free, low-information events by design. However, *White* changed the electoral game by opening the door in all states to issue-based discourse, including attack advertising that can be part of aggressive, well-financed campaigns.[7]

These recent developments only exacerbated criticisms that initially began to heighten in the 1980s as judicial elections were becoming "noisier, nastier, and costlier" (Schotland 1985: 78), trends that inspired a "blizzard of commentary" (Gibson 2008: 60) and a multitude of law review articles over the past several decades about "why judicial elections stink" (Geyh 2003: 43). But as Gibson (2009: 1285) aptly observed, "It is puzzling that observers are so certain of the consequences of electioneering . . . given that the scientific evidence of such effects is so scant." Indeed, while empirical scholarship on state supreme courts and judicial behavior within these institutions is advanced and complex,[8] few studies have investigated the exact nature of these campaigns or their effects on judges, courts, and state citizenries.[9]

This project helps to address this deficiency by taking a theoretically grounded empirical look at the effects of television advertising, including harsh attacks targeting incumbents, on two key aspects of state supreme court elections: the vote shares of justices seeking reelection and the propensity of the electorate to vote. As will be discussed in considerable detail in the following chapters, a burgeoning body of political science scholarship has investigated whether campaign negativity has harmful effects on candidate preference and citizen participation in legislative and executive elections, in response to rather alarming predictions about the toxic consequences of televised attacks. In this project, I examine these contentions within the context of state supreme courts.

As a prelude to this analysis, I provide an empirical description of state supreme court elections over the past several decades, with an emphasis on trends in the competitiveness of these races. In this regard, I test the hypothesis that the *White* decision and other aspects of highly competitive campaigns have altered key features of state supreme court elections in recent years. Similarly, I describe televised advertising in state supreme court elections, including the content, scope, and sponsors of attacks and other issue-based appeals. As with campaign politics generally, legal scholars and judicial reform advocates are deeply skeptical of the capacity for campaigns to provide meaningful information about candidates. As Brandenburg and Schotland (2008: 1241–1242) opine, "Unfortunately, TV ads are as likely to educate voters about judicial qualifications as they are to provide nutritional information about french fries." This study provides a systematic examination of this contention.

Generally, there are two compelling reasons to think that the concerns expressed by the American Bar Association, other reform organizations, and the legal academy about negativity in judicial elections may be merited. First, the legitimacy of judges may depend to some extent on an image of impartiality (e.g., Gibson 2008, 2009). Thus, negative advertising explicitly designed to disparage judges and their choices may have especially adverse effects in judicial elections. Second, many states do not list the partisan affiliations of judicial candidates on the ballot, thereby removing the most valuable heuristic in American elections. In these races, campaign messages, including scathing and repeated attacks, may constitute much of the information available to voters and thus may be a strong force in shaping the electoral fates of incumbents and the willingness of citizens to vote.

Alternatively, a theoretically sophisticated body of political science scholarship on campaign negativity in congressional and presidential elections predicts neutral or positive effects of these controversial messages. Though certainly not without contradiction (e.g., Ansolabehere et al. 1994; Ansolabehere and Iyengar 1995; Fridkin and Kenney 2011; Kahn and Kenney 1999), empirical evidence largely discounts the effectiveness of attack advertising in swaying voters (e.g., Lau et al. 1999; Lau, Sigelman, and Rovner 2007) or demobilizing the electorate (e.g., Brooks and Geer 2007; Finkel and Geer 1998; Jackson and Carsey 2007). In fact, quite a few studies (e.g., Finkel and Geer 1998; Jackson and Carsey 2007; Lau and Pomper 2001) show that negative ads *increase* voter turnout in some races.

Though currently lacking assessments of the direct effects of televised campaign messages in these races, empirical scholarship on state supreme courts likewise has documented that rather than being alienated by aggressive campaigns, the electorate is mobilized to vote by the very factors that intensify these races, especially partisan elections, hotly contested seats, and over-the-top spending (e.g., Baum and Klein 2007; Bonneau and M. G. Hall 2009; M. G. Hall 2007b; M. G. Hall and Bonneau 2008, 2013; Hojnacki and Baum 1992; Klein and Baum 2001). Generally, extant scholarship has failed to identify any observable behavioral manifestations of a disaffected electorate stemming from highly contentious races, at least in the form of the willingness to vote.

In short, a deep disjunction is evidenced between the assumptions underlying legal advocacy and much of the empirical evidence generated in studies of elections, including state supreme court elections. To bridge this gap, this research evaluates these two competing perspectives by capitalizing on the solid theoretical foundations of the scholarship on U.S. campaigns and elections and the analytical leverage of comparative research designs. Specifically, I examine all supreme court elections from 2002 through 2008 in the twenty-two states using partisan and nonpartisan elections to staff their highest courts. Although this study will provide a wealth of information about state supreme court elections and the campaigns of incumbents and challengers, five primary sets of questions are explored:

1. How competitive are state supreme court elections, and have the fundamental features of these races been transformed in the post-*White* era?

2. What is the exact nature and extent of televised campaign broadcasting?

3. Does the tone of broadcast advertising sway voters about candidates?

4. Does campaign negativity dampen citizen participation?

5. Are any impacts of campaign advertising contingent on the presence or absence of partisan ballots?

The Comparative Advantage of State Supreme Court Elections

State supreme court elections present an outstanding opportunity for systematic comparative inquiry into the question of how political institutions shape the impact of campaigns and mass electoral behavior, two of the discipline's most abiding concerns. Across the states, both partisan and nonpartisan ballots are used in supreme court elections, reflecting institutional variation that typically does not exist for other national or statewide offices in the United States. Likewise, judicial elections are low-salience, low-information events relative to many other important elections, including presidential, senatorial, and gubernatorial races. Assessing the effects of attack advertising and other campaign messages in these alternative contexts using single models that control for the wide range of other forces affecting elections can provide much needed insight into the role played by institutional arrangements and other contextual forces in democratic politics. This seems especially important given the relative inattention in the scientific literature to nonpartisan elections, despite their widespread use in many state and local elections across the nation (Schaffner, Streb, and Wright 2001).

As the results of this analysis will show, although the political controversy over electing judges is enormously complex and largely normative, the theoretical and empirical story about the impact of negativity in judicial campaigns is straightforward. Partisan state supreme court elections in many respects resemble their legislative and executive counterparts and present a striking challenge to the notion that this new era of intense televised campaigning necessarily threatens incumbents or weakens the participatory proclivities of the electorate. Generally speaking, partisan ballots and other institutional arrangements insulate supreme court justices and state citizenries from any adverse effects of short-lived events like televised attack ads.

However, when partisan labels are removed from ballots, campaigns have pronounced consequences. On the positive side, attack advertising and other factors related to aggressive competition increase voter participation in non-partisan elections. In fact, in nonpartisan and partisan state supreme court elections, there is no evidence whatsoever that attack advertising is a demobilizing force.

On the negative side from the perspective of the advocacy literature,[10] attack advertising serves to attenuate the incumbency advantage in nonpartisan elections. Although nonpartisan elections were adopted as a reform to insulate judges from external political events, removing partisan labels creates a strategic contingency within which some of the most damaging consequences of negative advertising can manifest. In short, nonpartisan elections render some of the most serious concerns about caustic campaigns into self-fulfilling prophecies.

A theoretical perspective drawn from neoinstitutionalism explains these results.[11] Nonpartisan judicial elections are influenced to a greater extent by hard-fought campaigns not because courts are intrinsically different from the other branches but because nonpartisan elections alter the rules of the game. These deliberate choices made by states about selection and retention mechanisms not only define the fundamental rules under which elections operate but also create alternative strategic contingencies that structure the manner in which voters receive and use information and the extent to which incumbents are insulated from external political forces. With regard to legal advocacy, court reformers are partially right about the harmful effects of negativity but for the wrong reasons. Through the lens of political science, those predicting the pernicious effects of negativity (e.g., Ansolabehere et al. 1994; Ansolabehere and Iyengar 1995) missed the institutions and the processes to which their arguments best apply.

The implications of this inquiry are significant. Understanding linkages between citizens and government is basic to a science of politics. By assessing judicial elections comparatively with a focus on the exact nature of the campaign messages broadcast to voters, this analysis helps to improve the current state of knowledge about judicial elections while facilitating the development of theory that captures the realities of these contests. Through the lens of democratic theory and the science of judging, ascertaining how citizens are drawn into the electoral arena and how voters select among candidates is essential for building theories of judicial choice that accurately reflect the complex task of balancing pressures from democratic processes with norms of judicial independence. Looking beyond the judiciary, this study helps to refine existing accounts of electoral politics, particularly with respect to ways in which institutional arrangements, especially the presence or absence of partisan ballots, shape citizen behavior.

The Practical Politics of Judicial Selection

From a practical perspective, this work helps to inform the debate about how best to select judges. Since 1960, twelve states have abandoned partisan elections for selecting their highest courts in favor of gubernatorial appointment plans, nonpartisan elections, or the Missouri Plan, which combines initial executive appointment with subsequent retention elections.[12] Another six states jettisoned nonpartisan elections for the Missouri Plan. In addition to the current claims about the harmful effects of campaign politics, reform advocates have asserted for decades that partisan elections are highly undesirable and should be replaced with other selection schemes.

Especially central to the initial case against partisan elections but still mentioned in the contemporary debate is the claim that judicial elections fail to achieve their goal of accountability, evidenced in part by purportedly incompetent voters and a widespread lack of participation.[13] The conventional wisdom (e.g., Dubois 1980; Schotland 1985), based largely on anecdotal evidence, is that voters "know nothing and care less" (Dubois 1980: 36), are plagued by "ignorance, apathy, and incapacity" (Geyh 2003: 63), are "only slightly affected" by close contests (Adamany and Dubois 1976: 743), and attach "limited importance to the work of the judicial branch of government" and thus decline to vote (National Center for State Courts 2002: 38). Geyh (2003: 76) summarizes the overall argument succinctly: "Judicial elections promote accountability so poorly that the minimal gains they engender on that score are offset by the losses to independence they cause."

These serious contentions formed one of the early cornerstones of the campaign against partisan judicial elections that began in earnest in the 1960s, long before attack advertising and other aspects of electioneering were a principal focus. However, these assertions have been shown to be overdrawn. Voters in state supreme court elections are not incapable of making informed, candidate-centered choices about the professional qualifications of judicial contenders. Previous studies of supreme court elections have demonstrated that state electorates prefer quality challengers to nonquality challengers (i.e., challengers who are judges rather than attorneys who lack judicial experience) (Bonneau and Cann 2011; Bonneau and M. G. Hall 2009; M. G. Hall 2001a; M. G. Hall and Bonneau 2006). Likewise, state electorates vote on issues relevant to judges even when partisan labels are not on the ballot (e.g., Baum 1987; M. G. Hall 2001a; Hojnacki and Baum 1992). Thus, the inability of state electorates to draw substantive distinctions between candidates or make issue-based choices has been exaggerated.

On the propensity to vote, studies of a wide array of political offices in the United States, including state supreme courts, document that citizen participation in elections is variable yet predictable. Among other things, voter turnout is influenced by the formal rules governing the conduct of elections and other regular features of these races (e.g., Baum and Klein 2007; Bonneau and M. G. Hall 2009; Dubois 1980; M. G. Hall 2007b; M. G. Hall and Bonneau 2008, 2013). Stated differently, serious deficiencies in citizen interest and involvement in elections are not intractable. Specifically with regard to judicial reform, eliminating partisan elections, which has been a long-standing and somewhat successfully achieved goal of the judicial reform movement, has had the unintended consequence of inhibiting voting in judicial elections (e.g., Bonneau and M. G. Hall 2009; Dubois 1980; M. G. Hall 2007b; M. G. Hall and Bonneau 2006, 2013), thus making criticisms about low citizen involvement in these races another self-fulfilling prophecy.

Whether these patterns have been altered by aggressive campaigns and televised advertising in the post-*White* era remains to be seen.[14] Thus, new empirical tests of some of the fundamental premises underlying judicial reform are essential. Beyond the judicial selection controversy, scientific research is critical for sorting out apprehensions about the harsh consequences of attack advertising from the realities of how these messages actually affect (or fail to influence) the justices, their courts, and state citizenries. As Geer (2006: 2) effectively summarizes and recommends:

> Worries about negativity lie at the very center of concerns about the health of our electoral system and whether that system promotes a process that can be thought of as democratic. These are serious concerns that warrant serious attention. The problem is that we are all too quick to criticize the system and wring our hands over the ill effects of negativity. We need to pause, reconsider starting

assumptions, and marshal systematic data that will allow us to assess more fully theses fears and concerns.

In short, science should inform any intelligent discussions of televised campaign negativity and the controversy over electing judges, including public policy decisions about which selection systems should be used to select and retain the state court bench.[15]

The Rising Profile of State Supreme Courts

Perhaps the best starting point for understanding state supreme court elections, including the impact of televised campaign politics on incumbent vote shares and citizen participation, is appreciating the power and function of state judiciaries. In the United States, state courts process staggering caseloads that collectively constitute about 98 percent of the nation's litigation (M. G. Hall 2013). The sheer volume of cases processed by state courts and the number of people actually involved in, or directly affected by, this litigation is considerable. Similarly, these conflicts span virtually the entire spectrum of human conflict endemic to personal, social, economic, and political intercourse. William J. Brennan (1966), a justice on the New Jersey Supreme Court prior to his appointment to the U.S. Supreme Court, observed that state courts actually are more important than federal courts because state courts resolve problems most directly relevant to citizens' day-to-day lives. Marriage and divorce, child support and child custody, tenant–landlord disputes, debt collection, the redistribution of estates, and other such matters, although seemingly mundane, are precisely the types of cases ordinary Americans are likely to be litigating and the types of disputes that will have an immediate and lasting impact on their lives.

Of course, not all cases brought to state courts entail such ostensibly routine matters as divorce or debt collection. State courts also decide some of the most salient and publicly visible issues on the American political agenda, generating heated debates and provoking accusations from political opponents and other dissatisfied parties of "judicial activism" and "legislating from the bench." These cases range from serious crimes to disputes over hot-button policy issues with far-reaching consequences. In recent years, for example, state courts have helped to define the law of same-sex marriage, access to abortion, the right to die, stem cell research, medical marijuana, voter identification requirements, tort liability, and affirmative action. Similarly, state courts play a vital role in interpreting and applying federal law, including federal constitutional law governing state felony prosecutions and a wide range of other types of disputes.[16]

From the perspective of state government, the power of state courts to thwart the will of the other branches of state government and to stand in direct contradistinction to the dominant political alliance is considerable. Through the power of judicial review, state courts, especially state supreme courts, decide some of the most significant and divisive issues of state politics and in doing so help to define the success or failure of legislative and executive agendas. These controversial cases can place state courts squarely into political conflict with the legislative and executive branches, requiring judges to act as countermajoritarian agents. Of course, governors and state legislatures can retaliate through such means as refusing to raise judges' salaries, altering court jurisdictions, and using subsequent legislation and state constitutional amendments to attack courts publicly and undo their rulings. Thus, when state courts are on the opposite side of the political fence from the other major players in state government, high political drama can quickly follow.[17]

In the vast majority of these various types of cases, state courts act relatively independently of the federal courts. Numerous areas of law remain largely within the purview of the states, including criminal law, education, and family law. Moreover, state court decisions are subject to review by the U.S. Supreme Court only when matters of federal law are involved or implicated. Decisions governed exclusively by state law are immune to federal scrutiny. However, even when cases can be appealed to the nation's highest court, the chances are remote of any particular case landing on the U.S. Supreme Court's docket. In the 2011 term (October 2011 through September 2012), which was not particularly distinctive relative to other terms, the Supreme Court decided only seventy-eight cases with full signed opinions and another fifty to sixty cases with per curiam opinions.[18] The majority of these cases came from the federal courts.

In short, state courts are major players in litigation in the United States, and state supreme courts, which sit at the apex of state judiciaries, have a great deal of power to shape law and policy. Overall, state supreme courts directly influence the lives of millions of people while setting the parameters of acceptable action by state governments. Most of these justices, who have tremendous influence over the distribution of wealth and power in the United States, are elected.

Particularly intriguing in recent decades is the rising profile of state supreme courts and the selection processes that surround these institutions. Explanations commonly cited to explain this trend include the polarization of the electorate, the decline of one-party domination in some states, the proliferation of single-issue groups, and the growing reliance in some states on state constitutions to expand civil rights and liberties beyond the lower limits set by the federal constitution and federal courts.

Fundamental changes in institutional design also have played a major role in this transformation, especially the fairly rapid diffusion of intermediate appellate courts starting in the 1960s (see, e.g., American Bar Association Commission on the 21st Century Judiciary 2003; M. G. Hall 1999). Intermediate appellate courts are designed to improve the capacity and efficiency of state judiciaries by handling the vast majority of appeals from the trial courts, leaving state supreme courts with the discretion to choose only the most significant cases for their dockets. In other words, intermediate appellate courts help to free state supreme courts from the drudgery of overburdened, highly routine caseloads, thereby elevating the policy-making role of state supreme courts while providing better opportunities to develop innovative solutions to the problems embodied in the cases. These two-tiered appellate structures produce complex and interesting dockets for state supreme courts but also increase the controversy surrounding these institutions, attracting sharper attention to, and scrutiny of, the justices' decisions.

At the beginning of the 1960s, only fourteen states had intermediate appellate courts (M. G. Hall 1999), but now all but ten states (Delaware, Maine, Montana, Nevada, New Hampshire, Rhode Island, South Dakota, Vermont, West Virginia, Wyoming) have these hard-working institutions.[19] A two-tiered appellate structure is not necessary in states with small populations and low litigation rates.[20]

Some observers describe these trends in the heightened power of courts, both in the United States and abroad, as the "judicialization" of politics, wherein crucial societal interests are ever more frequently decided by courts rather than the other branches of government. But regardless of the label one prefers, state supreme courts and judicial elections have moved to the forefront of American political discourse.

The Strategy of Negativity in American Politics

In discussions of American campaign politics, assaults on attack advertising and other forms of campaign negativity are loud and persistent. In the words of Geer (2006: 1), "We are . . . awash in a sea of negativity about negativity." Mayer (1996: 438) likewise observes that "whenever commentators compile a catalogue of the most heinous sins in current American politics, negative campaigning and attack advertising usually wind up near the top of the list." This is particularly apropos in discussions of judicial elections.

This trend raises a series of fundamental questions about the nature of American campaign politics, the answers to which provide an important context for this research. First and foremost, if negative advertising is so potentially damaging, destructive, and disliked by large segments of the American people, why is this practice so pervasive? There are numerous answers to this question, but the simplest and most basic response is that candidates and campaign firms believe that piercing attacks actually work. Other, more nuanced explanations relate to the necessity of providing information to voters and motivating them to go to the polls.

As studies (e.g., Ansolabehere and Iyengar 1995; Iyengar 2001/2002) based largely on analyses of presidential and congressional elections describe, candidates use short televised messages to advertise, and go negative, for multiple reasons, including bold attempts to persuade voters to reject opponents, to set the campaign agenda by focusing attention to a well-defined set of issues from which the candidates benefit, and to attract media attention, which in turn generates additional (and free) exposure.

Regarding the media, televised campaign ads are "made for TV news" (Ansolabehere and Iyengar 1995: 134). In fact, West (2010) documents that news coverage of televised campaign advertising in presidential elections by the *New York Times, Washington Post,* and the *CBS Evening News* has increased substantially since the 1980s.

Campaign advertising, and attack ads in particular, provide concise, sensational stories that fit easily within thirty-minute broadcasts and short news cycles, in many cases with a dramatic flare that generates suspense about who might win. These types of stories fall well within the proverbial horserace coverage of American elections (e.g., Patterson and McClure 1976), which is now a mainstay of contemporary televised news broadcasts.[21]

Another compelling question about attack advertising relates to its educational value: Are these brief televised campaign advertisements informative? Some scholarly accounts, as well as most popular accounts and descriptions provided by court reform organizations and the legal academy, certainly would suggest not. Recall Brandenburg and Schotland's (2008) remark cited earlier about the inability of televised ads to educate voters about the qualifications of judicial candidates. Indeed, many pundits and other political observers characterize television advertising, especially negative appeals, as inaccurate, deceptive, misleading, manipulative, and a host of other pejorative labels designed to convey their lack of value if not harmful impact on the electoral process. Others doubt the ability of fifteen- to thirty-second spots to educate or inform voters no matter how accurate the information.

In contrast, the answer typically given by scholars of campaign politics to questions about the information content of televised advertising is surprising and challenges widely held beliefs about the value of these messages. As Ansolabehere and Iyengar (1995: 12) summarize, "The conventional wisdom holds that advertisements are not educational and that exposure to campaign advertising impedes, rather than promotes, voter learning." However, Ansolabehere and Iyengar (1995: 12) provide evidence that "repudiates this claim overwhelmingly." Although their results were not derived from studies of state supreme court elections, Ansolabehere and Iyengar (1995: 8) conclude that advertising informs voters and that campaign messages, even attack spots, "are not a pack of lies." These results are consistent with other classic studies of campaigning, including Patterson and McClure's (1976) seminal study of the 1972 presidential election. One of Patterson and McClure's (1976: 11) most fundamental conclusions was that "spot commercials . . . educate the public."

Iyengar (2001/2002: 694–695) seconds this opinion by observing that "even when the message is delivered in the form of a thirty-second commercial, embellished with musical jingles and eye-catching visuals, viewers manage to acquire new and relevant information about the sponsoring candidate." In discussing judicial elections in particular, Iyengar (2001/2002: 695) argues that because of the low starting point of most citizens with respect to knowledge about the candidates, "exposure to campaign advertising cannot help but educate voters."

Ascertaining precisely whether televised ads are misleading, deceptive, or manipulative is difficult in some cases and ultimately may be in the eye of the beholder. But the thrust of the arguments about the educational value of campaign spots seems to suggest that these ads work to improve the information environment surrounding elections, especially in low-salience settings.

It also seems worthwhile to note that many of the concerns expressed about attack advertising apply equally well to positive messages.[22] As Finkel and Geer (1998: 592) aptly observe, "Dishonesty is not confined to negative appeals." An incumbent who claims to be fair, unbiased, nonpartisan, and a strict adherent to the rule of law may not be any of those things. Of course, these promotional ads lack the sensationalism and dramatic appeal that caustic attacks might provide, but exaggerations or outright falsehoods are quite possible in positive ads nonetheless. In fact, one scarcely can imagine an ad that does not cast its sponsor in a flattering light.

On the Benefits of Negativity

Several scholars (e.g., Geer 2006; Mayer 1996) have offered intriguing theoretical accounts of how and why harsh criticism, including attack advertising, is essential to the electoral process and a vibrant democracy. Many of these arguments, premised on the primacy of open and free expression and the value of information, are essential components of democratic theory. Paramount is the freedom for citizens to criticize the government and political leaders, debate the best approaches to pressing problems, and effectively determine who will hold the offices of government. Indeed, representative democracy, which places a profound responsibility on citizens, demands an informed and engaged electorate. By offering facts, assertions, and commentary on the virtues and flaws of incumbents and challengers, negative campaigning becomes an indispensable tool for enlightening voters. In describing these systemic benefits, Geer (2006: 1) goes so far as to suggest that "without negativity, no nation can credibly think of itself as democratic."

Geer (2006) also provides some evidence to support the notion that negative appeals in campaign advertisements are more effective than positive appeals in informing voters. Starting with the premise that issue appeals are more educational than appeals focused on values or traits, Geer (2006) documents that negative ads had significantly greater issue content than positive ads in presidential campaigns from 1960 through 2000. Geer (2006) also makes the provocative claim that attacks are more likely than positive ads to be supported by evidence and thus are more accurate.

West (2010) produces similar findings about the issue content of negative advertising in his analysis of presidential elections from 1952 through 2008. West (2010: 71) found that "the most substantive appeals actually came in negative spots" and argues that negative ads are more likely to be policy oriented because attacks require a basis for criticism.

There are other potential benefits of campaign negativity. Mayer (1996: 442) argues, as others have, that the threat of serious challenge, including the potential to draw attack advertising, has a preemptive effect:

> If candidates always knew that their opponents would never say anything critical about them, campaigns would quickly turn into a procession of lies, exaggerations, and unrealistic promises. Candidates could misstate their previous records, present glowing accounts of their abilities . . . all with the smug assurance that no one would challenge their assertions.

From this perspective, aggressive challengers, as well as the threat of televised attack advertising in response to campaign claims, keep candidates more honest than otherwise would be the case and thus improve the quality of the dialogue in American elections.

Overall, despite the disdain that some citizens may have for particularly harsh attacks, campaign negativity in some form is essential to robust elections and the democracy itself. The pivotal question is how far can these messages go before the beneficial effects translate into harms. As Jackson, Mondak, and Huckfeldt (2009: 55) summarize:

> A nation's citizens must walk a fine line when assessing elected officials and political institutions. On one hand, a degree of skepticism seems prudent. Were citizens to view the political arena with something approaching blind faith, the risk of elite malfeasance would be considerable. Although skepticism may be advisable, mass cynicism can be debilitating. If citizens conclude that government is damaged beyond repair, then little or no incentive exists for weighing pros and cons of new proposals or selecting between competing candidates.

The hypotheses tested in this project provide a systematic examination of some of the primary contentions about attack advertising within the context of state supreme courts. Is there evidence that these ads have detrimental consequences for the justices and state electorates, or might these ads have neutral impacts or even observable benefits for courts?

Issue Advertising in State Supreme Court Elections

One possible reaction to the work of Geer (2006) and other political scientists on the subject of negativity in American elections is that these arguments when applied to state judiciaries miss the point. Especially in law review articles and the advocacy literature, criticisms of campaign advertising in judicial elections focus not only on the positive or negative tone of the messages broadcast to state electorates but also on the substantive content of the ads themselves. Just as Geer (2006) argues that the most effective appeals for informing voters involve references to issues, many in the legal community decry the use of *any* issue appeals in judicial elections. References (positive or negative) to partisanship, judicial ideology, past decisions, and specific policy questions in judicial campaigns are considered evidence of the intrinsically harmful "politicization" (or even "hyperpoliticization") of the judicial selection process and state courts (e.g., Brandenburg and Schotland 2008; Geyh 2003; Tarr 2009). In this regard, the legal community and selection reform advocates are redefining the meaning of effective campaigns and informed electorates in judicial elections while remarkably at the same time are denouncing voters as unknowledgeable about candidates.

Instead, many legal academicians, legal advocacy organizations, and practitioners extol the virtues of "traditional" themes in judicial campaign advertisements, or positive messages that emphasize professional qualifications, experience, and judicial temperament. By definition, traditional appeals exclude any references to issues, allegiances, or decisions. A typical ad of this genre might have as a primary focus the candidate's years of service in legal practice or on the bench. These ads also invariably use an array of legally palatable terms to describe the candidate's values, traits, and approach to judicial power, including the standard claims that the judge or challenger is impartial, fair, involved in the community, a practitioner of judicial restraint, and strict adherent to the rule of law. In fact, before the *White* decision in 2002, state judicial codes of conduct in numerous states prohibited by law any campaign messages that stepped outside the parameters of traditional appeals.

Of course, others might question how useful traditional messages are in helping voters to evaluate judges given the absence of any specific information about the judges' decisions or even partisan-free or issue-free performance metrics. The U.S. Supreme Court took this stance explicitly in *White* (2002: 788) by referring to announce clauses as "state imposed voter ignorance."

For an excellent example of the typical framing of issue-based dialogue by organized interests, consider this assertion by the Justice at Stake Campaign (Sample, Jones, and Weiss 2007: 35–38), which offers a prescription for how to advertise appropriately based on their contentions about the 2006 state supreme court elections:

> Judicial candidates who sought to put disputed political and legal issues at the center of their candidacy lost more often than they won. In state after state, the more that judicial campaigns sounded like politics as usual, the warier the voters seem . . . American voters seem to be sending a strong message to would-be judges: tell us why you would be a good judge, not about your personal political views.

Thus, Sample, Jones, and Weiss (2007) intimate a preference for traditional appeals in state supreme court advertising while actually ascribing the same preference to voters.[23]

In fact, many court reform advocates and the legal academy have denounced issue-based campaigning as antithetical to judicial impartiality and independence, in the same manner that these political activists and scholars strongly oppose partisan elections. This helps to explain much of the fervor over the U.S. Supreme Court's decision in *Republican Party of Minnesota* v. *White* (2002). Stated well by Sample, Jones, and Weiss (2007: 29), "Telegraphing decisions in advance, explicitly or implicitly, would make a mockery of equal justice and undermine public confidence in the right to a fair trial."[24] Goldberg et al. (2005: 25) go so far as to describe judicial campaigns in the post-*White* era as a "New Dating Game—not a game of outright promises, but one of code words and coy signals" between candidates and interest groups.

To be sure, there are inherent tensions between some of the typical approaches to campaigning for legislative and executive office and the basic function of state judiciaries as independent arbiters of legal disputes. Promises by judges to decide particular cases in a specified way, to pledge to favor categories of litigants over others, or in any definitive way to prejudge specific disputes raise solemn concerns about fundamental fairness and due process. In recognizing this problem, federal court decisions after *White* have expressly upheld speech restrictions in judicial campaigns that otherwise would not be acceptable in legislative or executive elections. In *Siefert* v. *Alexander* (2010), for instance, the U.S. Court of Appeals for the Seventh Circuit refused to recognize the right of judicial candidates to endorse other candidates for political office or personally solicit campaign contributions.[25]

At the same time, as the *White* (2002) decision articulates, reporting one's ideological leanings or partisanship falls substantially short of specific promises to decide cases in a certain way. Likewise, various performance-based metrics seemingly central to evaluating the professional qualifications of judges are beyond the scope of the types of traditional and arguably vacuous messages favored by the reform community. Reversal rates by higher courts, for example, are quite relevant to judicial performance but constitute issue-based appeals to voters.[26]

Understanding the underlying premise of these arguments against the politicization of judicial elections is essential for understanding the controversy over electing judges and, in particular, the serious concerns of the legal community about issue-based appeals, attack advertising, and other forms of electioneering. The fundamental assumption is that judges must remain above the political fray to retain their legitimacy. Thus, issue advertising, especially in the form of televised attacks, and other campaign activities typical in legislative and executive elections are perceived as inherently dangerous for state judiciaries.

This assumption is derived largely from normative theories of judging, which dictate that judges should be free from political influence in order to uphold the rule of law. But this directive about what *should be* often is translated into highly debatable and contentious assertions about ostensibly what *is*: judges as highly trained technicians neutrally applying the law. The judges-as-umpires analogy articulated by Chief Justice John Roberts during his 2005 U.S. Senate confirmation hearing epitomizes this approach.[27] In the context of state courts, this fundamental theoretical premise leads to the inference that because partisanship, ideology, and other aspects of individual beliefs and preferences are poor guides to judicial performance, these extraneous factors should not be interjected into judicial election campaigns. Furthermore, doing so damages citizens' positive perceptions of judges, the judicial process, and state judiciaries, thereby posing a deep systemic threat to the nation.

Judicial politics scholarship offers a strikingly different perspective on judging. As a substantial body of empirical work on state supreme courts has shown, justices often have significant discretion in interpreting the law and, in the process of clarifying legal principles or extending established rules to new situations, are required to call on their own personal values and experiences to decide the cases (e.g., Bonneau and Rice 2009; Brace and M. G. Hall 1997; M. G. Hall 1987, 1992, 1995, 2014a; Langer 2002; Peters 2009; Savchak and Barghothi 2007).[28]

This is emphatically not to suggest that justices simply decide as they wish or that law is irrelevant to their decisions. In most empirical models, legal constraints often are the most powerful predictors of judicial voting behavior (e.g., Brace and M. G. Hall 1997; M. G. Hall 2014a). Even so, empirical judicial politics scholarship largely has discredited traditional notions that state supreme court justices are tightly constrained by law and lack a meaningful policy-making role. Thus, if judging is a political art as well as a legal science, some might reasonably conclude that judges, like other public officials with the power to shape public policy, should have their discretionary choices scrutinized by the electorate.[29]

In essence, there are seemingly intractable differences between the theories used in legal circles to oppose judicial elections and predict endemic harms of attack advertising and most political science depictions of political campaigning and decision making in the highest appellate courts as inherently preference based.[30] Chapter 2 continues to explore these differences within the context of a discussion of the evolution of the judicial reform movement over the past two centuries.

An interesting bottom line is that many in the legal community, although drawing on normative theories of judging, have offered the same excoriating criticisms of attack advertising as some political scientists concerned with U.S. elections generally. Across the academic and political spectrum, many have grave concerns about excessive attacks and other forms of political malevolence in modern elections. These serious misgivings merit systematic evaluation.

Primary Data Sources, Coding, and Model Specification

The purpose of this project is to test several key hypotheses about the impact of campaign negativity in American elections within the context of state supreme courts. In doing so, I rely on two primary data sources. First, I use information about state supreme court elections from 1980 through 2010, which I collected and coded from various official state sources, including reports from secretaries of state and state election commissions.[31] These data have been used extensively in previous research (e.g., Bonneau and Cann 2011; Bonneau and M. G. Hall 2009; Bonneau, M. G. Hall, and Streb 2011; M. G. Hall 2001a, 2007a, 2007b, 2011, 2014b; M. G. Hall and Bonneau 2006, 2008, 2013) and thus have been evaluated for reliability on an ongoing basis in multiple contexts.

Second, for specific details about campaign advertising, I rely on the storyboards collected by the Campaign Media Analysis Group (CMAG) and reports prepared collaboratively by the Brennan Center for Justice, the Justice at Stake Campaign, and the National Institute on Money in State Politics. CMAG, a commercial firm, captures storyboards and streaming video for every state supreme court campaign advertisement aired in the nation's 100 largest media markets. These storyboards and videos are posted on the webpage of the Brennan Center for Justice and are freely available for public use. For detailed information about each ad, I use editions of the *New Politics of Judicial Elections* series, which code all state supreme court advertisements for tone, sponsors, airings, cost, and specific subject themes. In these reports, the actual coding of the ads was done by researchers at the Brennan Center for Justice.[32]

With respect to tone and themes, state supreme court campaign advertisements have been classified using the same coding scheme as campaign ads in other types of elections. Specifically, the Brennan Center for Justice categorized each state supreme court advertisement by tone as "promotion of one candidate," "attack on the opponent," or "contrasting two or more candidates," which collectively constitute mutually exclusive and exhaustive categories. These ads also were classified using a series of subject categories, or "themes," including traditional appeals, civil justice, criminal justice, criticism for decisions, special interest involvement, civil rights, the role of judges, and conservative and family values. As described in Chapter 3, the Brennan Center subject categories fit readily within the coding scheme developed by Geer (2006) in his work on presidential elections. Overall, Geer (2006) classified the subject matter in presidential campaign advertising into three categories: traits personal to the candidates, broader values that do not involve specific issues or policies, and issues that are specific to controversial subjects or policies.[33] Taken together, discussions of state supreme court advertising by tone and substantive appeals will provide an interesting portrait of these campaigns in the post-*White* era and will serve as a means to assess the impact of different types of campaign messages, including attacks, on the electorate and incumbents.

The specific races to be analyzed in the hypothesis tests are supreme court elections from 2002 through 2008 in states using partisan or nonpartisan elections to staff their highest courts. The analysis begins in 2002 because data on television advertising in state supreme court elections are virtually nonexistent before 2002.[34] The analysis ends in 2008 only because of limits on the availability of campaign advertising data at the time of writing. Retention elections, which are part of the Missouri Plan, are excluded because of the complete absence of any televised campaign advertising in these races from 2002 through 2008.

Regarding model specification, I rely on well-established models of state supreme court elections (Bonneau 2007; Bonneau and Cann 2011; Bonneau and M. G. Hall 2003, 2009; M. G. Hall 2001a, 2007b, 2014b; M. G. Hall and Bonneau 2006, 2008, 2013), which include characteristics of the candidates, their campaigns, the state political context, and institutional arrangements. Essentially, I seek to replicate previous studies of citizen mobilization and the incumbency advantage while adding the unique component of campaign messages broadcast to state electorates.

Particularly important in these models are campaign spending and quality challengers. In this analysis, it is imperative to disentangle the effects of campaign spending from the effects of television advertising and to evaluate whether the races in some way indicate the ability of the electorate to select candidates based on their professional qualifications. In scientific studies of supreme court elections, quality challengers are defined as challengers who hold, or have held, judgeships and thus have the requisite professional experience for service on the states' highest courts.

As another unique contribution and as part of an emphasis on institutions, the models assess the potential for state supreme court professionalization to offset any adverse effects of particularly harsh ads. As the following chapters will document, opting for partisan or nonpartisan elections has important ramifications for state judiciaries, but determinations about how these courts are structured also are critically significant.

Overview of the Chapters

In the following chapters, I provide a great deal of descriptive information about state supreme court elections and television campaign advertising, as well as rigorous hypothesis tests of several central questions about the impact of campaign negativity on incumbents and state electorates. Chapter 2 maps the exact nature of state supreme court electoral competition from 1980 through 2010. As a prelude to the empirical analysis, I provide a brief historical review of how and why judicial elections were adopted in the first place, how states have modified their systems over the past several decades, and the extent to which selection systems vary across the nation. As a related matter, I offer an explanation for why electing judges is almost uniquely American. I also discuss the normative foundations of the judicial selection debate and the wide gap that persists between the legal academy and political scientists in approaches to fundamental questions of law and politics. These discussions highlight several notable differences between judicial elections and elections to the nation's most visible political offices in the nature of the public dialogue about campaign negativity.

Overall, Chapter 2 places an emphasis on the historically competitive nature of supreme court elections and the substantial variations both over time and across states in various indicators of electoral competition and citizen participation in these races. These data illustrate that state supreme court elections by several standard measures have actually become less competitive since the 1980s and in the aftermath of the *White* decision, findings that are inconsistent at the descriptive level with arguments about an increasingly threatening electoral climate for incumbents and voters. However, the 2008 and 2010 nonpartisan elections were quite competitive in some regard, suggesting the need for more systematic analysis.

In Chapter 3, I provide a comprehensive description of televised campaign advertising in state supreme court elections, especially the tone and themes of these messages and their sponsors. As Chapter 3 will reveal, television advertising is the norm in contested state supreme court elections overall, but sizable proportions of these races still do not draw any advertising from candidates, political parties, or organized interests. However, attack advertising is atypical, particularly for incumbents seeking reelection in partisan elections. Chapter 3 also categorizes the substantive content of attack, promote, and contrast advertising. These results show that attack and contrast ads are much more likely than promote ads to discuss issues rather than the traits or values of the candidates and consequently may have a greater capacity to provide meaningful information to voters. As with all discussions in this book, this chapter places an emphasis on comparing states and drawing distinctions between partisan and nonpartisan elections.

Chapter 4 and Chapter 5 offer systematic tests of several key hypotheses about the impact of televised attack advertising on the incumbency advantage and voter participation in state supreme court elections from 2002 through 2008. Both of these chapters utilize alternative model specification and measurement strategies to bolster confidence in the robustness of the statistical results and substantive conclusions. Both chapters continue to place an emphasis on the impact of institutional arrangements, including differences between partisan and nonpartisan elections. These chapters also focus on professionalization as a significant factor influencing the incumbency advantage and citizen participation in state supreme court elections.

Specifically, Chapter 4 assesses the influence of attack advertising and other types of campaign messages on the electoral performance of incumbents. Conventional wisdom suggests that television campaign advertising has a substantial influence on the election returns. For instance, a highly respected scholar deeply involved in judicial reform observed that "the existing data on judicial campaigns strongly suggest that television is very effective in generating votes for judicial candidates" (Champagne 2002: 684) and that "the strong correlation between television media markets and voting percentages should not be ignored" (671). The primary finding in Chapter 4 is that televised promotions do help the candidates but that attack advertising has harmful consequences for incumbents only in nonpartisan elections. Partisan elections are immune to these damaging effects.

Chapter 5 evaluates the influence of attack advertising and other types of campaign messages on the propensity of state electorates to vote. Standard accounts in the judicial reform literature suggest that campaigning negates citizens' positive attitudes, resulting in distrust and a loss of confidence in judges and courts. As extensive research on executive and legislative elections documents, the most pronounced symptom of such distrust and disillusionment is voter disaffection. However, the results in Chapter 5 sharply contradict the voter demobilization hypothesis. In nonpartisan state supreme court elections, attack advertising and other factors indicative of intense competition *improve* citizen participation. In partisan elections, attack advertising matters little in whether state electorates vote.

Finally, Chapter 6 summarizes the various findings in previous chapters and places them within the framework of extant scholarship. Particularly notable is the consistency in empirical findings between this study and earlier research (even studies going back to the 1980s) documenting how state supreme court elections actually work. Most of this evidence is inconsistent with normative assumptions about the harmful effects of televised negativity and other forms of intense competition in judicial elections. These findings also contradict claims about the inability of voters to select the most experienced candidates for office, even in the post-*White* era.

Much of the evidence reported in this study should help to alleviate some of the worst fears about the pernicious effects of attack advertising and other forms of campaign intensity in state supreme court elections. Attack advertising simply does not have the deleterious effects widely predicted on citizen participation in partisan or nonpartisan elections, findings that are strongly incompatible with assertions about the alienating impact of contemporary campaign politics on state electorates. And even in nonpartisan elections, where campaign negativity dampens the incumbency advantage, the deleterious effects of attack ads can be counterbalanced in numerous ways, including actions by states to professionalize their judiciaries and strategies by justices to run well-financed campaigns that include televised promotions.

Ultimately, the descriptions and analyses in this project are a testament to the power of institutions in American politics, including their ability to shape mass political behavior and the election returns. This work also illustrates the value of political science research in helping to inform some of the most significant debates on the American political agenda. Although many political choices are essentially normative and are premised on the values and instrumental goals of relevant political actors, empirical research can inform normative preferences by validating or invalidating the assumptions or conventional wisdoms on which these preferences are based. In this regard, scientific studies of state supreme court elections represent a perfect nexus between theoretically based empirical political science and the practical politics of judicial selection reform.

2 State Supreme Court Elections in Contemporary Democracy

ONE OF THE MOST ENDURING ISSUES OF AMERICAN POLI-
tics is how to select judges for the state court bench.[1] Because of
the intense controversy necessarily associated with decisions about who controls access to political power, the subject of judicial selection has produced
endless debate, replete with countless claims and counterclaims about the
various alternative selection schemes.

In recent decades, this debate has risen to a fever pitch as televised campaign advertising and various forms of issue-based discourse have become
institutionalized and as the costs of seeking office have escalated. "Why Judicial Elections Stink" (Geyh 2003), "Justice in Jeopardy" (American Bar Association Commission on the 21st Century Judiciary 2003), and "Justice in
Peril: The Endangered Balance Between Impartial Courts and Judicial Election Campaigns" (Brandenburg and Schotland 2008) are essay titles typify-
ing the deep concern that many, especially in the legal profession, have about
contemporary judicial elections. Of course, these trepidations are not unique
to the legal community or to state judiciaries but instead are part of a broader
national dialogue about campaign negativity and unrestrained money in
American politics.

Noticeably absent from discussions of judicial elections are political science theories and findings, particularly evidence about how elections and
campaigns for the nation's most visible offices actually work. To some extent,
this is because many legal academicians and policy advocates summarily

dismiss studies of elections to the legislative and executive branches, which constitute the largest proportion of this work, as irrelevant given the unique role of the judiciary. Instead, any obvious similarities between judicial elections and elections for nonjudicial offices are cited as examples epitomizing the deteriorating electoral climate for judges and the politicization of state courts (e.g., Geyh 2003; Goldberg and Sanchez 2003; Sample et al. 2010; Sample, Jones, and Weiss 2007; Tarr 2007).

Another factor is that some of the most fervent political activists shaping the judicial selection debate will not readily acknowledge even the most relevant and compelling research, including studies of judicial elections, when the evidence generated in these works contradicts their strategies and goals.[2] Value judgments about which selection systems are "better" are motivated in the political realm by numerous concerns, including the instrumental goals and basic self-interest of membership organizations, advocacy groups, and other political players.[3]

But at least part of the responsibility for the absence of much systematic empirical evidence in the judicial elections controversy rests with the discipline of political science itself. In fact, these races have received only limited scholarly attention, although there certainly are notable exceptions constituting a significant body of work (e.g., Baum and Klein 2007; Bonneau 2007; Bonneau and Cann 2011; Bonneau and M. G. Hall 2003, 2009; Dubois 1980; M. G. Hall 2001a, 2007b, 2014b; M. G. Hall and Bonneau 2006, 2008; Hojnacki and Baum 1992; Kritzer 2011, forthcoming). Nonetheless, relative to presidential and congressional elections, judicial elections remain largely unexplored.

This situation is quickly improving. In recent years, political scientists have produced valuable evidence about state supreme court elections, in many cases demonstrating that the conventional wisdom is overdrawn or inaccurate. Moreover, the pace of inquiry is increasing rapidly. In an interesting turn of phrase, Epstein (2013: 218) recently described this trend as an "assault on the assaulters of judicial elections." Indeed, scientific studies of state supreme court elections (and state court legitimacy) are beginning to highlight the substantial disconnect between empirical reality and many of the descriptions of judicial elections pervasive in the legal literature, popular press, and even in some political science accounts. On balance, much of this new evidence shows that vigorous electoral competition does not have the harmful impacts initially predicted or widely feared.

This chapter adds to these valuable insights by building an empirical picture of modern state supreme court elections. First, to place these races in historical perspective, I describe the circular route of the judicial reform movement that began in the early 1800s with arguments about the benefits of elections but now has shifted to dire concerns about them. I also discuss the normative paradigm that heretofore has framed the debate. In doing so, I highlight differences in the public dialogue between judicial elections and their legislative and executive counterparts. This chapter then describes the current practices used to select and retain state supreme court justices and illustrates how the distribution of state preferences for particular selection schemes has changed over the past five decades. Thereafter, this chapter provides detailed information about the key features of state supreme court elections from 1980 through 2010, including various aspects of electoral competition and the propensity for state electorates to vote in these races. In doing so, I compare nonpartisan and partisan elections, rank the American states, and compare trends in the pre- and post-*White* eras.

Overall, the evidence presented in this chapter challenges the accuracy of the prevailing stereotype of state supreme court elections as having remained electorally safe and politically dull until the turn of the twenty-first century. Generally speaking, supreme court elections have been expensive and competitive for decades and, in some significant ways, are becoming *less competitive*. Likewise, citizen participation has not declined substantially in recent years. At least at the descriptive level, these patterns contradict assertions about the alienating impact of televised attack advertising on state electorates and the diminution of the incumbency advantage.

This is not to suggest that attack advertising and other aspects of modern campaigns have no other potentially disturbing consequences or that all features of these races have remained fairly stable in recent years. However, this chapter definitively demonstrates that expensive, highly competitive elections are far from new. Incumbents and voters simply have not been recently blindsided by aggressive challengers and other aspects of intense competition in state supreme court elections and instead may have come to expect lively contests for the high court bench.

The Circle of Judicial Reform

After two centuries of political conflict, the debate over state judicial selection has come full circle. Historically, excoriating charges about the failings of appointment schemes gave rise to judicial elections. In today's dialogue, these arguments have been supplanted with equally disparaging claims about the deleterious effects of election schemes. In short, the American states have traveled the very rough route from appointment plans to election plans and may be circling back to appointment schemes again.

Initially, all judges in the American states were appointed by legislatures or governors, often with numerous devices for removing recalcitrant judges, including impeachment, joint legislative address, and short renewable terms subject to legislative approval (Hanssen 2004). However, judicial elections were introduced in the early nineteenth century as an innovation to raise the status of state judiciaries by providing them with independence from the legislative and executive branches and from the political cronyism that dominated the judicial selection process (e.g., K. Hall 1983, 2005; Hanssen 2004; Shugerman 2010).

As Kermit Hall (2005: 66) explains, because "cliques and circles of a few politicians . . . dominated the appointment of judges," well-qualified lawyers were precluded from judicial service and "could never hope to rise to the bench." Judicial elections were a reform to entrenched political party machines and political favoritism controlling the appointment process and diminishing the likelihood of any effective check on legislative and gubernatorial power. Placing judicial selection in the hands of state electorates "promised judges greater independence from the political branches by clothing them with the authority of the people to exercise judicial review" (K. Hall 2005: 66). With the practice of electing judges, the legitimacy of state courts flows directly from the citizens affected by the courts' decisions.

Evidence suggests that electing judges proved to be effective toward this goal. Numerous scholars (e.g., K. Hall 2005; Hanssen 2004; Shugerman 2010) have documented the rise of state judicial review as elected judges replaced appointed judges and began to take on state legislatures and executives in separation-of-powers conflicts.

An intriguing aspect of this story is the "legal profession's almost total control of the movement to elect judges" (K. Hall 2005: 65). The movement toward judicial elections was prompted, and then heralded, by the bar, which reflected to some extent a strategy by the legal community to elevate the practice of law (K. Hall 1983, 2005; Hanssen 2004). Not surprisingly, the legal profession has been at the center of each transformation in state judicial selection.

In 1832, Mississippi became the first state to establish a completely elected judiciary, although Vermont and Georgia already were using elections to select at least some of their judges (K. Hall 1984). Thereafter, every state entering the Union from 1846 through 1912 mandated the selection and retention of judges through popular election (K. Hall 1984). This trend did not last. Dissatisfaction with partisan elections led to a shift in preferences among lawyers and other court reform advocates for nonpartisan elections in the early twentieth century, and then disappointment with nonpartisan elections prompted a shift to the Missouri Plan in the mid-twentieth century (e.g., K. Hall 2005; Hanssen 2004). A recurring rhetorical theme in these movements is disenchantment with various manifestations of partisan politics and the politicization of the selection process.

These same arguments are driving the current campaign against partisan, nonpartisan, and—in some camps—retention elections. In the present debate, the features of modern judicial elections, including attack advertising and other issue-based discourse that can be part of aggressive, well-financed campaigns, are cast as serious threats to state courts, judicial legitimacy, and the rule of law. In this way, the focus has shifted away from protecting the power and integrity of state judiciaries from the other branches of government toward protecting the justices from the electorate, financial high rollers, and special interests seeking to control the outcomes of these races.

From the perspective of American constitutional theory, judicial selection represents a choice between the countermajoritarian difficulty ubiquitous to the federal courts and the majoritarian difficulty in most state courts. These constitutional quandaries lie at the center of the ever-present tension in the United States between law and democracy and represent two alternative approaches for structuring this tension.

Essentially, American constitutional democracy, with its system of judicial review, presents a choice between "how unelected/unaccountable judges can be justified in a political system committed to democracy" and how "elected and hence popularly accountable judges can be justified in a system committed to constitutionalism" (K. Hall 2005: 64). Kermit Hall notes that throughout the nation's history, this difficulty has been "at the center of the constitutional politics of most states" (K. Hall, 2005: 65). In fact, it seems reasonable to observe that because the decision has been made at the national level to opt for countermajoritarianism, the states have enjoyed greater latitude to experiment with the majoritarian difficulty. Nonetheless, both present intractable problems in the U.S. context.

Framing the Judicial Selection Debate

Rather than being discussed in theoretical terms as a fundamental question of democratic theory, debates about judicial selection typically are couched in normative terms as choices between the seemingly conflicting values of judicial independence versus accountability. Proponents of a strongly independent state judiciary tend to prefer that judges be appointed, while advocates for accountability tend to favor elections. However, both positions reflect basic beliefs about the best ways to promote the rule of law. As Tarr (2006: 3) effectively summarizes:

> Underlying the endemic conflict over judicial independence and judicial accountability are differing assessments of what are the most serious threats to the rule of law. Proponents of judicial independence emphasize the danger that pressures on judges may induce them to abandon their commitment to the rule of law in favor of what is popular or politically acceptable. But advocates of accountability see the danger primarily in the absence of checks on judges, which frees them to pursue their political or ideological or professional agendas at the expense of fidelity to law.

Geyh (2008: 86) frames the issue somewhat differently by identifying two primary aspects of judicial independence: (1) the ability of courts to act without encroachments from the legislative and executive branches and (2) the ability of courts to be free from "threats or intimidation that could interfere with their ability to uphold the rule of law." Thus, there must be a delicate balance "to ensure that judges are independent enough to follow the facts and law without fear or favor, but not so independent as to disregard the facts or law to the detriment of the rule of law and public confidence in the courts" (Geyh 2008: 86). Therein lies the extraordinarily complex and difficult challenge of state judicial reform.

These abiding concerns about promoting the rule of law and, specifically, how best to guard against illegitimate encroachments from both the popular will and the other branches of government while maintaining effective checks against unprincipled or incompetent judges, are not part of the public dialogue about legislative and executive elections. Quite obviously, the legislative and executive branches are designed to be majoritarian institutions closely connected to popular will, and in this regard citizens necessarily control the selection and retention of these officeholders. In the case of state judiciaries, many opponents of judicial elections raise fundamental questions about whether voters should play any role *at all* in the process. As with the debate about the propriety of issue- and partisan-based voting discussed in Chapter 1, the normative framing of the judicial selection debate introduces issues that are not part of the discussions about American elections generally. But at the heart of many of the concerns about judicial, legislative, and executive elections are attack advertising and other aspects of churlish campaigns.

A somewhat enigmatic aspect of the ongoing debate about state judicial selection is the fact that few reform advocates or members of the legal community have campaigned for the federal model of executive appointment, legislative confirmation, and lifetime tenure (Hanssen 2004). Even the American Bar Association's (2003) latest recommendations substantially modify the federal process by constraining executive appointments with nomination commissions and eliminating the legislative confirmation process. This reticence to endorse the federal model is complex and, as explained in the following discussion, relates in part to the goal of maximizing attorney influence in the judicial selection process. But until the ABA proposal in 2003, the reluctance to recommend appointment plans of any sort may have been a matter of sheer practicality. The American people overwhelmingly support electing the state court bench, even with today's concerns about campaign attacks and other aspects of highly competitive judicial elections (e.g., Geyh 2003; Gibson 2012).

Features of the Judicial Selection Debate

Several generalizations, all interrelated, are in order about the process of judicial selection reform. The first, just mentioned, is that the legal profession has been, and continues to be, chiefly responsible for designing and promoting the various plans for how state court judges are selected and retained. To some extent, this makes perfect sense given the centrality of the legal profession to the operations of these institutions. But this involvement also reflects the basic self-interest of state bar associations and other members of the legal profession in promoting their pivotal role in any selection scheme. This is particularly true of the Missouri Plan and commission-based appointment schemes.

Lawyers and bar associations are major players by design in judicial selection commissions, holding a formal role mandated by law in virtually every state.

Indeed, the dominance of attorneys and state bar associations is a long-standing criticism of the Missouri Plan. Fitzpatrick (2009) provides intriguing information about the composition of judicial nominating commissions across the states, including the minimum number of lawyers required by law. Of the twenty-four states (including a number of appointment states) using nominating commissions to screen high court justices and the District of Columbia (which also uses commissions), sixteen require that at least half of all commissioners be either lawyers or judges. In fifteen jurisdictions, at least half of the lawyer members are selected by bar associations, and in another ten states all of the attorney commissioners are selected by the bar. Lawyers and bar associations do not enjoy this strategic advantage in contestable elections.

The veritable monopoly over the public dialogue by the various segments of the legal community also has meant that many of the central arguments typically proffered about the advantages and disadvantages of the various selection schemes may lack empirical validity. Academicians and others in the legal community still tend to use logical reasoning and normative theories as primary tools, emphasizing what *should be*: judicial choices governed entirely by law. Although logic might tell us, for instance, that attack advertising may have especially pernicious effects on justices seeking reelection or that voters may be alienated by bruising campaigns, logical inference does not make it so. Many of these scholars likewise continue to rely on anecdotal observation, which also has serious limitations for generating robust inferences about complex political phenomena.[4]

In fact, many of the arguments used to support or oppose particular judicial selection systems are based on unverified assumptions and unsubstantiated claims. Among other things, for example, reform advocates have argued that nonpartisan and retention elections enhance the quality of the bench, provide a better basis for selecting judges than partisanship, and remove the stains of partisan politics. In practice, these promises have not been fulfilled. Judges do not vary in tangible qualifications across selection systems (e.g., Choi, Gulati, and Posner 2010; Glick and Emmert 1987; Hurwitz and Lanier 2008);[5] removing partisan labels suppresses voting, produces idiosyncratic outcomes, and raises the cost of seeking office[6] (e.g., Bonneau and M. G. Hall 2009; M. G. Hall 2001a, 2007a, 2007b; M. G. Hall and Bonneau 2008); and partisanship persists in nonpartisan and retention elections (e.g., M. G. Hall 2001a; Kritzer forthcoming; Squire and Smith 1988).

Specifically, empirical studies of state supreme courts have delineated the numerous ways in which nonpartisan and retention elections are intensely partisan. For instance, despite the claim that "judges not identified by party will escape the ebb and flow of partisan tides" (Herndon 1962: 67), the vote shares of the justices in both nonpartisan and retention elections are closely connected to patterns of state interpartisan competition and retrospective voting on the issue of violent crime (e.g., M. G. Hall 2001a; Kritzer forthcoming). In the same manner, retention elections may "easily be turned into partisan contests in the minds of voters" when the partisanship of an appointing governor becomes a surrogate voting cue for the incumbent's partisanship (Squire and Smith 1988: 70). Finally, nonpartisan elections show an underlying dimension of partisan voting that has increased substantially since the 1980s but is unrelated to recent trends in judicial elections, including television advertising and campaign negativity (Kritzer forthcoming). Specifically, county-level results in nonpartisan supreme court elections significantly correspond to partisan voting patterns in gubernatorial elections.

Perhaps even worse, the purported fixes to partisan elections—removing partisan labels (nonpartisan elections) and precluding challengers (retention elections)—exacerbated many of the most negative aspects of judicial elections, including voter disinterest, expensive campaigns, and interest group involvement (Bonneau and M. G. Hall 2009; M. G. Hall 2001a, 2007b, 2014b; M. G. Hall and Bonneau 2006, 2008). Thus, healthy skepticism is in order when thinking about the purported harms or benefits of any particular judicial selection scheme.

A somewhat different twist on the same problem is that, since the nation's inception, recommendations for reform have emphasized "depoliticizing" the selection process (e.g., American Bar Association Commission on the 21st Century Judiciary 2003; Schotland 1985; Tarr 2007). Although these arguments fit well with normative theories of judging, they seem largely out of touch with the political realities of judicial decision making and the judicial selection process, including appointments to the federal courts. A more realistic question in this regard is not how to remove politics from the process but rather which forms of politics are consistent with one's views about the proper role and function of state courts. Alleviating one set of problems by changing selection systems is no guarantee that worse consequences will not follow.

For instance, appointive systems (including the Missouri Plan) can be plagued by elitism, cronyism, and closed-door decision making, undesirable traits that also have the potential to undermine citizen confidence and judicial legitimacy (e.g., Dimino 2004, 2005; Fitzpatrick 2009; Schotland 1985; Tarr 2009; Ware 2009).[7] In reality, each selection system has advantages and disadvantages and, in large measure, reflects core beliefs about who should control access to the bench and monitor judicial performance.[8] Some selection processes give greater influence to political elites (the governor, state legislature, state bar association, and attorneys) while others place power in the hands of state citizenries. There are inherent drawbacks in both approaches.

In this regard, it is a long-standing belief of many in the legal community that voters, untrained in law, are not qualified to evaluate the performance of judges. As Geyh (2003: 59) asserts:

> It is one thing to expect voters with no training in the law to decide whether the policies favored by senators or governors (who may not be lawyers either) coincide with their own positions, and quite another to expect them to decide whether the rulings of judges coincide with the law.

This perspective illustrates well the clash between legal conceptualizations of the role of judges, voters, and elections in the judicial selection process and prevailing views about elections generally. According to at least some members of the legal community, because fidelity to law is the proper standard for evaluating judges, voters are unqualified to offer these assessments given their lack of legal technical skills and substantive knowledge of law. From this perspective, judges are characterized as highly specialized technicians applying law as a mechanical science. The corollary to this assertion is that because lawyers do possess the requisite skills, these professionals should play a critical role in the recruitment and retention of judges.[9] There are other implications flowing from the same set of theoretical principles. Attack advertising and issue-based discourse of any sort are evidence of system failure, as are electoral challenges and defeats of incumbents, who generally are presumed to be qualified. In fact, in order to highlight the perils of judicial elections and the need for radical reform, countless stories routinely are trotted out of judges being unfairly unseated, usually in response to some purported single cause such as a particularly derisive campaign attack ad or interest group sponsorship of advertising.

Of course, those who see the role of state supreme court justices as complex, including the ability of the justices to make both law and policy while interpreting and applying established legal rules, will question these assumptions and many of the inferences that follow. In fact, one hardly has to go so far as to view judges as mere politicians in robes to recognize that these officeholders, especially state supreme court justices, have considerable discretion to shape law and politics. But heretofore the public debate and the decisions of states about which selection schemes to adopt have been driven largely by normative assumptions, anecdotal evidence, and unverified contentions.

Why Electing Judges Is Almost Uniquely American

Many observers of judicial elections comment on the fact that the United States stands alone in electing state court judges.[10] The explanation for this is simple and straightforward. Few nations in the world share the unique confluence of institutional arrangements that give rise to state judicial elections. Foremost among these is federalism. To elect state court judges, there first must be states. Beyond this obvious point, federalism promotes "laboratories of democracy" in the states while guaranteeing fundamental rights and freedoms at the national level, supervised by electorally independent federal judges. Given the carefully engineered nexus between state governments and citizen preferences at the local level and the stringent guarantees of fundamental civil rights and liberties at the national level, the practice of electing judges emerged as a mechanism for insulating state judiciaries from legislative and executive encroachment while giving citizens a voice in the exercise of judicial power, including the authority to remove incompetent or arrogant judges.

Also contributing to the use of judicial elections are constitutional democracy, separation of powers with checks and balances, judicial review, and common law. Judges who act within this unusual configuration have extraordinary power and discretion that judges in other nations do not share.[11] Although not initially a primary motivation for adopting judicial elections, providing some measure of popular control of the bench is consistent with the modern trend toward the judicialization of politics and the recognition by a sizeable proportion of ordinary Americans that judges "make" law (e.g., Gibson and Caldeira 2011).

Justice Antonin Scalia acknowledged this point explicitly in *Republican Party of Minnesota* v. *White* (2002). As Justice Scalia argued:

> This complete separation of the judiciary from the enterprise of representative government might have some truth in those countries where judges neither make law themselves nor set aside the laws enacted by the legislature. It is not a true picture of the American system. Not only do state-court judges possess the power to make common law, but they have the immense power to shape the States' constitutions as well. Which is precisely why the election of state judges became popular.

Equally important, judicial elections are designed to safeguard the independence of the judiciary from the other branches of state government when serious conflicts endemic to separation of powers and checks and balances systems arise. On this score, elections are powerful legitimacy conferring institutions for state judiciaries. This also is true when the justices must weather occasional public dissatisfaction with unpopular court decisions.

Judicial Selection Systems in the American States

To provide a framework for assessing the use of judicial elections in the post-*White* era, Table 2-1 classifies the American states according to the current practices used to select and retain supreme court justices. As the table reveals, four basic types of systems currently operate in the fifty states: partisan elections, nonpartisan elections, the Missouri Plan (or "merit" plan), and appointment systems. Table 2-1 also includes terms of office, not only for states using elections but also for appointment plans with renewable terms.

Overall, thirty-eight states select and retain state supreme court justices in partisan, nonpartisan, or retention elections. As Table 2-1 also demonstrates, terms of office range from six to twelve years in elected courts and from six years to lifetime tenure in appointed courts. This reliance on fixed terms is one of the principal differences between state courts and the federal judiciary, where judges are appointed with lifetime tenure.

Most popular for selecting state supreme court justices is the Missouri Plan, of which retention elections are a part. This plan is still a recommended option by most court reform organizations, although the 2010 defeats of three Iowa Supreme Court justices in retention elections may change this.[12] Introduced formally in 1937 by the American Bar Association, with the enthusias-

TABLE 2-1. Selection systems and terms of office for state supreme courts, 2013.

Partisan elections	Term	Nonpartisan elections	Term	Missouri Plan (retention elections)	Term	Appointment systems	Term
Alabama	6	Arkansas	8	Alaska	10	Connecticut	8
Illinois*	10	Georgia	6	Arizona	6	Delaware	12
Louisiana	10	Idaho	6	California	12	Hawaii	10
New Mexico*	8	Kentucky	8	Colorado	10	Maine	7
Pennsylvania*	10	Michigan**	8	Florida	6	Massachusetts	Life
Texas	6	Minnesota	6	Indiana	10	New Hampshire	Life
West Virginia	12	Mississippi	8	Iowa	8	New Jersey	7
		Montana***	8	Kansas	6	New York	14
		Nevada	6	Maryland	10	Rhode Island	Life
		North Carolina	8	Missouri	12	South Carolina	10
		North Dakota	10	Nebraska	6	Vermont	6
		Ohio**	6	Oklahoma	6	Virginia	12
		Oregon	6	South Dakota	8		
		Washington	6	Tennessee	8		
		Wisconsin	10	Utah	10		
				Wyoming	8		

* Justices initially are selected in partisan elections but run in retention elections for subsequent terms (but only for uncontested seats in New Mexico).
** Partisan affiliations are not listed on general election ballots, but partisan methods (party conventions, partisan primaries) are used to nominate candidates.
*** Retention elections are used if the incumbent is unopposed.

SOURCE: American Judicature Society, *Judicial Selection in the States*, www.judicialselection.us; data are revised to reflect the coding rules in the notes designated above by asterisks.

tic endorsement of such organizations as the American Judicature Society, the Missouri Plan was first put into practice in Missouri in 1940.

The Missouri Plan is a hybrid system combining initial appointment with subsequent retention elections and, as Table 2-1 documents, is used in sixteen states. In this particular method, a nominating commission appointed by the governor screens candidates for each judgeship and ultimately recommends a short list of candidates for each vacancy. The governor then makes the official appointment, which must come from the commission's list. Once chosen by the governor, the nominee immediately assumes office but within a short time, usually the next general election, must win voter approval in a retention election. In these elections, challengers are not allowed, nor is the partisan affiliation of the candidate listed on the ballot. Instead, voters are asked to retain, or not retain, the incumbent. If successful, the judge begins a regular term of office and will come up for reelection as each term expires. If voters disapprove, the judge is removed and the selection process begins anew. In the states using retention elections, terms range from six to twelve years.

Almost as popular as the Missouri Plan are nonpartisan elections, which are used to select supreme court justices in fifteen states. The defining characteristic of nonpartisan elections is the absence of partisan labels on the ballot. But in two of these states (Michigan and Ohio), partisan processes are used to nominate candidates. In Michigan, supreme court candidates are nominated in party conventions. In Ohio, supreme court candidates are nominated in partisan primaries. Even so, partisan labels are not listed on general election ballots in Michigan or Ohio. Overall, terms of office in states using nonpartisan elections range from six to ten years.

Presently twelve states (Connecticut, Delaware, Hawaii, Maine, Massachusetts, New Hampshire, New Jersey, New York, Rhode Island, South Carolina, Vermont, Virginia) appoint their high court benches. Governors make these nominations except in South Carolina and Virginia, where state legislatures choose judges.[13] In some but not all gubernatorial appointment plans, the governor's nominations are restricted to the list of candidates forwarded by a nominating commission. Similarly, appointments must be confirmed by one or both houses of the state legislature except in Massachusetts and New Hampshire, where appointments are approved by an elected executive council. Only Massachusetts, New Hampshire, and Rhode Island provide lifetime tenure (subject to any mandatory retirement age provisions). In the remaining nine states, justices are appointed for terms ranging from six years (Vermont) to fourteen years (New York), with any subsequent terms subject to the approval of a judicial commission (Hawaii), governor, and/or one or both houses of the state legislature.[14]

Although appointive systems preclude any direct connection between voters and the bench, in nine of twelve states these plans authorize renewable terms rather than lifetime tenure. Justices in these states must be reappointed by the same process as their initial selection or by commission or state legislature.

Despite a deep commitment among modern judicial reform advocates to judicial independence, legislative selection and gubernatorial appointment plans have received scant attention or direct criticism. Currently nine states, a number that exceeds the number of states with partisan elections, use appointment systems in which supreme court justices must seek approval from the executive or legislative branch to continue in office. Structurally speaking, these courts are far from independent. In fact, some limited evidence suggests that justices subject to reappointment by other political elites act strategically to avoid retaliation (Brace, M. G. Hall, and Langer 1999; Langer 2002). At least on the hotly contested issue of abortion, these justices infrequently docket cases presenting constitutional challenges to state law and rarely invalidate legislation, ceteris paribus. In other words, appointment systems with fixed terms impair judicial review and undermine the system of separation of powers, which is precisely why judicial elections were adopted in the first place.

Finally, seven states use partisan elections in which the candidates' partisan affiliations are listed on the ballot. However, the picture is somewhat complicated. Illinois, New Mexico, and Pennsylvania use partisan elections for each justice's first term but then switch to retention elections for all subsequent terms. Consistent with other selection schemes, terms of office in partisan elections range from six to twelve years.

Interestingly, eight states use different methods to staff their trial courts. At the trial court level, the Missouri Plan is the least preferred method of judicial selection.[15] Indiana, New York, and Tennessee use partisan elections, and California, Florida, Maryland, Oklahoma, and South Dakota use nonpartisan elections. Overall, ten states use partisan elections, twenty states use nonpartisan elections, nine states use the Missouri Plan, and eleven states use appointment methods to recruit and retain the trial court bench.

There are other significant variations in judicial selection across the states beyond the four basic plans. For example, most retention elections require only a simple majority to win, but larger majorities are needed in Illinois (60 percent) and New Mexico (57 percent). Most elections are single member, but Michigan, Pennsylvania, and West Virginia hold some multimember elections. Most electoral constituencies are statewide, but some states (Illinois, Kentucky, Louisiana, Maryland, Mississippi, Nebraska) select supreme court justices from defined geographic districts within the state. Most elections are scheduled during the regular national election cycle, but Pennsylvania and Wisconsin conduct supreme court elections during odd years. As a final example, most states hold partisan primaries (separate elections for Democrats and Republicans) or nonpartisan primaries (all candidates run against each other without partisan labels) to nominate candidates. However, Louisiana holds blanket primaries, in which candidates of all parties run against each other but with partisan labels on the ballot.

In short, there is considerable variation across the states in how supreme court elections are conducted, including differences in timing, constituencies, nomination procedures, and votes needed to win. Generally speaking, these variations in institutional arrangements should influence the ways in which campaigns actually work, including the effectiveness of televised campaign advertising in shaping the election returns and the participatory propensities of the electorate. In this regard, anecdotal evidence is not sufficient for understanding complex processes across the great diversity of American states. Systematic comparative analysis is essential.

The Diffusion of Nonpartisan
Elections and the Missouri Plan

Since 1960, vituperative descriptions of judicial elections have motivated eighteen states to change the means by which they staff their supreme courts, including the most recent switch in North Carolina in 2004 (Council of State Governments 1960–2012). Of the twelve states abandoning partisan elections during this period, five adopted nonpartisan elections (Arkansas, Georgia, Kentucky, Mississippi, North Carolina), six opted for the Missouri Plan (Colorado, Florida, Indiana, Iowa, Oklahoma, Tennessee), and one state (New York) switched to gubernatorial appointment for state supreme court justices while retaining partisan elections for most trial court judges. Otherwise, six states moved from nonpartisan elections to the Missouri Plan (Arizona, Maryland, Nebraska, South Dakota, Utah, Wyoming). Currently, there are orchestrated efforts in Michigan, Minnesota, and Nevada to convince voters to abandon nonpartisan judicial elections, once a preferred method of selection.[16] In addition to these switches with elections, Rhode Island and Vermont changed from legislative to gubernatorial appointment plans.

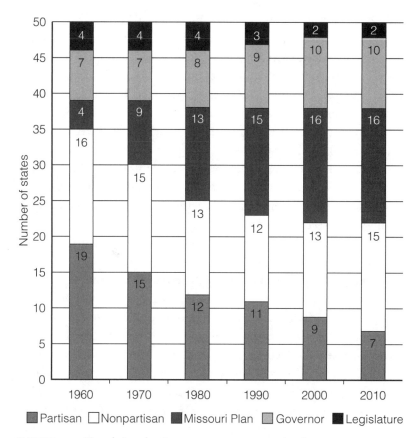

FIGURE 2-1. Trends in selecting state supreme court justices, 1960–2010.
SOURCES: Council of State Governments (1960–2008 editions of *Book of the States*), Hanssen (2004), and the American Judicature Society's *Judicial Selection in the States*, www.judicial selection.us.

Figure 2-1 illustrates these various trends well. Although the number of states electing judges has remained relatively constant since 1960, partisan elections have evolved from the most typical means for selecting state su-preme court justices to the least common electoral scheme. Nonpartisan elec-tions also have fluctuated but still survive as the second choice among states. The Missouri Plan has been the clear winner in popularity among selection schemes over the past six decades. Even so, the diffusion of the Missouri Plan appears to have stopped. No state has adopted this method since Tennessee made the switch in 1994.

Thinking about institutional change by decade, seven states (Colorado, Indiana, Iowa, Kentucky, Nebraska, Oklahoma, Utah) switched basic plans in the 1960s, five states (Arizona, Florida, Maryland, New York, Wyoming) changed in the 1970s, three states (Georgia, South Dakota, Vermont) transitioned in the 1980s, three states (Mississippi, Rhode Island, Tennessee) changed in the 1990s, and two states (Arkansas, North Carolina) switched in the 2000s.[17] Overall, the pace of institutional change has slowed considerably, but amid all of the institutional redesign taking place across the nation, no state has adopted a partisan election system in over a century. The last state to switch to partisan elections was Louisiana in 1904, although Oklahoma (in 1907) and New Mexico (in 1912) entered the Union with partisan judicial election plans in place (Hanssen 2004).[18]

In addition to fundamental system changes, Illinois and Pennsylvania retained partisan elections for initial terms but adopted retention elections for subsequent terms, and New Mexico opted to retain partisan elections for all contested seats but switched to retention elections for any uncontested seats. New Mexico's choice, which is the same type of system used in Montana with nonpartisan elections, is particularly interesting because the combination of partisan and retention elections actually increases the electorate's scrutiny of incumbents who are not challenged for reelection. Under typical circumstances, incumbents in partisan and nonpartisan elections have no possibility of losing if challengers do not enter these races. However, retention elections require voter approval even without challengers, so that unopposed incumbents still can lose their seats.

The Historical Record on State Supreme Court Electoral Competition

After what has been a decade-long halt in states making system-level changes in the way supreme court justices are selected and retained, the pressure is intensifying to eliminate contestable elections altogether. Fueling this renewed drive are misgivings about the nastier edges of campaign politics and other facets of aggressive competition in judicial elections.

But are state supreme court elections only recently competitive? Although scientific studies of state judicial elections in the earliest history of these races are rare, Kermit Hall (1984) provides some insight into this question with an intriguing description of state appellate court elections in California, Ohio,

Tennessee, and Texas from 1850 through 1920. In these races, 12.6 percent of incumbents who left office during this period were defeated and another 4.2 percent were denied renomination by their parties. These striking figures hardly suggest that these races were the equivalent of the oft-cited description of judicial elections as "about as exciting as a game of checkers, played by mail" (Bayne 2000).

Philip Dubois's seminal study of twenty-five non-Southern states from 1948 through 1974 provides additional insights. Dubois (1980) reported that defeat rates, which represent the most extreme form of electoral competition, were 19.0 percent in partisan elections and 7.5 percent in nonpartisan elections during this period. From a comparative perspective, the corresponding defeat rate in the U.S. House of Representatives, perhaps the nation's most representative institution by formal design, was 8.2 percent (Abramson, Aldrich, and Rohde 2012).[19]

These statistics reported by Dubois (1980) are comparable to those reported by M. G. Hall (2001a) for all states from 1980 through 1995, during which defeat rates averaged 18.8 percent in partisan elections and 8.6 percent in nonpartisan elections. The defeat rate for the U.S. House during this period was 6.5 percent (M. G. Hall 2001a). State supreme court election results shown in the following section for 1980 through 2010 tell the same story.

These facts were not unfamiliar to an astute group of political observers in the 1980s. Schotland's (1985: 78) iconic characterization of judicial elections as becoming "noisier, nastier, and costlier" was an observation about the 1970s and early 1980s. Similarly, after the 1986 and 1988 Ohio Supreme Court races, Hojnacki and Baum (1992: 944) described as "increasingly common" the "new style" campaigns that make "candidates and issues far more visible than in the average judicial contest."

Even in the popular press, an editorial in the *Los Angeles Times* (Chen 1988: 1) written in the aftermath of the famed 1986 defeats of three California Supreme Court justices observed the following:

> The intense public focus on [the California] high-stakes battle has all but obscured a trend that, some now say, threatens the independence and the moral foundations of the nation's judiciary. Throughout the country, judges increasingly are being forced to hit the campaign trail—to raise huge sums of money, often from special interest groups that have a tangible stake in the outcome of the cases before the courts . . . generating countless free-spending judicial campaigns all over the country.

The editorial specifically mentioned Ohio, Kentucky, Montana, Louisiana, North Carolina, Indiana, Oregon, Alabama, New York, Pennsylvania, Michigan, Texas, and California as states in which these expensive races were taking place. These thirteen states represent 34 percent of all states electing judges at that time and 60 percent of all states with contestable elections.[20] Generally speaking, it seems unlikely that these elections went entirely unnoticed by voters or were devoid of any electioneering by judges, challengers, political parties, or organized interests.

Despite these historical trends, many in the legal and advocacy communities would argue that past elections are largely irrelevant given transformative shifts in the nature of state supreme court elections after the U.S. Supreme Court's decision in *Republican Party of Minnesota v. White* (2002). Indeed, *White* is widely regarded as a "watershed" (Schultz 2006: 1011) that "significantly altered the landscape of judicial elections" (Caufield 2007: 39). The decision, derided in law reviews and the advocacy literature (e.g., American Bar Association Commission on the 21st Century Judiciary 2003; Caufield 2005, 2007; Geyh 2003; Goldberg and Sanchez 2003; Sample, Jones, and Weiss 2007; Schotland 2002; Schultz, 2006), has been predicted to have disastrous consequences for the state court bench by radically reshaping the conduct of elections.[21]

As Bonneau, M. G. Hall, and Streb (2011: 249) effectively summarize, "The basic argument is that by materially intensifying the politicization of state court elections by removing restrictions that helped to keep judicial candidates and their campaigns above the political fray, *White* will transform judicial elections into rancorous, below-the-belt exchanges dominated by special interests and other financial high rollers battling for undue influence in the judiciary." More specifically, Caufield (2005: 636) asserts that "there was (and is) general agreement [among legal scholars] that *White* is likely to produce longer, more contentious, and more costly judicial campaigns."[22]

These specific contentions are testable hypotheses. If Caufield (2005, 2007) and other pundits are correct, substantial shifts should be reflected in the key features of state supreme court elections after the *White* decision. Specifically, there should be discernable shifts in the propensity for challengers to take on incumbents, decreases in electoral support for incumbents, higher rates of defeat, and diminished voter participation. Indeed, these various features of supreme court elections are excellent indicators of a degenerating electoral climate for incumbents and free-for-all campaigns that pack a powerful punch.

Of course, these are not the only consequences that may have resulted from recent trends in campaign politics. However, the *White* decision, and the subsequent statutory revisions inspired by the decision (Caufield 2007), should have observable consequences for the justices and voters.

Contestation, Vote Shares, and Defeats in State Supreme Court Elections

To provide a detailed representation of modern state supreme court elections and to identify any temporal trends in electoral competition in recent years, the following figures and tables describe several defining features of these races from 1980 through 2010 in states using nonpartisan and partisan elections to staff their high courts. First consider Figure 2-2, which offers a graphical depiction of two different aspects of electoral competition: contestation rates for incumbents and rates of electoral defeat.[23] Defeat rates are measured in the standard way as the percentage of incumbents seeking reelection who lost, whether the race was contested or not. In Figure 2-2, contestation and defeat rates are shown for each election cycle from 1980 through 2010, separately for nonpartisan (n = 354) and partisan elections (n = 232). To simplify the presentation, I merged the small number of elections in odd years with elections in the prior year. Figure 2-2 also displays defeat rates for the U.S. House of Representatives, which provides a comparative baseline from which to gauge the competitiveness of state supreme court elections.

Overall, nonpartisan elections are far less competitive than partisan elections as evidenced by rates of contestation and rates of defeat. Average contestation over the entire series was 53.4 percent (189 of 354 incumbents seeking reelection) in nonpartisan elections and 72.8 percent (169 of 232 incumbents seeking reelection) in partisan elections. In only two election cycles (1980 and 1982) were justices in nonpartisan elections more likely to be challenged than justices in partisan elections.

Regarding electoral defeats, the overall defeat rate in partisan elections during this period was 20.7 percent (n = 48 of 232), compared with 8.2 percent (n = 29 of 354) in nonpartisan contests. In fact, defeat rates in partisan elections were higher than nonpartisan elections in twelve of sixteen election cycles. The exceptions are 1982, 1984, 2008, and 2010. Interestingly, in the last two election cycles shown (2008 and 2010), nonpartisan elections were considerably less electorally secure than partisan elections.

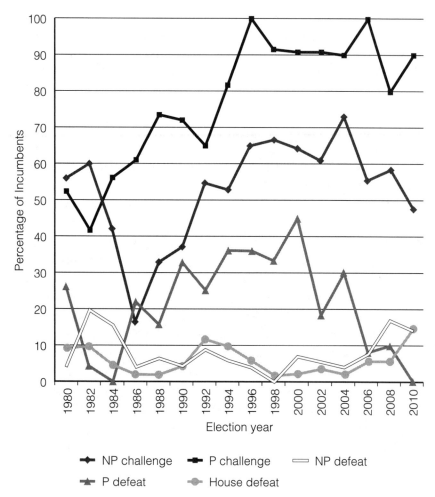

FIGURE 2-2. Contestation and defeat rates in state supreme court elections, 1980–2010.

SOURCE: For defeat rates in the U.S. House of Representatives: Abramson, Aldrich, and Rohde (2012).

In comparison, the defeat rate in U.S. House elections during this period was 5.9 percent (Abramson, Aldrich, and Rohde 2012). From 1980 through 2010, 375 of 6,359 members seeking reelection to the U.S. House were ousted from office. Thus, on average, both nonpartisan and partisan elections were less safe than House races.

Looking more specifically at temporal trends, Figure 2-2 indicates that rates of contestation in partisan state supreme court elections have increased dramatically, beginning with the pivotal year of 1984. Although only a bare majority (52.6 percent) of all incumbents seeking reelection were challenged in 1980, and even fewer in 1982 (41.7 percent), these rates have increased steadily and remain high. The most competitive years from the vantage point of challengers in partisan elections were 1996 and 2006, when all incumbents faced challengers during their reelection bids. But since 1996, contestation has remained at or above 90 percent except in 2008, when the rate fell to 80.0 percent.

In nonpartisan elections, temporal patterns in contestation are different. From 1982 to 1986, contestation declined precipitously (from 60.0 percent in 1982 to 16.7 percent in 1986) but then began to rise in 1988, up to 73.1 percent in 2004. In the last three election cycles, contestation rates have declined again. Interestingly, contestation in 1982 (60 percent) was higher than in 2006, 2008, and 2010. Likewise, 2010 (47.6 percent) was the least competitive year in nonpartisan supreme court elections challengers-wise since 1990 (37.5 percent).

Defeat rates also exhibit some interesting patterns. In partisan elections, the defeat rate in 1980 was 26.3 percent, but defeats then plummeted in 1982 and 1984. In fact, in 1984 all sixteen justices seeking reelection kept their seats. In 1986 defeat rates began to rise, peaking in 2000 at 45.5 percent. Since then, except for 2004, defeat rates in partisan elections have declined fairly steeply again. In fact, no justices seeking reelection in 2010 were defeated in partisan elections, only 8.3 percent lost in 2006, and only 10 percent were unseated in 2008. These are dramatic declines from the levels of the mid-1980s to 2000.

Nonpartisan state supreme court elections also had high defeat rates in the early 1980s. In 1982, 20 percent of all justices seeking reelection in these races were ousted, as were 15.8 percent in 1984. Afterward, defeats stayed below 10 percent to 2008 but then peaked again in 2008, to 17.2 percent. In 2010, the defeat rate declined somewhat to 14.3 percent. All things considered, nonpartisan elections were less electorally secure in 2008 and 2010 but still fell short of the 1982 levels.

From the perspective of recent change, pronounced increases are not evidenced in contestation and defeat rates since the U.S. Supreme Court's decision in *Republican Party of Minnesota* v. *White* (2002). Quite the contrary, trend lines in partisan contestation, nonpartisan contestation, and partisan defeats display downward trends. However, defeat rates in nonpartisan elections are consistent with the hypothesis of declining electoral security for incumbents starting in 2008. Nonpartisan defeat rates were higher in 2008 and 2010 than in election cycles after 1984 but generally have stayed under the ten percent mark except in 1982, 1984, 2008, and 2010.[24]

Defeat rates in the U.S. House (Abramson, Aldrich, and Rohde 2012), shown in Figure 2-2, illustrate well that both partisan and nonpartisan supreme court elections have been about as electorally insecure if not more so than elections to the nation's quintessential representative institution. Moreover, defeat rates in House races may be increasing as indicated by the 2010 rate, which was the highest over the series.

The Vote Shares of Incumbents

Figure 2-3 examines another dimension of state supreme court electoral competition: the percentage of the vote received by the incumbent. In Figure 2-3, these rates are displayed for all elections averaged and for contested races only, shown separately for nonpartisan and partisan elections for each election cycle from 1980 through 2010. Looking first at contested elections and overall averages, nonpartisan and partisan elections look very similar. Justices in contested nonpartisan elections received about 57.7 percent of the vote on average, and justices in partisan elections received 57.1 percent. Otherwise, looking across election cycles, average vote shares range from 52.7 percent to 65.6 percent in partisan elections, and from 53.0 percent to 63.6 percent in nonpartisan elections. Also, partisan and nonpartisan elections tie on the number of election cycles in which vote shares were lower (or higher) than the other election system. But what is particularly interesting about the trends in Figure 2-3 is that partisan contested elections have become more incumbent-friendly than nonpartisan elections in the last three election cycles.

When all elections are examined (both contested and uncontested races), partisan elections are more competitive than nonpartisan elections, in part because of their higher contestation rates. The only exception is the 1982 election cycle, when average vote shares were higher in partisan elections (a year in which the contestation rate was higher in nonpartisan elections, as Figure 2-2 indicates). Overall, vote shares averaged 76.6 percent in all nonpartisan elections from 1980 through 2010 and averaged 68.7 percent in partisan elections.

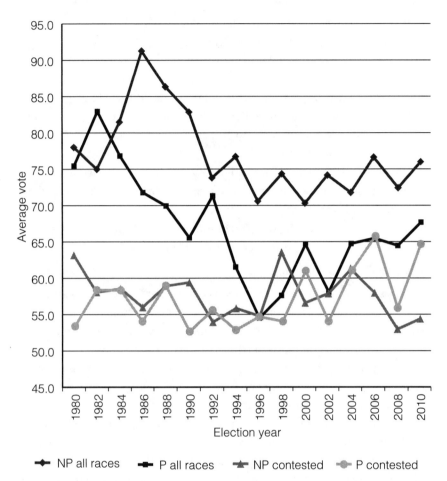

FIGURE 2-3. Average vote for incumbents in state supreme court elections, 1980–2010.

Turning to trends in recent years, Figure 2-3 indicates that partisan elections appear to be becoming safer for incumbents, in direct contradistinction to conventional wisdom about these races. In contested races, vote shares in partisan elections averaged at or less than 55 percent during the 1990s. The elections in 2002 and 2008 also hovered around the 55 percent benchmark. However, vote shares increased substantially in 2000, 2004, 2006, and 2010, reaching a peak of 65.6 percent in 2006.

Recent trends in contested nonpartisan elections are harder to discern. The lowest level of electoral support for incumbents was in 2008, at

53.0 percent. However, one of the highest rates was in 2004, at 61.4 percent. Although 2008 was a tough year for incumbents, 2004 and 2006 were average or better, especially 2004. In 2010, average vote shares looked fairly similar though slightly better than in 2008. Thus, there is some evidence that electoral insecurity has increased in contested nonpartisan elections in recent years, but this conclusion is driven by the 2008 and 2010 elections. Average vote shares actually improved in the first two election cycles after the *White* decision relative to 2000 and 2002.

In all elections, contested or not, Figure 2-3 shows that average vote shares in nonpartisan elections dropped precipitously from 1986 to 1992 but then have fluctuated since from about 70 to 77 percent. In partisan contests, there are steep declines in electoral support for incumbents from 1982 to 1996 but rising vote shares for the rest of the series except in 2002.

Electoral Competition for Open Seats

Open seats (not shown) in both nonpartisan and partisan elections are hotly contested.[25] From 1980 through 2010, average contestation in nonpartisan elections for eighty-two supreme court seats was 90.2 percent, hitting a low of 66.7 percent in 1998. In partisan elections, the contestation rate for 105 seats was 94.3 percent, with a low of 72.7 percent in 1990.[26] By this measure, partisan elections are somewhat more competitive than nonpartisan elections.

Vote shares received by the winning candidates in open-seat elections average 58.2 percent in nonpartisan elections and 59.3 percent in partisan elections, figures that are fairly close to average votes for incumbents in contested races in each system. By this measure, nonpartisan elections are slightly more competitive than partisan elections. There are no obvious temporal trends in any of these data or any significant differences between nonpartisan and partisan elections.

Electoral Competition in the American States

A different way of thinking about electoral competition is to examine differences across the states. Table 2-2 summarizes average rates of contestation, vote shares for challengers, unsafe seats (won by 55 percent of the vote or less), and defeat rates in state supreme court elections from 2000 through 2010. The vote shares variable is calculated for challengers rather than incumbents so that all four indicators are scaled in the same direction, with electoral insecurity for incumbents increasing as the values of each variable increase.

TABLE 2-2. Electoral competition for incumbents in state supreme courts, 2000–2010.*

State	N	Percentage contested	Percentage vote against	Percentage unsafe	Percentage defeated	2000–2010 score	1980–1999 score
Alabama	11	100.0	43.8	45.5	36.4	56.4	30.3
Arkansas	8	25.0	9.3	0.0	0.0	8.6	10.1
Georgia	14	35.7	12.6	0.0	0.0	12.1	12.3
Idaho	9	44.4	20.9	22.2	11.1	24.7	2.2
Illinois	3	66.7	39.7	66.7	33.3	51.6	NA
Kentucky	10	50.0	24.5	40.0	20.0	33.6	42.4
Louisiana	5	40.0	14.9	0.0	0.0	13.7	30.6
Michigan	12	100.0	42.4	41.7	16.7	50.2	45.2
Minnesota	14	71.4	25.0	7.1	0.0	25.9	15.7
Mississippi	14	92.9	45.8	57.1	35.7	57.9	26.2
Montana	3	66.7	28.7	33.3	0.0	32.2	51.0
Nevada	10	60.0	38.8	50.0	10.0	39.7	27.0
New Mexico	2	50.0	21.2	0.0	0.0	17.8	35.4
North Carolina	9	100.0	44.5	55.6	33.3	58.4	43.2
North Dakota	7	14.3	6.2	0.0	0.0	5.1	12.7
Ohio	12	83.3	37.0	33.3	8.3	40.5	50.1
Oregon	11	18.2	7.8	0.0	0.0	6.5	7.2
Texas	35	97.1	33.6	22.9	5.7	39.8	53.8
Washington	15	73.3	30.2	20.0	6.7	32.6	18.3
West Virginia	4	100.0	48.6	75.0	50.0	68.4	50.0
Wisconsin	5	40.0	18.3	20.0	20.0	24.6	24.8

* Pennsylvania is not included because all races were for open seats.

Additionally, Table 2-2 presents a composite electoral insecurity score for each state based on the formula used to generate Holbrook–Van Dunk (1993) state electoral competition scores. Specifically, Holbrook and Van Dunk (1993) used four indicators of district-level state legislative competition—contestation, vote shares, unsafe seats (55 percent or less), and margins of victory—to generate a composite score for each American state. Basically, they calculated a separate score on each of the four different dimensions of competition, added the four scores, and divided by four for each state.

I replicated this process with one exception. Because state supreme court elections have much higher defeat rates than state legislative elections, I replaced margins of victory (which are closely related to vote shares) with defeats. As Holbrook and Van Dunk noted (1993), any one of these indicators could serve as a robust measure of electoral competition, but with all four indicators averaged together the measure is more valid and reliable.

For state supreme court elections, I calculated competition scores separately for 2000–2010 and 1980–1999, to facilitate temporal comparisons within states. For those who prefer other approaches to conceptualizing competition, the data in Table 2-2 can be used to rank states separately on each dimension or in whatever combination is preferred.

As the figures in Table 2-2 document, states vary considerably on multiple dimensions. Regarding contestation rates, states range from contexts in which most justices avoid challengers (as evidenced by contestation rates of 25 percent or less in Arkansas, North Dakota, and Oregon) to all incumbents having to face challengers (in Alabama, Michigan, North Carolina, and West Virginia). With the vote shares of challengers (shown for all races, whether contested or not), average percentages range from less than 20 percent in Arkansas, Georgia, Louisiana, North Dakota, Oregon, and Wisconsin to over 40 percent in Alabama, Michigan, Mississippi, North Carolina, and West Virginia. From the perspective of unsafe seats, or winning with 55 percent of the vote or less, the least competitive states are Arkansas, Georgia, Louisiana, New Mexico, North Dakota, and Oregon. These states had no marginal wins from 2000 through 2010. At the other extreme are Illinois, Mississippi, North Carolina, and West Virginia. On the issue of incumbents being ousted, eight states have never had a supreme court justice voted out of office. Alternatively, in West Virginia half of all incumbents lose.[27]

Thinking about temporal trends by comparing composite competition scores for 1980–1999 and 2000–2010, Table 2-2 indicates that nine states (Alabama, Idaho, Michigan, Minnesota, Mississippi, Nevada, North Carolina, Washington, and West Virginia) have become less electorally secure, nine states (Arkansas, Kentucky, Louisiana, Montana, New Mexico, North Dakota, Ohio, Oregon, and Texas) are safer, and two states (Georgia and Wisconsin) have stayed virtually the same.[28]

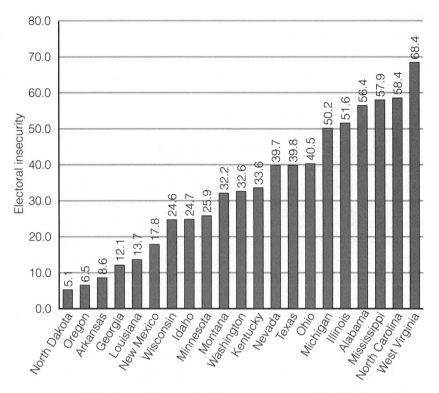

FIGURE 2-4. The electoral insecurity of state supreme court justices by state, 2000–2010.

Figure 2-4 provides a useful visual depiction of the states based on their composite competition scores for 2000–2010. The states are arrayed in Figure 2-4 from least to most electorally insecure. Notably, there is little to suggest a tendency toward electoral insecurity in a sizeable number of states. At less than the 30 percent mark are North Dakota, Oregon, Arkansas, Georgia, Louisiana, New Mexico, Wisconsin, Idaho, and Minnesota. These scores and rankings should not be interpreted to mean that no seats in these states were ever intensely contested or that incumbents were not occasionally unseated, but on average high-intensity contests are far less likely in these states than in others. At the other end of the spectrum are Michigan, Illinois, Alabama, Mississippi, North Carolina, and West Virginia. In the middle, from least to most competitive, are Montana, Washington, Kentucky, Nevada, Texas, and Ohio. Of the six partisan election states being ranked, two (Louisiana and

New Mexico) are relatively uncompetitive, one (Texas) is moderately competitive, and three (Illinois, Alabama, West Virginia) are at the highest end of the scale. Likewise, nonpartisan elections are distributed along the continuum and are found at both ends of the scale.

Citizen Participation as Ballot Roll-Off

Although electoral competition is a vital aspect of state supreme court elections, citizen participation also is a primary feature of these races and is closely connected to the most serious concerns about the consequences of piercing campaign negativity. Indeed, most scientific studies of attack advertising (e.g., Ansolabehere and Iyengar 1995; Finkel and Geer 1998; Jackson and Carsey 2007) focus on voters and their propensity for civic engagement.

In this project, I examine citizen participation by assessing ballot roll-off, defined as the percentage of voters who go to the polls who do *not* vote in the state supreme court election. With this measure, higher values indicate lower levels of citizen participation in state supreme court races. As discussed in greater detail in Chapter 5, measuring citizen participation as ballot roll-off rather than voter turnout has distinct analytical advantages in down-ballot elections, primarily by sidestepping complex specifications related to the most visible races driving voter mobilization.

For an interesting visual depiction of citizen participation in state supreme court elections over the past three decades, Figure 2-5 displays average roll-off rates for each election cycle from 1980 through 2010 in both incumbent–challenger races and open-seat contests, shown for all elections and for contested races only.[29] Because the concern with ballot roll-off is with voters rather than justices seeking reelection, both incumbent–challenger and open-seat races are relevant. As in other presentations, nonpartisan and partisan elections are shown separately for each election cycle.

As Figure 2-5 reveals, and as we would expect, average ballot roll-off in both partisan and nonpartisan elections tends to be higher when contested and uncontested races are considered together. Naturally some of these differences shrink or disappear as rates of contestation rise. Overall, ballot roll-off averaged 25.8 percent in nonpartisan elections ($n = 288$) and 17.1 percent in partisan elections ($n = 229$) from 1980 through 2010. When only contested races are counted, average roll-off rates fall to 21.0 percent in nonpartisan elections ($n = 193$) and 13.4 percent in partisan elections ($n = 200$). As a size-

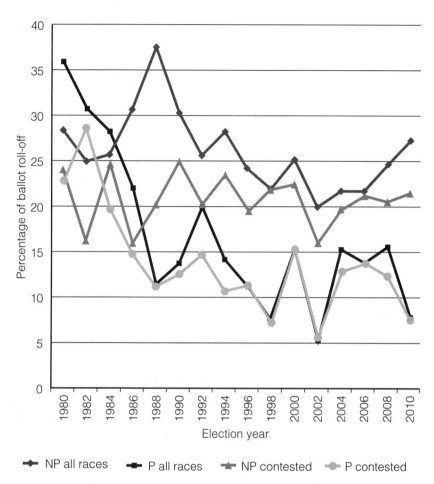

FIGURE 2-5. Ballot roll-off in state supreme court elections, 1980–2010.

able body of research suggests, nonpartisan elections and the absence of competition dampen citizen participation in state supreme court elections, as in
elections to other offices in the United States.

In contested races, no temporal shifts are immediately apparent in nonpartisan elections. Contrary to serious concerns about the harmful effects
of contemporary campaigns and other developments in state supreme court
elections, there is no evidence that ballot roll-off has increased in recent election cycles. Instead, average roll-off rates in the last few election cycles look
very similar to those in the 1980s and 1990s. Generally, in contested nonpartisan elections, the highest and lowest peaks in ballot roll-off were in earlier

decades, with the exception of a big dip in 2002 (indicating higher levels of citizen participation).

In all nonpartisan elections (contested and uncontested), we see an overall decline in ballot roll-off since 1988 but increases in 2008 and 2010. Even so, the 2008 rate falls at or below the levels of the 1980s and 1990s. The 2010 rate, which approaches 1994 levels, is likely strongly connected to a low contestation rate (47.6 percent).

Partisan elections are another matter. Ballot roll-off has decreased substantially in these races, particularly from the early 1980s. This trend is clearly evidenced in all state supreme court races and in contested elections in particular. In other words, larger proportions of the electorate on average now vote in partisan elections than in earlier decades, a pattern inconsistent with the demobilization hypothesis and claims about the dangers of modern election campaigns for state electorates.

Testing for Post-*White* Trends Systematically

The various tables and figures just presented about state supreme court elections reveal some surprising truths. Contrary to conventional wisdom, these races have not been staid affairs from the perspective of the willingness of challengers to take on incumbents and the electorate's propensity to vote against sitting justices or oust them from office. In fact, state supreme court elections were competitive long before the onslaught of televised campaigns, vicious attack advertising, exorbitant spending, or the *White* decision. The exception seems to lie with contestation rates in nonpartisan elections, which have been significantly lower than contestation rates in partisan elections and appear to be declining. Similarly from the perspective of civic engagement, there is little evidence of widespread alienation or the disinclination of state electorates to vote in recent years.

Although descriptive tendencies are interesting and provide valuable insights, systematic tests are essential for drawing robust inferences about any temporal trends in the data. To this end, I replicate Bonneau, M. G. Hall, and Streb (2011) by examining differences in various indicators of competition and citizen involvement before and after the *White* decision.[30] *Republican Party of Minnesota* v. *White* (2002) is widely regarded as having marshaled in a new era of campaign politics, including the widespread reliance on televised campaigns and harsh negativity targeting state supreme court justices.

The logic of the empirical tests is straightforward. If trends in the electoral climate are as profound as generally expressed, these effects should be evidenced in the principal features of state supreme court elections, including an attenuated incumbency advantage and diminished citizen participation after 2002. To analyze changes in recent election cycles, and consistent with the strategy employed by Bonneau, M. G. Hall, and Streb (2011), I examine differences in various indicators of electoral competition and ballot roll-off in the four election cycles prior to *White* (1994, 1996, 1998, 2000) and the four election cycles after *White* (2004, 2006, 2008, 2010).[31] Because *White* was decided in June 2002, after the primaries but before the general election, I treat the 2002 elections as a separate category, which avoids having to make a value judgment about whether 2002 should be considered pre- or post-*White*.

In analyzing the presence or absence of challengers and the electoral success or defeat of incumbents, both of which are dichotomous variables, I use probit to estimate models that include as independent variables a dummy variable for the 2002 election cycle and a dummy variable for the post-*White* period. To assess trends in incumbent vote shares and ballot roll-off, both of which are continuous variables, I use ANOVA (analysis of variance) with the same independent variables. As a robustness check, I also employ OLS (ordinary least squares) regression as an alternative estimation technique. In all of the tests, I omit pre-*White* to avoid perfect collinearity.

Table 2-3 shows the mean values of each measure of electoral competition and ballot roll-off for each of the three periods being analyzed: pre-*White* (1994–2001), *White* (2002), and post-*White* (2003–2010). Table 2-3 also indicates which variables attained statistical significance in the hypothesis tests.

In nonpartisan elections, there are no statistically discernable changes in contestation, defeats, vote shares, or ballot roll-off in the post-*White* period. In fact, none of the post-*White* variables is significant in any of the models for nonpartisan elections. In partisan elections, the only statistically significant results are *opposite* to those predicted by most commentators, especially the scathing reviews of the *White* decision in the mountain of law review articles and political advocacy on this topic. As Table 2-3 shows, electoral defeats have declined while vote shares have increased in partisan elections in the post-*White* period. Stated differently, on two key dimensions, state supreme court elections have become more electorally secure for incumbents and more interesting to voters when partisan ballots are used to select judges.

TABLE 2-3. Features of state supreme court elections, pre-*White* and post-*White*.

	Nonpartisan elections	Partisan elections
Contestation[a]		
Pre-*White* (1994–2001)	63.5% (85)	91.1% (45)
2002	61.1% (18)	90.9% (11)
Post-*White* (2003–2010)	59.2% (103)	90.5% (42)
Defeat[a]		
Pre-*White* (1994–2001)	4.7% (85)	37.8% (45)
2002	5.6% (18)	18.2% (11)
Post-*White* (2003–2010)	10.7% (103)	11.9% (42)*
Vote shares[b]		
Pre-*White* (1994–2001)	57.6% (54)	55.5% (41)
2002	57.6% (11)	53.9% (10)
Post-*White* (2003–2010)	57.1% (61)	62.1% (38)*
Ballot roll-off		
Pre-*White* (1994–2001)	21.6% (58)	11.3% (52)
2002	16.0% (8)	5.4% (13)*
Post-*White* (2003–2010)	20.4% (58)	11.8% (43)
Total candidate spending[c]		
Pre-*White* (1996–2001)	$ 790,675 (55)	$1,226,406 (50)
2002	$1,109,959 (12)	$ 992,046 (12)
Post-*White* (2003–2008)	$ 762,568 (56)	$1,492,871 (32)

$* = p < 0.05$
[a] All races in which incumbents are seeking reelection
[b] Contested incumbent–challenger races only
[c] All contested elections, including incumbent–challenger and open-seat races. These figures are taken from Bonneau, M. G. Hall, and Streb (2011).

These results are entirely consistent with Kritzer's (forthcoming) study of all state supreme court elections from 1946 through 2012. In this intriguing new work, Kritzer systematically tests for temporal trends in a variety of ways, including comparisons between the first eleven years (1946–1956) and the last eleven years (2002–2012) of the series. Perhaps the most distinctive finding is that the electoral security of incumbents has *not* changed appreciably since the 1940s–1950s. Kritzer attributes any modest changes to trends in partisan elections in the South but concludes that the overall pattern of electoral competition in state supreme court elections since the 1940s is "one of relative stability."

Even if *White* has had no immediate electoral consequences for incumbents or voters, the decision still may be altering the campaigns themselves though no manifestations of these effects are yet apparent in the election returns. But how prevalent are attack ads, and are they "metastasizing" across the nation? This issue is considered in Chapter 3, and the effects of campaign negativity are evaluated systematically in Chapter 4 and Chapter 5.

Campaign Spending

One final aspect of state supreme court elections merits attention: campaign spending. In fact, the rising costs of campaigns and the involvement of various organized interests, including wealthy single-issue groups, are a central concern in the contemporary judicial reform movement.[32] Closely related are trepidations about the costs of television advertising, including the use of attack advertising to challenge incumbents and remove them from office. As with campaign negativity, these apprehensions about money are not unique to judicial elections. Instead, the undue influence of special-interest money is a highly salient and growing concern in American politics generally.

Of course, some campaign spending is essential to efficacious elections. Money is used in campaigns to educate and motivate voters and to transform races from lackluster events into meaningful electoral contests. Without some spending by the candidates and other political activists including political parties, voters are likely to know little and care less, particularly when partisan labels are removed from ballots.

That the costs of campaigns have risen in the past few decades is a well-documented trend in the scholarly and advocacy literatures. For example, Bonneau (2007) and Bonneau and M. G. Hall (2009) have shown that campaign costs for the candidates have increased steadily since 1990, one of the first election cycles for which systematic data have been gathered for all states. Likewise, Bonneau (2007) and Bonneau and M. G. Hall (2009) have provided comprehensive multivariate models that explain rising campaign expenditures by state supreme court candidates. Among the most important factors reducing the costs of campaigns, ceteris paribus, are multiple seats being contested in the same election cycle and multimember elections. Factors that raise the costs of seeking office are nonpartisan elections, longer terms of

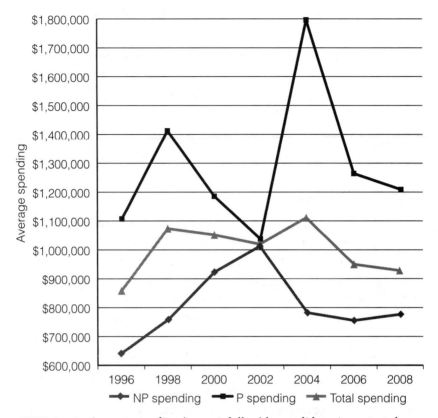

FIGURE 2-6. Average spending (in 2008 dollars) by candidates in contested state supreme court elections, 1996–2008.

office, dockets with larger proportions of tort cases, and close margins of victory. Finally, Bonneau, M. G. Hall, and Streb (2011) have demonstrated that any increases in campaign spending by supreme court candidates began long before the *White* decision or televised campaign advertising and did not shift appreciably in or just after 2002.

To provide a brief update on campaign spending in recent campaigns beyond the work already available on this topic, Figure 2-6 displays average total expenditures by state supreme court candidates in contested elections from 1996 through 2008. These figures are reported in 2008 dollars, to adjust for inflation.

A significant limitation of these figures is that they do not include independent spending by organized interests or other parties outside the candidates' campaigns. There simply is no reliable way to estimate these costs given significant variations across the states in reporting and disclosure requirements. As we would expect, information about independent spending also is not part of the candidates' financial disclosure reports, which are the basis for this analysis. Regarding the costs of televised advertising, I consider these figures separately in Chapter 3, which discusses advertising in detail, including the sponsorship of ads by organizations and interests independent of the candidates' campaigns.

As Figure 2-6 documents, average spending per race has increased from 1996 through 2008 but not monotonically and, in numerous election cycles, not more than in 1998. In nonpartisan elections, average campaign spending by candidates rose from 1996 to 2002, declined substantially from 2002 to 2004, and leveled off steadily to 2008. In contrast, average candidate spending in partisan elections rose from 1996 to 1998, decreased in 2000 and 2002, peaked sharply in 2004, and declined again through 2008. The steep increase in 2004 was largely the result of two unusually exorbitant races in Illinois and West Virginia, which grossly inflate the statistic.

As with the previous discussions of electoral competition and citizen participation, I ask whether any differences in pre- and post-*White* spending are statistically significant. To answer this question, I applied the same basic methodology to candidate spending that was just used with contestation, defeats, vote shares, and ballot roll-off. Specifically, I compare the three election cycles prior to *White* (1996–2000) to the three election cycles after (2004–2008) using ANOVA and OLS regression. These results also are reported in Bonneau, M. G. Hall, and Streb (2011).

As Table 2-3 illustrates, in both nonpartisan and partisan elections, there are no significantly discernable differences in candidate spending between the pre-*White* and post-*White* periods. These results are robust regardless of whether ANOVA or OLS regression is used, and when spending is measured in per capita terms (not shown), as previous work demonstrates (Bonneau, M. G. Hall, and Streb 2011).

These findings comport well with those reported by Kritzer (forthcoming), who shows that changes in campaign spending in state supreme court elections parallel trends in other elections starting in the 1980s and then increasing substantially in the 1990s.

As an alternative, some readers reasonably might ask whether 2000 rather than 2002 was the pivotal year in campaign financing (Brandenburg and

Caufield 2009; Brandenburg and Schotland 2008), or a "dangerous turn-ing point for . . . the growing, systematic, and unprecedented infusion of big money . . . pressure into the election of Supreme Court justices across the country" (Goldberg, Holman, Sanchez 2001: 4). Brandenburg and Schotland (2008: 1237) argue that money was seeping into judicial elections back into the 1980s but that "the breakthrough year for big-money campaigns was 2000," so that the "growth in total spending was sudden and dramatic." To explore this assertion, I analyzed differences in candidate spending in the 1996–1999 elections compared first with the 2000–2003 elections and then with the 2000–2008 elections. Nothing was statistically significant.

Thus, the interjection of outside money into state supreme court elections has not been met with any radical changes in campaign spending by the can-didates or observable shifts in various forms of electoral competition or citi-zen participation in these races. This is not to say that scholars, pundits, prac-titioners, and citizens should not be concerned about unrestrained campaign spending independent of the candidates, which may have increased consid-erably, or that there are no other possible adverse effects than those tested above. However, the very good news is that any financial involvement in state supreme court elections by well-heeled political activists has yet to alter some of the most basic and politically significant features of these races.

Conclusion

In somewhat surprising ways, both partisan and nonpartisan state supreme court elections fall substantially short of the pejorative stereotype of having been politically uninteresting before the advent of televised campaign adver-tising, changes in the campaign dialogue brought about by *Republican Party of Minnesota v. White* (2002), and soaring spending by candidates and other political activists. The evidence shown in this chapter, as well as other empiri-cal studies of state supreme court elections going back to the 1940s, reveals a more complex reality. In fact, state supreme court elections have been highly competitive for decades, which casts serious doubts about the validity of the earliest charges that judicial elections were institutional failures with regard to their ability to promote a reasonable degree of electoral accountability.

In this regard, this chapter did not find any evidence of the portended transformative effects of the *White* decision on the most basic features of state supreme court elections. As Bonneau, M. G. Hall, and Streb (2011) noted, the impact of this decision has been exaggerated, at least with regard to observable consequences for the ability of incumbents to run well and win, the willingness of voters to participate, and levels of actual spending by the candidates to promote their chances of success. If *White* has altered the nature of campaign dialogue or the ways in which state supreme court candidates engage the electorate, these changes are not evidenced in adverse ways in some of the defining features of these races.

Of course, the American states are not equally competitive. Additional work is needed to explain patterns across the states and to devise better measures of electoral insecurity. Similarly, care must be taken in multivariate models to capture these important state-level variations and to assess their impact on the effectiveness of campaigns and other significant aspects of judicial elections.

Concerning the incumbency advantage and the primary hypothesis to be tested in Chapter 4, any heightened efforts in recent years by interest groups and other political heavyweights to oust incumbents through the use of punishing televised attacks and other tactics associated with gutter politics are not evidenced in partisan elections. Although contestation rates in partisan elections have risen over the past few decades, average vote shares are up and defeat rates are down. In other words, the electoral security of incumbents has increased in recent years in partisan elections, in statistically significant ways. However, nonpartisan elections exhibit somewhat mixed trends. In 2010, the contestation rate in nonpartisan elections was at its lowest since 1990, but defeat rates increased and vote shares declined in 2008 and 2010. Nonetheless, these changes are not statistically significant when compared with the election cycles immediately preceding the *White* decision. Multivariate tests are needed to facilitate more robust inferences, but evidence just presented does not clearly indicate an increasingly hostile climate for incumbents in nonpartisan elections.

Regarding citizen participation and the empirical tests in Chapter 5, the overall body of evidence at the descriptive level does not support the contention that expensive highly competitive elections inhibit voting in state supreme court elections. Quite the contrary, the propensity of state electorates to vote in these elections has increased since the 1980s. Rather unpredictable at this point is how those in the legal community will view higher levels of citizen participation, particularly if influenced by televised attack campaigns. However, in the political science literature, stronger levels of citizen engagement are sharply inconsistent with arguments about losses of citizen confidence in state judiciaries and the deleterious effects of aggressive campaigning.

Through the lens of judicial politics scholarship, it is essential to observe that state supreme court electoral competition and ballot roll-off are not random events. Numerous studies have documented that electoral competition in numerous forms is a systematic response to the candidates, the political context, and institutional arrangements (e.g., Bonneau and Cann 2011; Bonneau and M. G. Hall 2003, 2009; M. G. Hall 2001a, 2014b; M. G. Hall and Bonneau 2006; Hojnacki and Baum 1992). The same is true of citizen participation (e.g., Baum and Klein 2007; Bonneau and M. G. Hall 2009; M. G. Hall 2007b; M. G. Hall and Bonneau 2008, 2013). The results in Chapter 4 and Chapter 5 provide additional evidence of this essential fact while testing hypotheses about televised attack advertising and other forms of campaign messages broadcast to voters.

Finally, although some (e.g., Brandenburg and Caufield 2009) argue that the biggest shifts in campaign financing and big money in judicial elections began in 2000, there is evidence to suggest that substantial changes began to occur in the nature of both candidate spending and independent spending starting in the early 1980s. Shugerman (2012: 241) points to the 1980s as the time when "businesses returned to trying to win judicial elections outright, and they did so by . . . pouring money into key races." Kritzer (forthcoming) also observes that, although "it has long been common for those with strong interests in the decisions of courts—trial lawyers, labor organizations—to contribute to campaigns and otherwise be active in judicial selection at the state level," it was in the 1980s that business groups started to become involved.

Nonetheless, independent spending in state supreme court elections and the parties who engage in these activities may be changing. Whether these trends are evidenced in the sponsorship of televised campaign advertising is examined in Chapter 3, along with other trends in the use of the airwaves in state supreme court elections.

3   Campaign Advertising in State
Supreme Court Elections

I N A 2006 RACE FOR THE GEORGIA SUPREME COURT, THE FOL-
lowing televised message was broadcast to voters:

[Announcer]: "Mike Wiggins was sued by his own mother for taking her
money. He sued his only sister. She said he threatened to kill her while she was
eight months pregnant. A judge ordered Wiggins never to have contact with her
again. Mike Wiggins. The wrong experience. The wrong values for the Supreme
Court."[1]

This blistering advertisement, sponsored by incumbent Carol Hunstein in
her bid against challenger Mike Wiggins, illustrates well the controversy over
televised attack advertising in American politics. Thoughtful viewers wit-
nessing such a hard-hitting personal attack reasonably might have numerous
immediate concerns, including questions about whether this startling information is accurate, whether these accusations will determine who wins the
election, and whether these types of caustic ads will diminish citizens' positive perceptions of judges and courts. Indeed, withering assaults on opposing
candidates and the reactions these ads provoke are at the heart of the controversy over televised campaigns for state judiciaries and the ongoing debate
about the practice of electing judges.[2]

Of course, not all televised campaign advertisements, including attack ads,
are as damning and vitriolic as the 2006 Georgia ad. Televised advertisements
in state supreme court elections run the gamut from lighthearted and funny

to brutal. At the innocuous end of the scale are cheerful messages designed to facilitate name recognition and portray candidates as having esteemed values or close connections to the community. An excellent example is a spot in the 2008 West Virginia multimember races that distinguished challenger Menis Ketchum from the "Ketchup guy running for the Supreme Court." "Ketchum, not ketchup" was repeated throughout the ad.[3] Another comes from the 2008 Mississippi races featuring challenger Jim Kitchens's wife asking voters to keep Jim Kitchens out of her kitchen by electing him to the Supreme Court.[4]

At the other end of the spectrum are claims of egregious conflicts of interest and deficits of integrity, including accusations of candidates being in the pockets of special interests or otherwise beholden to campaign donors who are unpopular in the state. The 2008 West Virginia races are legendary for featuring photographs of Chief Justice Elliot "Spike" Maynard together with Don Blankenship, CEO of Massey Energy, on the French Riviera. The ad, sponsored by challenger Bob Bastress, asserted that "later the justice ruled in favor of the coal baron's company in a $50 million dollar case."[5] Chief Justice Maynard was ousted from office in the primary.

Despite the objectionable nature of some campaign advertisements to some viewers, classic studies have shown the surprising ability of very short messages to educate voters. In a seminal study on this topic, Patterson and McClure (1976) examined every broadcast of the evening news on ABC, CBS, and NBC and every campaign ad in the 1972 presidential election. Their astonishing conclusion was that news coverage was not very informative because of the focus on horserace politics but that the ads actually did serve a valuable educational function. In discussing judicial elections, Iyengar (2001/2002: 694–695) similarly observed that even in short commercials, voters "acquire new and relevant information" about the candidates. Indeed, Iyengar (2001/2002: 695) argued that campaign advertising may be particularly important in judicial elections given the limited knowledge most voters have about the candidates.

These educational benefits do not necessarily translate directly into influence over the electorate's choices. As studies of nonjudicial elections have shown, advertising tends to reinforce partisan predispositions (e.g., Ansolabehere and Iyengar 1995).[6] However, the information in broadcast ads, including harsh attacks, may stimulate the electorate to vote (e.g., Finkel and Geer 1998; Jackson and Carsey 2007).

As an important prelude to testing whether these findings are generalizable to state supreme court elections, this chapter takes an in-depth look at televised campaign advertising from 2002 through 2008, the period covered by the empirical tests in Chapter 4 and Chapter 5. The primary goal is to describe the extent to which televised advertising is used in supreme court elections, the tone of these messages, whether they appear to be issue based, who sponsors them, and their cost. Of particular significance are differences between nonpartisan and partisan elections.

Glimpses of Bygone State Supreme Court Campaigns

Campaign negativity in state supreme court elections often is described as an emerging trend in American politics, justifying renewed efforts to end the practice of electing judges. Although there have been no systematic accounts in the political science literature that provide reliable information across states or over time about the nature of state supreme court campaigns in earlier years, there is some scattered evidence that these campaigns in some states have been, from the very start, hotly contested and often issue based, with raucous attacks against incumbents and challengers. Perhaps the best evidence about the late nineteenth and early twentieth centuries was provided by Kermit Hall (1984, 2005), who wrote fascinating histories of appellate court campaigns and elections held from 1850 through 1920 in four states: California, Ohio, Tennessee, and Texas.[7] Contradicting conventional wisdom, these studies (K. Hall 1984, 2005) show that some of these races in several regards were intense, with partisan, issue-based campaigns that inspired significant involvement from state electorates.[8]

Specifically, "At least through 1920, voters in California, Ohio, Tennessee, and Texas demonstrated a greater interest in state appellate court contests than voters do today" (K. Hall 1984: 356). In fact, about one-third of all judicial elections in these four states produced voter turnout rates that exceeded those for the most visible statewide offices, including gubernatorial elections. As Kermit Hall (1984: 361) observes:

> During the period from 1880 to 1899, voters in California, Ohio, and Tennessee regularly gave fuller attention to judicial than to nonjudicial contests, and this pattern continued in the latter two states until 1910. Roll-off persisted in Texas, but the vote in judicial elections as a percentage of the total vote reached

new highs . . . During the period 1910 to 1920, voters cast ballots in judicial and nonjudicial contests in equal numbers, something that had never happened before in Texas.

However, when nonpartisan ballots were introduced in Ohio and Tennessee, citizen participation declined significantly (K. Hall 1984).[9]

These impressive levels of citizen participation were largely the consequence of high contestation rates, tight margins, and electoral defeats.[10] Overall, only three of 138 appellate court elections (2.2 percent) in California and Ohio were uncontested, and 76.8 percent of these races were decided by five or fewer percentage points (K. Hall 1984). Tennessee and Texas were less competitive by this standard, with rates of contestation at 80 percent in Tennessee and 81.5 percent in Texas. However, as shown in Chapter 2, these rates are still respectable by contemporary standards. The contestation rate in partisan supreme court elections in 2008 was 80 percent for incumbents seeking reelection.

Of the judges who left the bench in California, Ohio, Tennessee, and Texas from 1850 through 1920, 12.6 percent (twenty-eight of 220 incumbents) were ousted from office (K. Hall 1984). Ohio topped the list at 19.3 percent while Texas was lowest at 4.0 percent. However, this study also shows that a sizeable proportion of incumbents failed to be renominated by their parties, for an overall rate of 4.2 percent but up to a sizable 11.1 percent in Tennessee.

Most importantly for this discussion, these close calls for incumbents and outright defeats took place "often after bruising campaigns" (K. Hall 2005: 67). "Controversial issues could and did become part of judicial campaigns, and this frequently worked to the disadvantage of incumbent judges forced to run on their records" (K. Hall 1984: 363). Among the examples given is an emotionally charged 1898 campaign in which a California Supreme Court justice was lambasted for his majority opinion reversing a ruling in a publicly visible tort case arising from the death of a child run over by a train. This justice was branded a callous elitist who valued the interests of wealthy railroad owners over the life of a child from a family of modest means.

Other examples include the politically complicated 1910 Tennessee Supreme Court races, in which Democrats seeking reelection were unseated over a decision to vacate a ruling involving the killing of Edward Carmack, a former U.S. Senator and newspaper editor (K. Hall 1984). Senator Carmack was killed by Duncan Brown Cooper, a Democratic politician and staunch political opponent. As the story goes, Senator Carmack vilified Mr. Cooper in a series of newspaper articles and editorials and then on a public street fired gunshots at Mr. Cooper and his son, wounding the son. Mr. Cooper shot back, killing the Senator, but both Coopers were convicted of murder. Later, the Tennessee Supreme Court overturned the son's conviction and ordered a new trial.[11]

As Kermit Hall (1984: 363) describes the nature of electoral defeats:

> Invariably, public and partisan rejection stemmed from the judges' courtroom behavior. Incumbents were safe so long as they operated within the prevailing majoritarian norms on major public issues. If their grasp of public policymaking exceeded the reach of their popular support, they were made to feel the sting of partisan-imposed democratic accountability.

These intriguing historical accounts of several judicial campaigns sound markedly similar to descriptions of some contemporary campaigns, particularly with their attacks and issue-based dialogue. However, though interesting and in many ways quite extraordinary, these studies (K. Hall 1984, 2005) examined appellate court races in only four states. We do not know to what extent the descriptions are representative or what typical campaigns for office may have been during this period. Nonetheless, this limited historical evidence supports the contention that highly charged campaigns, including attack advertising centered on the decisions of judges, are not a twenty-first century invention. In fact, it seems reasonable to posit that the various trends just described are among the most influential factors giving rise to subsequent changes in the electoral process, including nonpartisan elections and the Missouri Plan.

Today's accounts of judicial campaigns focus on television advertising, especially blatant attacks against incumbents seeking reelection, and on interest group involvement in these races. Generally, although the advocacy literature (e.g., Goldberg, Holman, and Sanchez 2001; Goldberg and Sanchez 2003) typically describes the 2000 and 2002 election cycles as the turning point in state supreme court electoral politics, some scholars point to trends toward politically volatile televised campaigns starting some time in the 1970s. In this regard, Champagne (2002: 669) lists Alabama, California, Illinois, Kentucky, Michigan, Montana, Ohio, Pennsylvania, Texas, and Wisconsin as states in which "big money" started flowing into judicial elections in the late 1970s, increasing interest group involvement and campaign spending independent of the candidates. Champagne (2002) observes that much of this outside money was used to purchase television advertisements.

Schotland (1985: 66) provides additional insights, observing about the campaigns of the 1970s and early 1980s that "campaigning judicial candidates often express[ed] their views on general political or social issues." Schotland (1985: 66) provides as an example the 1982 Ohio Supreme Court elections in which Justices Ralph Locher and William Sweeney, along with the challenger for a third seat, James Celebrezze, ran a television spot stating the following: "Thirty million dollars—that's what the Democratic Supreme Court saved us in just one year by saying no to utility tax hikes . . . Let's keep the people's court Democratic." This was followed in 1984 with the defeat of Justice Celebrezze and Democrat John Corrigan, who was seeking an open seat. These defeats came in the aftermath of a heated campaign criticizing the court majority—and the Democrats in particular—for a 1984 ruling about gas utility rate increases.

Schotland's (1985: 76) landmark study, which coined the modern court reform movement's battle cry "noisier, nastier, and costlier," also observed that California elections in the 1970s and early 1980s (including trial court elections) frequently involved televised campaign advertising. As Schotland (1985) noted, "A *bête noire* of campaigns has long been, for many people, spot ads." In fact, campaign ads broadcast on television and radio prompted Schotland (1985: 125) to recommend that states discourage or ban spot ads in judicial campaigns. Schotland (1985) also described a 1982 survey of Oregon and Washington voters, which showed clearly that television advertising was among the sources used to obtain information about the candidates.[12]

Also writing about the 1980s, Hojnacki and Baum (1992: 944) called our attention to "new-style" supreme court campaigns that were becoming "increasingly common." According to Hojnacki and Baum (1992: 921), these new-style campaigns are those in which "candidates undertake large-scale efforts to reach the voters and emphasize substantive issues in their appeals." In the context of their particular study, Hojnacki and Baum (1992) described the 1986 and 1988 Ohio Supreme Court campaigns as issue-based campaigns, centering on economics with vigorous involvement by labor unions. The results of their analysis caused Hojnacki and Baum (1992: 945) to conclude that "voters increasingly are choosing judges on the basis of what judicial candidates seem to stand for." Interestingly, Hojnacki and Baum (1992, 945) appeared to welcome this development, pointing out that "it is not just the most emotional and dramatic issues in new-style campaigns that can reach voters effectively. Under the right conditions, voters can respond to more prosaic issues such as tort law."

From reports in the popular press, many will recall Republican strategist Karl Rove's campaigns on behalf of Republican candidates for the Alabama Supreme Court in 1994 and 1996, particularly the race in which incumbent Kenneth Ingram ran a statewide ad against challenger Harold See likening him to a skunk. "Some things you can smell a mile away" (Poovey 1996) was the tag line in this personally disparaging attack.

Retired Chief Justice Tom Phillips, a long-time advocate for judicial election reform who served as Chief Justice of the Texas Supreme Court from 1988 through 2004, tells a similar story about elections to his court. Chief Justice Phillips reports that televised attack advertising began in Texas no later than 1986 but may have appeared as early as 1980.[13] As the Chief Justice recalls, Oscar Mauzy filed grievances in 1986 with the Judicial Conduct Commission against his three opponents in the primary and then ran a televised spot claiming that all of his opponents were under investigation for ethics violations. All complaints were dismissed.

Chief Justice Phillips also reports that in 1988 he and challenger Ted Z. Robertson ran negative ads against each other. In the same election cycle, an independent group launched attacks against Governor Clements's three appointees to the Supreme Court (Chief Justice Phillips and Justices Barbara Culver and Eugene Cook). Likewise, Justice Bill Kilgarlin aired televised attacks against challenger Nathan Hecht.

In 1990, Oscar Mauzy and Tom Phillips attacked each other over the airwaves in the race for the chief justiceship. More campaign negativity was broadcast in 1992 in the race between Craig Enoch and Oscar Mauzy, and again in 1994 between Raul Gonzalez and Rene Haas. Ms. Haas attacked Justice Gonzalez for never having handed down a death sentence on the Texas Supreme Court, which has civil jurisdiction only. This prompted an acerbic counterattack from Justice Gonzalez that his opponent was unknowledgeable because she read law rather than going to law school.

Overall, accounts of the Texas Supreme Court from 1980 through 1994 reveal that eight of twenty-six contested races (of twenty-nine total races) involved televised attack advertising. Not included in these totals are possible attacks in 1980 (a race in which newly appointed Justice Will Garwood spent over a million dollars but still lost) and a 1984 race between C. L. Ray and Shelby Sharpe that was negative but may have been by mail only. In contrast, *none* of the contested elections for the Texas Supreme Court from 2002 through 2008 drew televised attacks, and only five used television ads of any sort, of fifteen contested elections (sixteen elections total). Additionally, there were no televised campaigns for the Texas Supreme Court in 2000 (Goldberg, Holman, and Sanchez 2001). If we were to examine the Texas Supreme Court from 2000 through 2008 only, we would reach patently inaccurate conclusions about the nature of televised campaign advertising and negativity for this court historically.

Thus, statements about historical trends in judicial elections should be offered carefully. As Brandenburg and Schotland (2008: 1236) reported, "At least back into the 1980s, [televised] ads run in judicial campaigns have been so disturbing that they are presented as horror cases when legislators and others consider changes in judicial selection methods." To my knowledge, there have been no systematic or large-scale attempts to examine the historical record before the advent of television or to create an accurate trend line on televised campaign advertising (or even radio ads) in state supreme court elections starting in the 1970s or earlier.

Modern State Supreme Court Election Campaigns

Although the historical record is sparse, extensive information is now becoming available about state supreme court campaigns across the nation. In this chapter, I rely on reports in the *New Politics of Judicial Elections* series[14] and advertising data coded by researchers at the Brennan Center for Justice to assess the exact nature of these campaigns in recent election cycles.[15] Included in all of the counts is advertising for both the Texas Supreme Court and the Texas Court of Criminal Appeals. Also, in the following graphs and tables, all televised advertisements are analyzed regardless of sponsor. Thus, unlike campaign spending discussed in Chapter 2, these ads are not limited to candidate-sponsored messages but also include spots purchased by political parties and organized interests. Likewise, all of these advertisements are included in the empirical tests in Chapter 4 and Chapter 5.

In this regard, it is imperative to note that incumbents, challengers, political parties, and outside interests can sponsor any type of advertisement. Concerning negativity, attack and contrast advertising should not be interpreted as directed solely at incumbents. Incumbents air vitriolic attack ads against their challengers, just as political parties and organized interests attack both incumbents and challengers.

Ideally, rigorous before-and-after tests would be used to measure the impact of the *White* decision on state supreme court campaigns, which also would help to pinpoint exactly when any trends in contemporary campaigns may have started. Although the absence of systematic campaign data before the *White* decision does not permit such investigations, it is possible to examine key features of these campaigns now and to observe any trends in the most recent election cycles.

State Supreme Court Advertising by Seat

Judicial reform advocates (e.g., American Bar Association 2003; Brandenburg and Schotland 2008; Geyh 2003; National Center for State Courts 2002; Sample et al. 2010) are forcefully arguing that state judiciaries are facing crises of legitimacy brought about by rapid changes in the campaign context, including the rise of television campaign advertising and the excoriating attacks that can be part of expensive, hotly contested races. But just how prevalent are these practices, and do there appear to be any upward trends in these figures?

Figure 3-1 begins this exploration by summarizing the presence (not volume) of televised campaign advertising on a race-by-race basis. All elections, both with incumbents and for open seats, are counted. For each election cycle, Figure 3-1 shows the total numbers of elections, contested seats, races with television ads, and races with promote, contrast, and attack ads. Consistent with standard practice, promote ads are defined as those promoting one candidate, contrast ads compare two or more candidates, and attack ads criticize the opponent (incumbent or challenger). These categories are mutually exclusive and exhaustive. Overall, promote ads are positive, attack ads are negative, and contrast ads are both positive and negative.

As in Chapter 2, data in an odd year are merged with the prior year to simplify presentation. Included in the totals for 2006 are three supreme court races from 2007 described briefly in the *New Politics of Judicial Elections* report for the 2000–2009 elections cycles (Sample et al. 2010). Although the Sample et al. (2010) report does not provide enough information for these three campaigns to be disaggregated by tone, themes, or sponsors, the authors mention the high cost of televised advertising for two contested seats in Pennsylvania

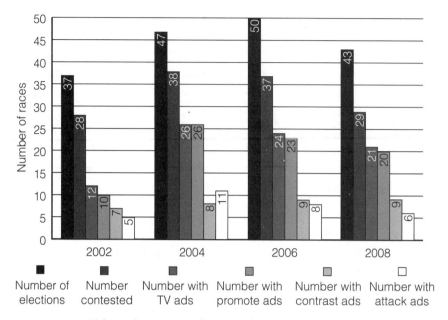

FIGURE 3-1. Televised campaign advertising by seat and election cycle in state supreme court elections, 2002–2008.

SOURCE: Compiled by the author from data reported in the *New Politics of Judicial Elections* series and by the Brennan Center for Justice.

(not disaggregated by race) and another in Wisconsin in 2007. Thus, to avoid undercounting, I include these three elections in Figure 3-1 and Figure 3-2 and assume that promote, contrast, and attack ads aired in each race.

Perhaps the most unanticipated aspect of the information reported in Figure 3-1, even with the addition of three 2007 elections, is that television advertising still is not used in a sizable proportion of state supreme court campaigns even when these races are contested. In 2002 through 2008, the percentage of contested races with television ads is 42.9 in 2002, 68.4 in 2004, 64.9 in 2006, and 72.4 in 2008. Certainly television broadcasts were used more commonly to campaign for state high courts in 2008 than in 2002, proportionally speaking, and a significant change appears to have occurred between 2002 and 2004, perhaps reflecting the impact of the *White* (2002) decision. But even in the most active year, about one of every four contested elections did not motivate any candidates, political parties, or groups to engage in televised campaigning.[16]

The most recent election cycles manifest a downward trend in televised campaigning. Kritzer (forthcoming) shows that only 61 percent of all contested races in 2010 and 62 percent in 2012 involved television advertising. Thus, 2008 appears to have been the peak so far in this trend, and substantial proportions of contested elections even now do not involve candidates, political parties, or organized interests taking to the airwaves. Given the importance of state supreme courts and claims in the advocacy literature that "candidates and groups now almost invariably rely on the airwaves to boost—or bash—contenders for judicial office" (Sample, Jones, and Weiss 2007: 1), this is an unexpected finding.[17]

Thinking about the tone of messages broadcast to voters, Figure 3-1 shows that races with promote ads are the most common in any given election cycle, followed by races with contrast and attack ads. An exception is the 2004 election cycle, in which attacks exceeded contrasts from the vantage point of numbers of elections with these messages.

More specifically, promote ads aired in 35.7 percent of the contested races in 2002, 68.4 percent in 2004, 62.2 percent in 2006, and 69.0 percent in 2008. The percentage of races with contrast or attack ads is much lower. By election cycle, contrast ads were broadcast to voters in 25.0 percent of the contested elections in 2002, 21.1 percent in 2004, 24.3 percent in 2006, and 31.0 percent in 2008. Attack advertising appeared in 17.9 percent of the contested races in 2002, 28.9 percent in 2004, 21.6 percent in 2006, and 20.7 percent in 2008. Of these four election cycles, 2004 was the most negative in terms of the numbers and proportions of races with attacks. Overall, the large majority of contested state supreme court elections do not involve attack advertising. From 2002 through 2008, only 32 of 132 (22.7 percent) contested elections involved these controversial messages.

In the most recent elections, Kritzer (forthcoming) shows that attacks in 2010 and 2012 were used, respectively, in 18 percent and 21 percent of all contested supreme court elections. Thus, there is no upward trend in recent election cycles in the use of attack advertising on a race-by-race basis. In fact, the high point of this trend was in 2004.

Figure 3-2 takes a different look at supreme court campaign advertising by comparing nonpartisan incumbent–challenger races, partisan incumbent–challenger races, and open-seat races. Figure 3-2 displays the numbers of races, contested races, races with television advertising, and races with

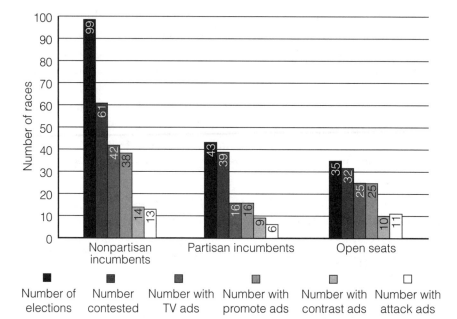

FIGURE 3-2. Televised campaign advertising by seat and incumbency in state supreme court elections, 2002–2008.

SOURCE: Compiled by the author from data reported in the *New Politics of Judicial Elections* series and by the Brennan Center for Justice.

promote, contrast, and attack ads disaggregated by selection system and incumbency status.

As Figure 3-2 indicates, the largest proportion of contested elections with televised advertising involves open seats, followed by nonpartisan elections and then partisan elections with incumbents. Overall, 78.1 percent of all contested open seats, 68.9 percent of all contested nonpartisan elections with incumbents, and 41.0 percent of all contested partisan elections with incumbents drew televised campaign advertising from 2002 through 2008. The figure for contested partisan elections is unexpected. Fewer than half of these races resulted in televised advertising during the four election cycles being examined even though sitting justices were being challenged for reelection. From this perspective, advertising is not the norm in partisan races with incumbents though it clearly is so in nonpartisan and open-seat contests.

These same rankings are evidenced in the extent to which promote ads are used on a race-by-race basis. Overall, promote ads were broadcast to voters in

78.1 percent of contested open-seat races, 62.3 percent of contested nonpartisan elections with incumbents, and 41.0 percent of contested partisan elections with incumbents. When television advertising is employed as a strategy, these campaigns almost always involve positive messages.

Contrast and attack ads are used much less frequently. Proportions of contested elections with attack ads for open seats, nonpartisan incumbent–challenger races, and partisan incumbent–challenger races are, respectively, 34.4 percent, 21.3 percent, and 15.4 percent. From 2002 through 2008, sizeable majorities of contested elections simply did not prompt televised attacks by candidates, political parties, or organized interests. Interestingly, partisan elections are the least likely to go negative.

With contrast advertising, nonpartisan and partisan elections with incumbents are almost identical (23.0 percent versus 23.1 percent), while open seat races are the most likely to involve these types of campaign messages (31.3 percent). As with attack advertising, most races do not attract contrast advertising from any sponsor even when challengers are seeking to unseat incumbent justices.

State Supreme Court Advertising by Volume
A different way to conceptualize the scope of televised campaign advertising is to think in terms of volume, or saturation of airings, both with regard to average airings per race of promote, contrast, and attack spots and as the percentage of airings devoted to each category. Figure 3-3 provides this information by showing average airings by tone for the 2002, 2004, 2006, and 2008 election cycles, as well as percentages of total campaign effort dedicated to each of the three types of messages. These figures are calculated only for races with broadcast airings and are not averaged over all contested races. Otherwise, average airings would be considerably lower in all categories.

Looking first at average numbers of airings for all contested state supreme court elections, Figure 3-3 indicates that the volume of airings has increased substantially in the races in which television advertising is used. However, this trend has not been monotonic. Total average airings are higher in 2002 (2,056 average airings) and 2008 (with 3,010 average airings) than in 2004 (1,757 average airings) and 2006 (1,724 average airings). Thus, although the proportion of races with televised ads does not appear to be rising, the volume of airings may be increasing in those races in which broadcast advertising is employed.

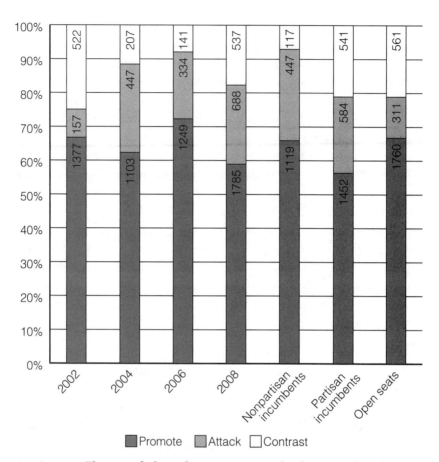

FIGURE 3-3. The tone of televised campaign airings by election cycle and incumbency status in state supreme court elections, 2002–2008.
SOURCE: Compiled by the author from data reported in the *New Politics of Judicial Elections* series and by the Brennan Center for Justice.

Regarding tone, average airings of promote ads are substantially higher than attack or contrast airings in all four election cycles. Generally, campaign airings tend toward the positive rather than the negative, even in 2008. This finding is consistent with the previous figures counting races rather than airings. However, when campaigns go negative, average attack airings outnumber average contrast airings in each election cycle except 2002.

From the perspective of the percentage of campaign effort, Figure 3-3 shows that promote airings are the most common messages broadcast to voters when television advertising appears in state supreme court elections. Average promote airings relative to total airings in televised campaigns are 67.0 percent in 2002, 62.8 percent in 2004, 72.4 percent in 2006, and 59.3 percent in 2008.

The proportion of attack airings shows no distinct temporal trend except for a substantial change between 2002 and later election cycles. Figure 3-3 indicates that average attack airings were 7.6 percent in 2002, 25.4 percent in 2004, 19.4 percent in 2006, and 22.9 percent in 2008. Thus, 2004 was the most negative year for average attack airings, but there have been substantial increases in televised attacks, proportionally speaking, in all three election cycles since 2002.

Contrast airings evidence different patterns. Generally, contrast advertising constituted a larger share of campaign advertising in 2002 than in any other election cycle. In 2002, contrast airings were 25.4 percent of the airings broadcast to voters on average, compared with 11.8 percent in 2004, 8.2 percent in 2006, and 17.8 percent in 2008. However, when attack airings and contrast airings are considered together, 2008 was the most negative election cycle of the four being examined, though promotions still were the most typical. Also from this perspective, 2004 and 2008 look similar, as do 2002 and 2006. This suggests that political actors adjust their campaign strategies in presidential election years versus midterm cycles.

Figure 3-3 offers additional insights by displaying information about average airings of promote, attack, and contrast ads categorized by selection system and incumbency status rather than election cycle. As Figure 3-3 documents, airings are higher on average in open-seat races, followed by partisan elections with incumbents and nonpartisan elections with incumbents. On this dimension, partisan elections look a lot more like open-seat elections than their nonpartisan counterparts.

Regarding tone, although the average airings of promote ads in all three types of races substantially outweigh negative airings, partisan elections in which justices are seeking reelection are less positive by this standard than nonpartisan elections or open-seat races. The highest levels of average promotions are in open-seat races (1,760 airings per race), compared with partisan elections at 1,452 average airings and nonpartisan elections with 1,119 airings. Partisan elections have higher average levels of outright attacks (584 airings per race) than nonpartisan elections (447 airings per race) or open-seat elections (311 airings per race). With contrasts, average airings are highest in open-seat races (561 airings per race), compared with partisan elections at 541 average contrast airings per race and nonpartisan elections with 117 average contrast airings per race.

When airings are examined as proportions of campaign advertising in each type of election, rankings on campaign positivity remain the same. In partisan elections, 56.3 percent of televised campaign airings were, on average, promotions, compared with 66.5 percent in nonpartisan elections and 66.9 percent in open-seat contests. However, average attack airings are highest as a proportion of overall campaign advertising in nonpartisan incumbent–challenger elections, although the difference with partisan elections is not large. The percentage of average airings of attacks in nonpartisan elections is 26.6 percent, compared with partisan elections at 22.7 percent and open seat races with 11.8 percent. Alternatively, contrast airings are a small part of televised campaigns, proportionally speaking, when incumbents are seeking reelection in nonpartisan elections (7.0 percent of all airings in these types of races). These messages are much more common in partisan elections with incumbents (21.0 percent of all airings) and open-seat races (21.3 percent of all airings). Overall, there are some notable differences in the use of promote, attack, and contrast airings in nonpartisan incumbent–challenger elections, partisan incumbent–challenger elections, and open-seat contests. On balance, partisan elections are the most negative when the volume of airings is taken into account. Fewer partisan elections attract advertising and fewer have attack ads, but when televised advertising is introduced, partisan elections are nastier and noisier than nonpartisan elections.

Substantive Appeals in State Supreme Court Advertising

Although the tone of campaign messages is a central concern in discussions of modern-day judicial elections, the themes, or substantive appeals, of these ads also are of vital interest. Recall that political science scholarship, especially Geer (2006), generally regards negativity as a way to enhance the information environment surrounding each election, in part because attack ads are more likely to contain references to issues rather than traits or values, which are considered less useful to voters. However, many in the legal community are sharply critical of issue-based appeals in judicial elections and view these messages as a major threat to the power and integrity of state judiciaries (e.g., American Bar Association Commission on the 21st Century Judiciary 2003; Brandenburg and Schotland 2008; Sample, Jones, and Weiss 2007; Tarr 2009).

To examine the extent to which promote, contrast, and attack advertising facilitates issue-based campaign discourse, I adapted the coding scheme developed by Geer (2006) in his pathbreaking work on presidential elections to state supreme courts using information reported in the *New Politics of Judicial Elections* series. Geer categorized televised presidential campaign ads into three distinct types of appeals: traits personal to the candidates, broader values that do not involve specific issues or policies, and issues that are specific to controversial subjects or policies. Geer's codes are readily adaptable to state supreme courts and provide interesting insights into why attack advertising may have, or may not have, its predicted effects in the post-*White* era. Please note that unlike tone, which is described using mutually exclusive and exhaustive categories, each ad can contain any or all of these three types of appeals.

Specifically, the Brennan Center for Justice classified all state supreme court advertisements by themes using the following coding scheme reported on their webpage at www.brennancenter.org/analysis/buying-time-2004-methodology:

- *Traditional:* Does not discuss issues or allegiances; discusses the personal and professional qualifications of the candidate (e.g., statements about the candidate's education/training/experience/background, family/community involvement, fairness/impartiality, character/temperament)
- *Civil Justice:* Protection/rights of injured, dangerous/defective products, accidents, personal injury lawyers/trial lawyers, health maintenance organizations (HMOs), doctors, corporations/big business, drug/insurance companies, puts people first, right to trial by jury, lawsuit abuse
- *Criminal Justice:* Death penalty, overturns convictions, tough/soft on crime/criminals, victims' rights, technicalities/loopholes/appeals
- *Special Interest Influence:* For sale/sold, supporters are buying a seat on the court, in the pocket of/influenced by special interests, campaign financing
- *Criticism for Decision(s):* In a specific case or type of case
- *Family/Conservative Values:* Protects children/families/community/religion

- *Role of Judges:* How judges should act while on the bench and when presiding over cases
- *Civil Rights:* Voting rights, minority rights

The Brennan Center themes fit remarkably well into Geer's (2006) typology of appeals. Specifically, I categorized all ads labeled by the Brennan Center as traditional advertisements into the traits category, given their direct references to the candidates and, by definition, the absence of issues or partisanship. Additionally, I classified all advertisements involving family/ conservative values and the role of judges as values. The "role of judges" category involved campaign slogans such as interpreting the laws rather than making them, serving as a referee rather than a player, and respecting the law. Finally, all advertisements involving civil justice, criminal justice, special interest influence, criticism for decisions, and civil rights were classified in the issues category.

Additionally, a handful of advertisements were coded by the Brennan Center as "other" or as "attacks," with no other themes identified. For all of the ads with available storyboards, I read and coded these ads using the issues, values, and traits categories developed by Geer (2006). Additionally, I conducted reliability tests to verify the accuracy of this new coding. Overall, twenty-three advertisements resulted in new information.

Each of the traits, values, and issues categories are dichotomous only; each trait is coded as 1 if any mention was made of the type of appeal constituting the category and 0 otherwise. Although it would be preferable to count the exact number of appeals in every ad, the Brennan Center coding scheme does not allow for this more refined approach.[18]

Figure 3-4 displays this information, classifying promote ads, contrast ads, and attack ads according to the percentage of each type of appeal present. In these data, the ads are the unit of analysis. Overall, there were 718 types of appeals in 563 unique ads from 2002 through 2008.[19]

As Figure 3-4 indicates, contrast ads and attack ads are much more likely than promote ads to present issue-based information to voters. In fact, only 29.2 percent of all promote ads have any issue content; instead, promote ads focus on traits (43.6 percent) and values (27.2 percent). Contrast ads also contain a sizeable proportion of traits (31.6 percent) and values (12.7 percent) but mostly (55.7 percent) are issue based. In attack ads, discussions of traits and values are unusual. Only 14.9 percent of attack ads in state supreme court

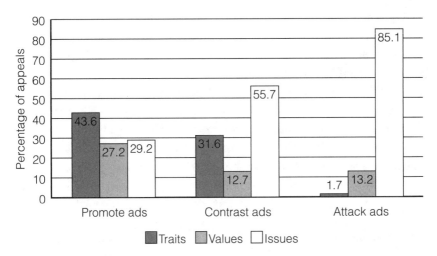

FIGURE 3-4. Shares of traits, values, and issues appeals in televised campaign advertising by tone in state supreme court elections, 2002–2008.
SOURCE: Compiled by the author from data reported in the *New Politics of Judicial Elections* series and by the Brennan Center for Justice.

elections make appeals to voters about the traits or values of the candidates. Instead, 85.1 percent of all attack ads focus on issues. If issue appeals are more effective in educating and mobilizing voters, attack advertising in state supreme court elections seems to hold the most promise for advancing informed and active electorates.[20]

Whether one considers the relatively high issue content of contrast and attack advertisements to be good news or bad news will depend on the reader. Many in the legal community consider partisan or other issue-based dialogue in judicial elections sterling evidence of total system failure. Others do not share these concerns but instead view issues and partisanship as critical to American elections, including judicial elections. Either way, promote, contrast, and attack advertisements make different types of substantive appeals to voters; therefore, promote, contrast, and attack spots may have different impacts on justices seeking reelection and the civic engagement of state electorates in supreme court races.

State Supreme Court Advertising by Sponsors

One of the most serious concerns about state supreme court elections is the involvement of organized interests, including single-issue groups and other financial high rollers, in the process of selecting and retaining state court judges. These concerns have become even more pressing in the aftermath of the U.S. Supreme Court's decision in *Citizens United* v. *Federal Election Commission* (2010). In this highly contentious decision, the Supreme Court invalidated federal campaign finance reform legislation that prevented corporations and labor unions from advertising independently of the candidates within thirty days of an election. The Supreme Court viewed these restrictions as unconstitutionally impinging on First Amendment rights guaranteed to these groups. Seen by critics as unleashing a storm of unrestrained special interest influence in the electoral process, this decision was openly condemned by President Obama in his 2010 State of the Union Address, which inspired a whispered (yet visible to the cameras) defense from Justice Alito that the President's criticisms were "not true."

Just months before the *Citizens United* decision, the Supreme Court ruled in *Caperton* v. *Massey Coal Company* (2009) that state supreme court justices who benefit from significant campaign contributions or independent expenditures have a constitutional obligation to recuse themselves from any cases involving those parties. Although the *Citizens United* and *Caperton* decisions brought squarely into the political limelight the complexities of balancing fair democratic processes with moneyed special interests, *Caperton* also illustrates the high profile of state supreme court elections and the desire for powerful organizations and other political players to seek to influence who serves in these vitally important institutions.

Trepidations along these lines continue. In April 2014, the U.S. Supreme Court decided *McCutcheon* v. *Federal Election Commission*, which invalided on First Amendment grounds federal regulations imposing aggregate biennial limits on individuals contributing to political candidates and committees (party committees and political action committees).[21] Many fear that the *McCutcheon* decision is just one more step down the path of unregulated big money in all American elections, and the decision is being universally derided by judicial reform advocates as having potentially deleterious consequences for state judicial elections.

Figure 3-5 provides insights into the role of organized interests in state supreme court elections by reporting, in the aggregate, the overall share of state supreme court airings by tone and by sponsor from 2002 through 2008. For each category, Figure 3-5 shows the percentage of total airings sponsored by incumbents, challengers, political parties, and interest groups. These figures are shown separately for nonpartisan incumbent–challenger races (69,000

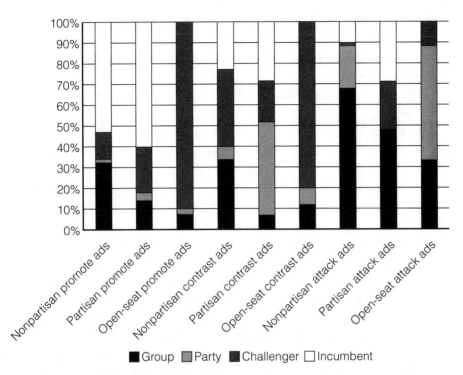

Group **Party** **Challenger** □ Incumbent

FIGURE 3-5. Total televised campaign airings by sponsor and tone in state
supreme court elections, 2002–2008.
SOURCE: Compiled by the author from data reported in the *New Politics of Judicial Elections*
series and by the Brennan Center for Justice.

airings in forty-two elections), partisan incumbent–challenger races (36,706
airings in sixteen elections), and open seats (51,204 airings in twenty-two
elections).[22] In open-seat contests, which lack incumbents, all candidate airings are reported in the "challenger" category. Overall, these data reveal the
extent to which interest groups are responsible for what many consider to be
the dirty politics of campaign negativity and controversial policy discourse in
state supreme court elections.

As Figure 3-5 indicates, most of the promote airings, which all are positive in tone, have been sponsored by the candidates. In nonpartisan elections,
52.7 percent of the promotions have come from incumbents and 13.3 percent
from challengers, for a combined total of 66 percent. In partisan elections, the
numbers are higher. In these races, 60.5 percent of all promote airings were
sponsored by incumbents, along with another 21.7 percent from challengers,

for a total of 82.2 percent. In open-seat races, 89.0 percent of all promote airings were sponsored by the candidates. Thus, campaign positivity is largely a product of the candidates, although interest groups play a greater role in nonpartisan elections than in the other two types of races and are much more active in promoting candidates than political parties in all three election scenarios.

Contrast airings do not reflect these same patterns. In nonpartisan elections in which incumbents are seeking reelection, contrast airings are sponsored for the most part by challengers (36.5 percent) and interest groups (33.9 percent). In these elections, only 22.9 percent of all contrast airings were aired by incumbents while only 6.7 percent came from political parties. However, collectively incumbents and challengers dominate these messages, at 59.4 percent, rather than organized interests. In partisan elections, interest groups contribute little to these messages. Only 6.1 percent of all contrast airings were sponsored by interest groups, compared with 45.8 percent by political parties. Otherwise, 28.1 percent of contrast airings were from incumbents, and 20.0 percent were from challengers, which together just outweigh the airings of political parties. In open-seat races, the large majority (78.9 percent) of contrast airings came from candidates. Political parties (10.1 percent) and interest groups (11.0 percent) aired only small shares of these messages.

The participation of interest groups in supreme court election campaigns is most evidenced, and is of the greatest concern, in their sponsorship of attack airings. As expressed by Goldberg, Holman, and Sanchez (2001: 17), "More than any other phenomenon, the aggressively negative tone of television ads sponsored by independent groups defines the new style of judicial campaigns." In the advocacy literature, interest groups, along with political parties, are described as "the attack dogs of judicial elections" (Goldberg et al. 2005: 3).

As Figure 3-5 reveals, in nonpartisan elections with incumbents, 67.9 percent of all attack airings in these races were sponsored by interest groups, compared with 47.9 percent in partisan elections and 33.4 percent in open-seat contests. In nonpartisan elections, political parties come in second, with 20.8 percent of attack airings, followed by incumbents at 10.3 percent and challengers at 1.0 percent. The incredibly small proportion of attack airings by challengers is surprising. However, it may well be to the advantage of challengers not to attack when groups and parties have decided to assume this unpleasant task. The downside is that the challengers then cannot control the content of these messages.

Partisan elections with incumbents are different. Most of the attack airings in these elections are candidate sponsored (28.9 percent by incumbents plus 23.3 percent by challengers). In fact, political parties did not sponsor any attack airings in partisan elections during this period. Consistent with attacks in nonpartisan elections, incumbents attack more than challengers as a proportion of these airings. Organized interests sponsored a sizeable share of attacks (47.9 percent) in partisan elections but not in the same proportions as in nonpartisan elections.

In open-seat elections, most of the attack airings have been sponsored by political parties (55.1 percent), followed by interest groups (33.4 percent) and candidates (11.5 percent). In short, attack airings are largely the product of interest groups in nonpartisan elections with incumbents, candidates in partisan elections with incumbents, and political parties in open-seat races. Of course, attacks by interest groups and parties can be directed at incumbents or challengers. These figures should not be interpreted as attacks solely against incumbents.

Figure 3-6 displays information about substantive appeals (i.e., traits, values, issues) by sponsor. For each category, Figure 3-6 shows the percentage of total appeals during this period sponsored by incumbents, challengers, political parties, and interest groups. These figures are shown separately for nonpartisan incumbent–challenger races (89,671 appeals in forty-two elections), partisan incumbent–challenger races (54,574 appeals in sixteen elections), and open seats (63,272 airings in twenty-two elections).[23] Because there are no incumbents in open-seat contests, all candidate airings are reported in the "challenger" category. Collectively, these data reveal the extent to which interest groups and political parties are responsible for issue-based dialogue in state supreme court elections, which are closely associated with attacks.

Looking first at the sponsorship of traits appeals, Figure 3-6 shows that these types of messages are largely the product of candidates. In nonpartisan and partisan elections in which justices are seeking reelection, the lion's share of traits appeals come from incumbents, especially in nonpartisan races. Overall, 71.6 percent of all traits appeals in nonpartisan elections and 60.3 percent in partisan elections are from the justices. Challengers also contribute, with 10.0 percent in nonpartisan races and 30.3 percent in partisan races.

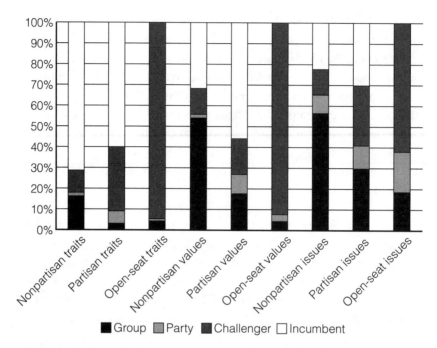

FIGURE 3-6. Total televised campaign airings by sponsor and appeals in state supreme court elections, 2002–2008.

SOURCE: Compiled by the author from data reported in the *New Politics of Judicial Elections* series and by the Brennan Center for Justice.

In open-seat elections, virtually all of the traits appeals (94.8 percent) are sponsored by candidates. Political parties and interest groups do not appear to use these types of messages nearly in the same proportions as the candidates.

Values appeals are different. In nonpartisan elections with incumbents, interest groups sponsor the biggest share of these airings, at 54.3 percent. Incumbents follow with 32.3 percent. In partisan elections, interest groups make smaller contributions to values appeals. Instead, the majority (55.5 percent) of values appeals in partisan elections come from incumbents. Interest groups (at 17.8 percent) and challengers (at 17.5 percent) come in next. In open-seat elections, values appeals come from candidates overwhelmingly, at 91.8 percent.

Patterns of sponsorships of issues appeals in nonpartisan elections look somewhat similar to those of values appeals. Most issue appeals (56.6 percent) are made by interest groups, followed by incumbents (22.0 percent), challengers (12.6 percent), and political parties (8.8 percent). In partisan and open-seat races, interest groups play a lesser role. Only 29.9 percent of all issue appeals in partisan elections and 18.4 percent in open-seat races are controlled by interest groups. Instead, candidates sponsor the majority of issue-based advertising in partisan and open-seat elections.

In sum, organized interests actively sponsor attacks and issue-based appeals in partisan incumbent-challenger races and in open-seat elections, but their biggest efforts on these fronts have been in nonpartisan elections in which justices are seeking reelection. Overall, interest groups sponsor larger shares of attack airings and broadcast larger proportions of issue appeals in nonpartisan elections than do other major political actors, including the candidates. This may reflect the practical reality that attacks against any state's partisan majority are less effective when partisan labels are on the ballot or when there are no incumbents to criticize. Regardless, those concerned with the pernicious effects of organized interests and other big-money players in state supreme court elections should be looking most carefully at nonpartisan elections.

These same patterns are reflected in spending by organized interests on television advertising. Based on state supreme court elections in the 2004 election cycle, Goldberg et al. (2005: 7) asserted that "campaign cash from special interest groups is fast becoming an important fixture in state supreme court elections. Both the number of interest groups sponsoring television ads . . . and the amount spent by these groups continues to grow exponentially."

Figure 3-7 examines this contention about interest group sponsorship of televised campaign advertising from a cost perspective for each election cycle from 2002 through 2008, displayed for nonpartisan elections with incumbents, partisan elections with incumbents, and open seats. The advertising costs shown in Figure 3-7, and also in Table 3-1, should be interpreted cautiously. These figures, which come directly from the Campaign Media Analysis Group as reported in the *New Politics* series, have not been adjusted to reflect population size or the varying prices of broadcast markets across and within states. Also, these costs are only for airtime and do not include charges for media consultants, production, and other expenses associated with televised campaigning. However, the data do provide some basis, though far from perfect, for comparing the costs of airtime by sponsors across the states and over election cycles.

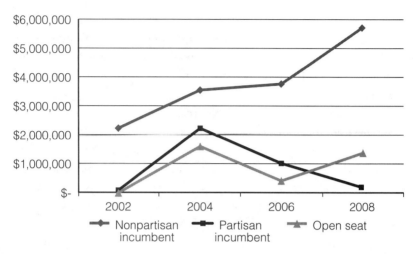

FIGURE 3-7. The total cost of airtime purchased by interest groups in state supreme court elections, 2002–2008.

SOURCE: Compiled by the author from data reported in the *New Politics of Judicial Elections* series and by the Brennan Center for Justice.

As Figure 3-7 indicates, total interest group spending on televised advertising has increased substantially since 2002 in nonpartisan elections with incumbents. In fact, total spending on airtime by outside interests tripled over the four election cycles in these races. Similar patterns are not evidenced in the other two types of elections. In open-seat contests, interest group spending was highest in 2004, although 2008 looks very similar. In 2002 and 2006, interest group spending on airtime was minimal. In partisan elections with incumbents, spending by interest groups has been substantially less than nonpartisan elections and shows a pronounced downward trend.

Overall, interest groups spent about $22.1 million on campaign airtime in state supreme court elections from 2002 through 2008, which is roughly 32 percent of the total cost of airtime of $68.6 million. As with airings, nonpartisan elections with incumbents are the primary target for interest group involvement in state supreme court elections.[24]

State Supreme Court Advertising by State

As the final step in this exploration of televised campaign advertising in state supreme court elections, Table 3-1 provides an interesting comparison of the American states from 2002 through 2008. For each state during four election

TABLE 3-1. Television campaign advertising by state in supreme court elections, 2002–2008 (all races: candidate–challenger and open-seat contests).*

State	N races with ads/ races contested	N unique ads	Average promote airings per race	Average contrast airings per race	Average attack airings per race	Total cost of advertising	Average cost of advertising
Alabama	10 /10	89	3,109	482	686	$14,383,221	$1,438,322
Arkansas	4 / 4	10	82	0	0	$ 161,540	$ 40,385
Georgia	2 / 4	10	540	225	662	$ 3,128,572	$1,564,286
Idaho	2 / 2	3	240	67	0	$ 69,159	$ 34,580
Illinois	2 / 2	31	1,531	1,204	1,752	$ 7,141,130	$3,570,565
Kentucky	5 / 6	49	511	49	20	$ 1,007,886	$ 201,577
Louisiana	3 / 3	42	654	118	133	$ 1,223,342	$ 407,781
Michigan	6 / 7	26	972	178	864	$ 6,723,233	$1,120,539
Minnesota	0 / 4	0	0	0	0	0	0
Mississippi	8 / 9	48	779	8	153	$ 2,313,569	$ 289,196
Montana	1 / 4	3	571	0	0	$ 60,801	$ 60,801
Nevada	6 / 8	46	828	104	50	$ 2,859,192	$ 476,532
New Mexico	1 / 2	4	326	0	0	$ 383,023	$ 383,023
North Carolina	7 / 9	21	771	0	0	$ 1,569,648	$ 224,235
Ohio	9 / 9	79	3,283	976	462	$16,350,006	$1,816,667
Oregon	2 / 3	5	557	31	0	$ 576,304	$ 288,152
Pennsylvania[a]	2 / 3	NA	NA	NA	NA	$ 4,555,196	$2,277,598
Texas	5 / 27	11	753	1,252	0	$ 2,533,538	$ 506,708
Washington	3 / 10	7	91	77	296	$ 1,158,431	$ 386,144
West Virginia	3 / 3	57	1,887	24	1,359	$ 3,189,764	$1,063,255
Wisconsin[b]	2 / 3	22	4,688	328	6,944	$ 5,897,343	$2,948,672

* Average airings figures are calculated using races with television advertising only. There were no contested elections in North Dakota during this period.

[a] Airings by tone are not available for Pennsylvania. The two elections reported are two open seats in 2007.

[b] Airings by tone are available in Wisconsin for the 2008 election only.

SOURCE: Compiled by the author from data reported in the *New Politics of Judicial Elections* series and by the Brennan Center for Justice.

cycles, Table 3-1 shows the numbers of contested races, races with televised advertising, and unique ads broadcast to voters. Table 3-1 also indicates the average airings of promote, contrast, and attack airings, the total cost of advertising, and the average cost of advertising.

As these data clearly illustrate and as we would expect, the American states differ considerably on multiple dimensions where campaign advertising is concerned. Looking first at the proportion of contested supreme court races with television advertising, seven states (Alabama, Arkansas, Idaho, Illinois, Louisiana, Ohio, West Virginia) have experienced televised campaigns in all of their contested races from 2002 through 2008, while four states (Minnesota, Montana, Texas, Washington) are relatively unfamiliar with television as a campaign strategy. The figures for Texas are especially surprising and misleading given what we know about the televised campaigns of the 1980s and early 1990s for the Texas Supreme Court. Also interesting is the fact that Minnesota did not have any televised campaigns in their state supreme court races during these four election cycles. Generally, both nonpartisan and partisan election states are represented in the upper and lower brackets of the use of televised advertising in contested state supreme court elections.

From the perspective of tone as indicated by average airings, five states have not experienced contrast advertising (Arkansas, Minnesota, Montana, New Mexico, and North Carolina), and eight states have had no attack airings (Arkansas, Idaho, Minnesota, Montana, New Mexico, North Carolina, Oregon, and Texas). At the other end of the spectrum, Georgia, Illinois, Washington, and Wisconsin have averaged more attack airings than contrast or promote airings when televised campaigning is used, and coming in close with relatively high levels of negativity are Michigan and West Virginia. As with the use of televised advertising, attack airings at both extremes are found in nonpartisan and partisan elections.

Regarding the average cost of campaign advertising, states in which average spending has exceeded $1 million are Alabama, Georgia, Illinois, Michigan, Ohio, Pennsylvania, Washington, and Wisconsin. At the other extreme are Arkansas, Idaho, and Montana, where televised campaigns average less than six figures. As with advertising tone, expensive advertising is found among partisan and nonpartisan states. However, the least costly campaigns have been run in three nonpartisan systems, two of which (Idaho and Montana) have among the lowest populations of the states using judicial elections.

Conclusion

Until recently, judicial election campaigns may have been politically uninteresting and largely invisible to state electorates but there are numerous exceptions, as the various examples provided from the historical literature and recent accounts indicate. This is not a trivial matter. Voters in some states may have become desensitized long ago to aggressive campaigning, much more so than is widely appreciated. This would reduce significantly the impact of *Republican Party of Minnesota* v. *White* (2002) and complicate theories about the effects of various types of electoral processes on state electorates and justices seeking reelection. These theories also may have made inaccurate assumptions about states electorates. As Gibson (2012) suggests, voters may *prefer* policy talk by judicial candidates to the types of arguably vacuous messages previously mandated by state codes of judicial conduct. A longer-term trend starting in earlier decades in aggressive campaigns, including attack advertising or other issue-based advertising, also would deflate the crisis-based framing of the contemporary judicial reform movement, which holds as axiomatic that dramatic, sudden, and transformative changes in the current campaign context demand immediate political action to end the practice of electing judges and/or contestable elections.[25] Much more research is needed on this fascinating and critically important topic.

Some very interesting and unexpected patterns are present in state supreme court election campaigns from 2002 through 2008. Although television advertising is the norm in contested elections, popular accounts have exaggerated the extent to which televised campaign advertising is used in state high court elections. Even in the most competitive election cycle, about one of every four contested races still failed to result any televised advertising by the candidates, political parties, or interest groups. Likewise, some states have had few races, or even no races in the case of Minnesota, in which televised advertising was employed as a campaign strategy. There also is some interesting evidence that the proportion of contested elections with broadcast advertising may be declining. According to Kritzer (forthcoming), only 62 percent of the contested races in 2012 involved taking to television airwaves.

Televised advertising campaigns typically do not involve attacks. The most negative election cycle so far has been 2004, in which 28.9 percent of the contested races drew these types of pejorative messages. Generally, there are no trends toward increasing reliance on the airwaves or campaign negativity when measured in terms of the number and proportion of races. However, the airings of televised messages generally, and attacks in particular, have increased when television is used as a campaign tactic. In races with advertising, the 2008 elections were the noisiest yet. Alternatively from the perspective of the states, eight states have not experienced campaign negativity at all in the form of attack airings.

Significant differences also are evidenced between nonpartisan and partisan elections when these elections are contested and incumbents are seeking reelection. Nonpartisan elections are more likely than partisan elections to have televised campaigns. In fact, taking to the airwaves is not the norm in partisan elections. Similarly, nonpartisan elections are more likely to go negative than partisan elections. Nonpartisan elections have higher numbers of races, and higher proportions of races, with attack ads than partisan elections, although partisan elections average higher numbers of airings overall and attack airings in particular once televised advertising is employed. Finally, attack airings and issue airings in nonpartisan elections are the product of interest groups to a greater extent than in partisan elections or open seats. These same patterns are reflected in the dollars spent directly on airtime by organized interests.

Given the patterns evidenced to date in televised campaign advertising, promoting nonpartisan elections as a way to shield incumbents from the dangers of harsh negativity, issue-based campaign rhetoric, and interest group influence in the judicial selection process seems counterproductive. Although the National Center for State Courts (2002: 14) has argued that "nonpartisanship in judicial races will reduce dependence on interest groups and parties and lead to less negative campaigning," nonpartisan supreme court elections do not appear to conform to these predictions.

Despite the fact that televised attack advertising remains atypical in state supreme court elections, even small doses could be critical if stark negativity actually packs the devastating punch predicted by many in the legal community. To contribute to the dialogue about campaign negativity and to assess some of the principal claims about its pernicious effects, Chapter 4 assesses whether attack advertising diminishes the electoral performance of justices seeking reelection, and Chapter 5 evaluates whether attacks dampen the willingness of citizens to vote. These questions have profound implications for American democracy and go directly to the center of the disciplinary debate in political science about the nastier edges of contemporary campaign politics.

4 Attack Advertising and Electoral Support for State Supreme Court Justices

A S NEGATIVITY IN AMERICAN POLITICS, INCLUDING MUD-slinging and other outrageous attacks, become an entrenched component of many campaigns for the nation's most visible offices, scholars and other political observers have speculated about the potentially deleterious consequences of these controversial messages for candidates, voters, and political institutions. From the perspective of predicted harms delineated in the conventional wisdom among the public, pundits, and some political scientists, "The indictment of negative advertising is alarming" (Jackson, Mondak, and Huckfeldt 2009: 59). In this regard, judicial reform advocates and the legal academy are not alone in their trepidation about attack advertising.

The specific charges against negative campaign politics are many and range from fairly amorphous normative concerns to theoretical and empirical questions of considerable scientific import. In scientific accounts, two sets of claims, which constitute testable hypotheses, have attracted a great deal of scholarly attention over the past several decades. First, political scientists have assessed the widely held assumption that attack advertising actually works; that is, negativity influences the preferences of voters when selecting among candidates. In this regard, negative campaign messages are believed by many to reduce electoral support for the targeted candidates, which may be especially threatening to incumbents seeking reelection. Second, scholars have evaluated the popular contention that by debasing political discourse and demeaning the electoral process, attack advertising alienates voters and undercuts the legitimacy of elections and governmental institutions.

Perhaps the most influential treatment of the consequences of campaign negativity in the political science literature was offered by Ansolabehere et al. (1994: 835) and Ansolabehere and Igyengar (1995), who not only presented a plausible argument but also provided empirical evidence generated largely through experiments that "attack advertising extracts a toll on electoral participation" and engenders a "cynical" electorate. In fact, Ansolabehere et al. (1994) and Ansolabehere and Iyengar (1995) argued that campaign negativity was the single biggest cause of declining voter turnout in the United States. These studies also suggested that the disaffection brought about by negativity poses "a serious threat to democracy" (Ansolabehere and Iyengar 1995: 12). In essence, Ansolabehere et al. (1994) and Ansolabehere and Iyengar (1995) claimed that the effects of negativity certainly are discernable with regard to specific elections but that the damage extends far beyond the immediate to long-term systemic harms to American political institutions. According to these pathbreaking studies, campaign negativity demoralizes citizens, demobilizes the electorate, and delegitimizes government.

This thesis is remarkably akin to the most fundamental predictions from the legal and advocacy communities about the effects of caustic ads in judicial elections. In speaking about legislative and executive elections, Ansolabehere and Iyengar (1995: 111) argued that "people infer from negative advertisements that the entire process, not just the targeted candidate, is deeply flawed."[1] Judicial reform advocates similarly assert that attack advertising poisons the electoral climate for incumbents and reduces citizens' positive perceptions of judges and courts, resulting in crises of legitimacy for state judiciaries.

The Ansolabehere (Ansolabehere et al. 1994; Ansolabehere and Iyengar 1995) studies inspired a considerable body of research testing these and other contentions about the effects of negativity on American voters. But despite the plausibility of the initial claims and some subsequent findings consistent with the Ansolabehere assertions (e.g., Kahn and Kenny 1999), the weight of the evidence to date supports the conclusion that negativity does not demobilize the electorate or threaten individual attitudes essential to democracy. In fact, quite a few studies (e.g., Finkel and Geer 1998; Goldstein and Freedman 2002; Jackson and Carsey 2007; Jackson and Sides 2006; Lau and Pomper 2001; Niven 2006) show that negative ads *increase* voter turnout. In short, "Despite all the hand-wringing about incivility and its pernicious effects on politics, it is not at all clear that such concerns are warranted or under what conditions they are warranted" (Brooks and Geer 2007: 2).[2]

These same conclusions describe studies that assess whether attacks are effective in persuading voters about which candidates to prefer. Although there is far less research on this important topic than on voter turnout, the consensus among political scientists is that negativity does not convince voters to favor or disfavor particular candidates, including incumbents (e.g., Lau et al. 1999; Lau, Sigelman, and Rovner 2007).[3] In fact, any effects that do occur tend to reinforce preexisting partisan loyalties (e.g., Ansolabehere and Iyengar 1995) or otherwise "dissipate rapidly" (Gerber et al. 2011: 135). Summarized well by Ansolabehere and Iyenger (1995: 17), "Campaigns in general and campaign advertising in particular are relatively unimportant determinants of electoral outcomes," despite the primacy that campaigns are believed to hold by candidates, political strategists, and popular conventional wisdom.

Whether these fascinating and, in many ways, counterintuitive findings about the impact of attack advertising on voter persuasion and voter mobilization are generalizable to judicial elections remains to be seen, particularly for incumbents not insulated by partisan ballots and for voters unassisted in their voting decisions by the partisan cue. Thus, in this chapter and the next, I examine the effects of campaign negativity within the context of state supreme court elections. First, this chapter assesses the impact of attack ads on the electoral performance of state supreme court justices seeking reelection. Does campaign negativity significantly diminish electoral support for incumbents, or do state supreme court elections more closely resemble their executive and legislative counterparts?[4] Chapter 5 then follows with an investigation of the demobilization hypothesis. Does attack politics shrink the active electorate in state supreme court elections, effectively reducing citizen participation in the judicial selection process, or do state supreme court elections essentially reflect the same patterns as elections to the other branches?

In both chapters, I synthesize the scientific and advocacy literatures and offer generalizations about American elections based on the lessons of state supreme courts. Both chapters also place a sharp focus on the institutional rules governing state supreme court elections, particularly differences between nonpartisan and partisan elections. When partisan labels are removed from ballots, bruising attack ads and other aspects of campaign politics may have more pronounced consequences. Thus, any dissimilarities between judicial elections and those for legislative and executive offices may have less to do with differences in fundamental institutional functions than with variations in the principal rules structuring the elections process.

Judicial Reform Advocacy and Judicial Politics Scholarship

Among legal pundits and court reform organizations, there is little doubt that expensive, hard-fought judicial elections are widely presumed to have serious consequences for incumbents. Consider the following contention by the Justice at Stake Campaign, one of the premier lobbying organizations driving the movement against contestable elections:

> Candidates increasingly rely on TV ads to reach voters who get little other information about judicial candidates, while interest groups appreciate the "cut-through value" that explosive negative ads can have in an otherwise low-profile election. The information deficit and the low turnout in judicial elections mean that TV ads have considerable power to shape the outcome of the races (Goldberg et al. 2005: 1).

This same report (Goldberg et al. 2005: 1) claims that "Big Spenders on TV Usually Win," a relatively common theme in the biennial *The New Politics* series that reflects the conventional wisdom about the power of advertising on candidate choice in judicial elections. Similarly, Tarr (2007: 55) observed that "because of the limited information available from candidates even today, voters in judicial elections often lack a basis on which to evaluate the claims of television ads, and thus they are especially vulnerable to manipulative characterizations of a few decisions by interest groups." Tarr (2007: 55) goes even further by asserting that "the accusations against particular judges may have consequences beyond the particular race . . . because the public makes little distinctions among Judges."

These same observers call into question the capacity for campaigns to provide meaningful information about candidates. As Sample, Jones, and Weiss (2007: 1) opine, "In an ideal world, television ads would help arm voters with information they can use to elect the most qualified, experienced judges. But in reality, television advertising is often used to misrepresent or distort facts, and mislead or scare voters."[5]

As mentioned in Chapter 2, judicial reform advocates have been quite successful in convincing states of the dangers of partisan elections. Since 1960, twenty states have changed the means by which they staff their supreme courts, and twelve of these twenty switched from partisan elections to other selection plans (Council of State Governments 1960–2012). Currently, there are orchestrated efforts in Michigan, Minnesota, and Nevada to convince voters to abandon nonpartisan judicial elections, and the American Bar Association has denounced the use of judicial elections in any form, including retention elections.

Although much of the current case against judicial elections rests with assumptions about the harmful effects of aggressive campaigns and the various forms of electioneering that accompany intensely contested seats, the fundamental premise underlying these concerns is that judges must avoid the ugly stains of politics to retain their legitimacy. In this regard, any form of campaigning or electoral politics, including negative advertising, intrinsically is perceived as injurious to judges and courts. In the minds of citizens, as conventional legal wisdom goes, judges cannot remain respected arbiters of disputes and neutral interpreters of law while behaving like ordinary politicians in the electoral arena.

This assumption about the deleterious impact of democratic politics on the state court bench will continue to be debated. However, recent evidence challenges the legal account of hard-hitting campaigns and their consequences for judicial legitimacy. Gibson (2009) found that neither issue-based discourse nor outright attacks have harmful effects on legitimacy in states that elect judges.[6] More importantly, Gibson et al. (2011; Gibson 2012) show that although some campaign messages can dampen citizen support for courts, the strongly legitimizing effects of elections outweigh the adverse effects of caustic ads. Even with the nastiest attacks, judicial elections are a legitimizing force.

Studies of state supreme court elections also contradict the thesis that voters are alienated by aggressive campaigns and rough-and-tumble elections. A substantial body of work documents that state electorates actually are mobilized rather than demobilized by a variety of factors that increase the salience of the races and improve the information available to voters (e.g., Baum and Klein 2007; M. G. Hall 2007b; M. G. Hall and Bonneau 2008, 2013; Hojnacki and Baum 1992; Klein and Baum 2001).[7] Particularly effective as agents of mobilization are partisan elections, hotly contested seats, and substantial spending (Baum and Klein 2007; M. G. Hall 2007b; M. G. Hall and Bonneau 2008, 2013). Assessing empirically whether political behavior in the form of support or opposition to incumbents will reflect these same patterns is the primary purpose of this chapter.

Campaign-Based Models of the Electoral Performance of Incumbents

This research capitalizes on the solid theoretical foundations of scientific studies of judicial politics, campaigns, and elections, as well as the analytical leverage of comparative research designs, to examine the effects of negative advertising on the electoral performance of state supreme court justices in this new era of television advertising and in the aftermath of *White*. Thus, the dependent variable is each incumbent's vote share, measured as the percentage of the vote received by the incumbent (*incumbent vote*) in each race.[8]

Specifically, I examine ninety-five supreme court elections from 2002 through 2008 in nineteen states[9] using partisan and nonpartisan elections to staff their highest courts. In doing so, I ask two primary questions. First, is attack advertising effective? Second, are any impacts of campaign advertising contingent on the institutional arrangements governing the elections? Indeed, the analysis devotes considerable attention to the various institutional contingencies within which these elections occur while incorporating other campaign-related, candidate-specific, and contextual factors identified as important in previous research (e.g., Bonneau 2007; Bonneau and Cann 2011; Dubois 1980; M. G. Hall 2001a, 2014b; M. G. Hall and Bonneau 2006).

There are two fundamental theoretical tenets underlying this research. First, vigorous criticism and open public debate are valuable democratic assets enhancing the electorate's ability to make informed choices (e.g., Finkel and Geer 1998; Geer 2006). Generally speaking, these advantages accrue disproportionately to incumbents.[10] Among other things, incumbents receive more extensive media coverage, enjoy greater name recognition, raise and spend more money, and have added experience on the job and with campaigning (e.g., Bonneau 2007; Bonneau and Cann 2011; M. G. Hall and Bonneau 2006). Also, state supreme court justices tend to mirror the preferences of their constituencies (Brace, Langer, and M. G. Hall 2000), especially given that many of the most electorally vulnerable incumbents retire strategically to avoid being ousted (M. G. Hall 2001b).

Second, institutional arrangements have a powerful impact on the conduct of American elections (e.g., Baum and Klein 2007; Bonneau 2007; Bonneau and Cann 2011; Bonneau and M. G. Hall 2003, 2009; Dubois 1980; M. G. Hall 2001a, 2007a, 2007b, 2014b; M. G. Hall and Bonneau 2006, 2008, 2013; Hojnacki and Baum 1992; Peters 2009). These deliberate choices made by states not only define the fundamental rules under which elections operate but also create alternative strategic contingencies that structure the manner in which voters receive and use information and the extent to which incumbents are insulated from external political forces. Particularly important among these is the partisan ballot. Partisanship provides a low-cost yet effective vote cue, especially in lower ballot races (e.g., Dubois 1980; M. G. Hall 2001a, 2007b; Schaffner, Streb, and Wright 2001), and shields incumbents from the vicissitudes of short-term political events.

Given these theoretical constructs, this study posits that negative campaigns will have disparate impacts in partisan and nonpartisan elections. Incumbents in partisan elections should be relatively immune to negativity because partisanship mitigates the impact of brief events like campaign ads. However, because nonpartisan elections significantly reduce the information immediately available to voters and expose incumbents to idiosyncratic forces (e.g., M. G. Hall 2001a, 2014b; Schaffner, Streb, and Wright 2001), negativity should have a more pronounced impact in these types of elections. In fact, even newspaper coverage of nonpartisan elections appears to lag behind reporting about partisan elections, or at least this was the case in supreme court elections from 2000 through 2004 (Schaffner and Diascro 2007).

Stated differently from the perspective of theories of American elections, scholars concerned with the pernicious effects of negativity may have been correct about their assumptions but may have missed the institutions to which their arguments best apply. Regarding reform, nonpartisan judicial elections may facilitate some of the most serious consequences of hard-fought campaigns, not because courts are intrinsically different from the other branches but because these judicial elections alter the rules of the electoral game.

In testing these propositions, my specific empirical focus is on the fifty-six supreme court justices in nonpartisan elections and thirty-nine justices in partisan elections who were challenged for reelection from 2002 through 2008.[11] The analysis begins in 2002 because television advertising in state supreme court elections may have been limited before 2002 (e.g., Goldberg et al. 2005) and because systematic data on campaign ads before 2002 are not available. The analysis ends in 2008 only because of data availability at the time of this project.[12]

Because the models in this chapter include television advertising and campaign spending, this analysis is restricted to contested races only (e.g., Bonneau 2007; Bonneau and Cann 2011; M. G. Hall and Bonneau 2008). With uncontested seats, either the states do not consistently report spending or the amounts are so small that their inclusion would threaten valid inference by giving disproportionate weight to the uncontested cases. This also is true of television advertising; ads do not air if races are not contested. From a different perspective, nonpartisan and partisan elections without challengers are not really contests and thus pose no threat to incumbents.[13]

For information about television advertising, I rely on campaign advertisements gathered by the Campaign Media Analysis Group (CMAG) and presented in various reports by the Brennan Center for Justice, the Justice at Stake Campaign, and the National Institute on Money in State Politics.[14] CMAG, a commercial firm, collects storyboards and streaming video for television ads aired in state supreme court elections, and these ads are then classified by tone by Brennan Center researchers as "promotion of one candidate," "attack on the opponent," or "contrasting two or more candidates," which collectively constitute mutually exclusive and exhaustive categories. The exact number of airings of each ad also is reported, along with their sponsors.

Regarding model specification, I rely on well-established models of state supreme court elections (Bonneau 2007; Bonneau and Cann 2011; Dubois 1980; M. G. Hall 2001a, 2007b, 2014b; M. G. Hall and Bonneau 2006, 2008, 2013). Essentially, I seek to replicate previous studies of the incumbency advantage while adding the unique component of campaign advertising and the specific types of messages broadcast to voters.

State Supreme Court Campaigns

In models of contemporary judicial elections, important features of campaigns should figure prominently. Regarding attack advertising, the advocacy and political science literatures, with some exceptions, predict opposite effects for these controversial messages. Although groups like the American Bar Association and the Justice at Stake Campaign have deemed attack ads to be destructive for incumbents and politically alienating to voters, political science largely has failed to identify any harmful effects of negativity on candidate preference, voter turnout, or citizen attitudes essential to the civic culture. Given the empirical evidence generated to date from legislative and executive elections (which use partisan ballots) and the compelling theoretical story explaining why negativity does not have the effects initially predicted, this study hypothesizes that attack ads in state supreme court elections will reduce vote shares only in nonpartisan elections.

In measuring attack advertising, I follow the standard practice (e.g., Jackson and Carsey 2007; Jackson, Mondak, and Huckfeldt 2009) of counting the total number of airings in each race, separately against the incumbent (*attack airings against incumbent*) and the challenger (*attack airings against challenger*). Also consistent with convention, I transform the airings variables into their natural logarithms because of an expected diminishing marginal impact on incumbent support at higher levels of airings.[15] This same strategy is followed with promote ads (*promote airings for incumbent, promote airings for challenger*) and contrast ads (*contrast airings for incumbent, contrast airings for challenger*). All ads in each race are counted, regardless of their sponsors, which include candidates, political parties, interest groups, and other organizations.

Although there is little theoretical or empirical guidance in the scientific literature about what to expect with regard to the effects of promote or contrast ads, it may be that positive messages in promote ads and mixed messages in contrast ads will not have the same impact as outright attacks, even in nonpartisan elections. Citizens appear to weigh negative messages more heavily when evaluating candidates (Jackson and Carsey 2007). Also, positive messages may not effectively differentiate candidates and are less likely to mention specific issues or policies (Finkel and Geer 1998; Geer 2006). In fact, Jackson, Mondak, and Huckfeldt (2009) failed to find any consistent patterns in whether and how contrast and promote ads affect congressional approval and political efficacy. In state supreme court elections, Chapter 3 documents that both contrast and promote ads have less issue content than attack ads and thus may not be as useful to voters, although contrast ads should be better than promote ads on this score.

In addition to measuring the direct impact of attack, promote, and contrast ads separately for incumbents and challengers, I also gauge the relative impact of these three types of ads between incumbents and challengers. Specifically, I generate a variable measuring the difference in attack airings against the incumbent and attack airings against the challenger (*net attack airings against incumbent*). Similarly, I generate variables that subtract challenger airings from incumbent airings of promote ads (*net promote airings for incumbent*) and contrast ads (*net contrast airings for incumbent*).

Aside from advertising, another key aspect of campaigning is spending by the candidates. In fact, campaign spending is the principal indicator of overall campaign activity in American election studies. Generally, campaign expenditures capture the scope and intensity of campaigning, which is quite distinct conceptually from the tone and saturation of messages. Also, campaign advertising is but a part of overall spending in any race.[16]

In the models, campaign expenditures are measured two different ways. First, spending is measured in relative terms as the difference between the incumbent and challenger (*spending differences*). Generally, positive disparities should generate support for incumbents (Bonneau 2007; M. G. Hall and Bonneau 2006). However, as challengers outspend incumbents, support for incumbents should decline. Consistent with standard practice and the airings measures, I log the values of incumbent and challenger spending before calculating differences because of expected diminishing marginal returns. These figures also are recalculated into 2002 dollars to control for inflation.

Because of the central importance of this variable, I also measure spending separately for incumbents (*incumbent spending*) and challengers (*challenger spending*) and adjust these figures by each state's voting age population so that the values are comparable across states. As with the *spending differences* variable, I transform actual dollars into 2002 dollars and take the log of these figures. As Bonneau and Cann (2011) expertly have shown, spending by incumbents and challengers can have differential effects in supreme court elections.[17]

Candidate-Specific Variables
Various characteristics of the candidates themselves should be important determinants of their electoral fates. And of all the candidate-specific factors that should influence the ability to do well, first and foremost is the relative strength of the incumbent. Generally, candidates already occupying their positions enjoy an extraordinary advantage. However, the incumbency advantage is attenuated for those who were elected by relatively narrow margins or who initially were appointed to fill ad interim vacancies and are seeking their first electoral victories as supreme court justices (Bonneau 2007; M. G. Hall 2001a; M. G. Hall and Bonneau 2006).

To capture these effects, the models include a dummy variable (*unsafe seat*) to identify seats narrowly won with 55 percent of the vote or less. Consistent with previous research (e.g., Bonneau and Cann 2011; M. G. Hall 2001b,

2014b; M. G. Hall and Bonneau 2006, 2008), this variable is coded as dichotomous because of an anticipated threshold effect rather than a linear association. Theoretically, the effect of a change in previous vote share from 55 percent to 70 percent, for example, should differ from a 70 percent to 85 percent shift.

Similarly, the models distinguish between incumbents who successfully have campaigned for the high court bench and their novice counterparts (*new appointee*) who initially were appointed and have yet to face voters in supreme court races. This variable is dichotomous, coded 1 if the incumbent initially was appointed and is facing his or her first election and 0 otherwise. Generally, new appointees seeking the electorate's approval for the first time should perform less well than their more seasoned colleagues. These appointees will be less familiar to voters, will lack the experience of campaigning for the state high court, and may not have the credentials—political or otherwise—to be acceptable to the electorate, especially in states with unpopular governors or vigorous interpartisan competition (Bonneau 2007; M. G. Hall 2001a, 2014b; M. G. Hall and Bonneau 2006, 2008).

The final candidate characteristic to be evaluated is whether challengers are quality challengers (*quality challenger*), or candidates who already are judges or have been judges and thus represent qualified alternatives from the singular perspective of experience on the bench. Consistent with a voluminous literature on legislative elections, studies of state supreme courts (Bonneau 2007; Bonneau and Cann 2011; M. G. Hall 2014b; M. G. Hall and Bonneau 2006) have shown that the electorate favors challengers who are current or former judges over challengers who lack such experience (i.e., lawyers).[18] This choice arguably represents a meaningful substantive preference but also reflects the fact that these candidates benefit from the expertise and name recognition garnered from successful campaigns to the lower courts. *Quality challenger* is coded 1 if the challenger holds, or has ever held, a judgeship and 0 otherwise.

Institutional Context

In addition to campaigns and candidates, the institutional context within which the elections are held should affect the electoral performance of incumbents. Among these important variables is whether the state supreme court is experiencing the "new politics" of judicial elections. As M. G. Hall (2001a, 2007a) has shown, some states historically have been much more competitive than others, creating varying levels of electoral security for the high court bench. However, in a period of potentially rapid change, a dynamic measure is needed to identify states that in the past may have been safe for incumbents but now are experiencing keen competition and the electioneering that accompanies these races.

To this end, a marginal win in the previous election cycle has been shown to be an excellent predictor of ballot roll-off (Bonneau and M. G. Hall 2009; M. G. Hall 2007b; M. G. Hall and Bonneau 2013), vote shares (Bonneau 2007; Bonneau and M. G. Hall 2009; M. G. Hall 2014b; M. G. Hall and Bonneau 2006), challenger emergence (Bonneau and M. G. Hall 2003), and strategic retirement (M. G. Hall 2001b). Thus, I follow the conventional practice of including a variable (*competitive court*) coded 1 for states in which an election was won by 55 percent or less in the previous election cycle or 0 otherwise. Although this measure is not perfect, there are no other measures of electoral competition in state supreme courts capturing this dynamic that have been shown to have greater validity or reliability, including continuous variables rather than dichotomies.

Also, it is important to note that this measure is not related to each incumbent's previous electoral margin. The bivariate correlation between *competitive court* and *unsafe seat* is 0.013. This makes perfect sense given that terms of office range up to twelve years and a considerable number of electoral cycles can occur within a justice's term. Also, the electoral security of incumbents varies considerably within courts.

A second institutional feature that should play a critical role in the election returns is the professionalization of state supreme courts.[19] Studies of state legislative elections consistently have found that professionalization significantly increases the likelihood of challengers but decreases their effectiveness (e.g., Berry, Berkman, and Schneiderman 2000; Hogan 2004). In fact, the incumbency advantage is greatest in professionalized legislatures, where incumbents garner larger percentages of the vote and are much more likely to win (Carey, Niemi, and Powell 2000). Berry, Berkman, and Schneiderman (2000: 859) provide a compelling theoretical explanation for this interesting phenomenon by positing that "professionalism promotes institutionalization by establishing boundaries that shield members from external shocks." In other words, professionalism insulates individuals from the political, economic, and social context surrounding the institution.

The usual components of legislative professionalization are the "five S's": space, salary, session length, staff, and structure (Berry, Berkman, and Schneiderman 2000). In the judicial context, these factors have been adapted by Squire (2008) to include salary, staff, and docket control, all standardized against the U.S. Supreme Court. As applied to state supreme courts, these indicators "gauge a court's ability to generate and evaluate information" (Squire 2008: 223) and overall institutional capacity. Importantly, this measure does *not* include method of judicial selection, which has little to do with the information or performance capacity of courts.[20]

The Squire index of state supreme court professionalization ranges from 0 (least professionalized) to 1 (most professionalized) and should be strongly related to support for incumbents.[21] Generally, professionalized courts (*professionalization*) have a greater capacity to attract quality members, decide cases more efficiently and effectively, and use dockets strategically to minimize political controversy. Indeed, evidence has shown that highly professionalized state supreme courts allocate docket space differently than less professionalized courts, at least with tort cases involving power-asymmetric litigants (Brace and M. G. Hall 2001). Moreover, professionalized supreme courts have better strategic opportunities to promote incumbency. These institutions can avoid some controversial issues altogether by denying review and have greater flexibility to control the timing of sensitive decisions that otherwise cannot be dodged. Thus, professionalization provides a strategic advantage in the electoral process for incumbents seeking reelection.

A third institutional feature potentially affecting vote shares concerns the timing of the races in the electoral cycle. In some states, the electoral fates of incumbents are determined in primaries, either because the incumbent is defeated or wins with an absolute majority (thereby avoiding the general election). Excluding these races would interject systematic bias against largely one-party states and nonpartisan elections (e.g., Bonneau and M. G. Hall 2006; M. G. Hall 2001a, 2014b; Kritzer 2011). To control for these types of situations, the models include the variable *primary*, coded 1 for elections decided outside the national general election cycle and 0 otherwise.

Finally, this study places a sharp focus on ballot type. Research on state supreme courts has identified significant differences between partisan and nonpartisan elections in ballot roll-off and electoral competition for incumbents and candidates for open seats (e.g., Bonneau and M. G. Hall 2009;

M. G. Hall 2001a, 2007b; M. G. Hall and Bonneau 2006). Accordingly, this study hypothesizes that partisan elections without television advertising (*partisan*) will be more competitive than nonpartisan elections without advertising (the omitted baseline category), but it is not clear to what extent these effects will be present once features of campaigns and candidates are controlled.

Equally important, and as discussed as a central focus, partisan elections should condition the impact of attack ads on the vote shares of incumbents. Thus, the variable *partisan* is included as a multiplicative term in the models with each of the various types of televised messages.

Temporal Controls

To control for any temporal effects, the models include dummy variables for the year in which each election was held (2002, 2004, and 2006). The 2008 election cycle is excluded as the baseline category.

Estimation Technique

Because the dependent variable (*incumbent vote*) is continuous, ordinary least squares regression is used to estimate the models. Additionally, I use robust variance estimators clustered on state, which are robust to assumptions about within-group (i.e., state) correlation.

To provide a substantive context and to illustrate similarities and differences between nonpartisan and partisan elections, Table 4-1 shows the mean values of each variable for all elections and, separately, for nonpartisan and partisan elections. These statistics are based on the partisan and nonpartisan elections included in the statistical analysis in this chapter, which are contested nonpartisan and partisan elections in which incumbents are seeking reelection and for which there are no missing data values. In other words, these are the actual observations being analyzed.

As Table 4-1 indicates, nonpartisan and partisan elections look quite similar on multiple dimensions. Regarding the dependent variable, the average percentage of the vote in contested nonpartisan elections is 57.9 percent, which is close to the 59.5 percent in partisan elections. Likewise, nonpartisan and partisan elections are similar in levels of past competition for supreme court seats, justices in unsafe seats, professionalization of the state high court, and the proportion of elections decided outside the November general election cycle. Bigger differences are evidenced with new appointees and quality challengers. New appointees are more common in partisan elections, while quality challengers are more typical in nonpartisan elections.

TABLE 4-1. Variable means, overall and by election type, in campaign-based models of incumbent vote shares.*

Variable	All elections	Nonpartisan elections	Partisan elections
Incumbent vote	58.56	57.91	59.49
Attack airings against incumbent	145.07	160.58	122.80
Attack airings against challenger	79.88	51.09	121.22
Promote airings for incumbent	546.99	605.16	463.47
Promote airings for challenger	140.28	135.60	147.00
Contrast airings for incumbent	31.01	25.44	39.01
Contrast airings for challenger	109.39	56.30	185.62
Net attack airings against incumbent	65.19	109.49	1.58
Net promote airings for incumbent	383.77	469.56	260.57
Net contrast airings for incumbent	−12.85	−30.86	13.00
Spending differences	234,063	229,372	240,800
Incumbent spending (per capita)	173.08	182.84	159.06
Challenger spending (per capita)	120.35	130.75	105.41
Unsafe seat	0.2632	0.2679	0.2564
New appointee	0.2105	0.1607	0.2821
Quality challenger	0.4632	0.5536	0.3333
Competitive court	0.5895	0.6071	0.5641
Professionalization	0.6406	0.6231	0.6657
Primary	0.1789	0.1964	0.1538
Partisan	0.4105	0	1
2002	0.2211	0.1964	0.2564
2004	0.2947	0.3393	0.2308
2006	0.2842	0.2679	0.3077
2008	0.2000	0.1964	0.2051
N	95	56	39

* Means shown for the advertising and spending variables are actual values (airings or dollars) rather than natural logarithms.

These races also are fairly similar with regard to spending per capita, although nonpartisan elections are more expensive on average, both for incumbents and challengers, than partisan elections. When spending is viewed as differences between incumbents and challengers, these figures are fairly similar in nonpartisan and partisan elections. In both types of elections, incumbents tend to outspend challengers, with somewhat larger differences in partisan elections.

Regarding advertising, nonpartisan and partisan elections are closely comparable with regard to the average number of airings of promote ads for challengers and contrast ads for incumbents. However, there are some interesting differences in the use of advertising themes between nonpartisan and partisan elections. Attack advertising targeting incumbents is more common on average in nonpartisan elections than partisan elections. Negative ads attacking incumbents air, on average, 161 times in nonpartisan elections versus 123 times in partisan elections. Likewise, nonpartisan campaigns average higher levels of promote advertising for incumbents. In fact, in both nonpartisan and partisan elections, promotions of the incumbent are more prevalent than any other type of campaign message. On the other hand, attacks aimed at challengers are much more common in partisan races than nonpartisan elections, as is contrast advertising favoring challengers.

These intriguing patterns merit systematic evaluation. What effects do these variables, including attack airings, have on the electoral performance of incumbents, and are any campaign effects conditioned by the presence or absence of partisan ballots?

Results

The results of estimating campaign-based models of state supreme court elections in this new era of aggressive televised campaigns and open public dialogue across all states are reported in Table 4-2, which includes two alternative measures of campaign spending and models estimated only with those interactions that attain statistical significance.[22] Models with all interaction terms are reported in Table 4-3 as a robustness check. As Table 4-3 illustrates, the central inferences about attack advertising are not biased by choices about whether to include or exclude all possible theoretically relevant conditional relationships for advertising tone in the equations even if these relationships are not statistically significant. Table 4-3 also shows that the only significant statistical interaction among the campaign advertising variables is with attack ads targeting incumbents. Thus, it does not appear that institutional design plays much of a role in structuring the impact of other aspects of state supreme court advertising campaigns on the electoral margins of incumbents.

TABLE 4-2. Televised campaign advertising and the electoral performance of state supreme court incumbents, 2002–2008.

Variable	Model 1			Model 2		
	Coefficient	Robust standard error	P > |t|	Coefficient	Robust standard error	P > |t|
Campaign features						
Attack airings against incumbent	−0.8288	0.3028	0.014	−0.7453	0.3210	0.032
Attack airings against incumbent × partisan	1.5233	0.5184	0.009	1.7520	0.5526	0.005
Attack airings against challenger	−0.8543	0.5038	0.107	−0.9356	0.5370	0.099
Promote airings for incumbent	0.3779	0.1773	0.047	0.5231	0.1975	0.016
Promote airings for challenger	−0.8718	0.4152	0.050	−0.8079	0.4056	0.062
Contrast airings for incumbent	0.3526	0.4354	0.429	0.3820	0.4310	0.387
Contrast airings for challenger	−0.3421	0.3703	0.368	−0.3178	0.3580	0.386
Spending differences	1.1691	0.2441	0.000	—	—	—
Incumbent spending	—	—	—	0.4638	0.2366	0.066
Challenger spending	—	—	—	−1.3137	0.3726	0.002
Candidates						
Unsafe seat	−7.5017	1.3641	0.000	−7.0199	1.2866	0.000
New appointee	−4.2734	1.7092	0.022	−3.8384	1.8444	0.052
Quality challenger	−3.3806	1.1424	0.008	−2.8219	1.2256	0.033
Institutional context						
Competitive court	−3.5093	1.6163	0.044	−2.2635	2.0893	0.293
Professionalization	22.9901	3.9805	0.000	19.1938	5.3041	0.002
Primary	−3.0571	1.5548	0.065	−3.2710	1.7794	0.083
Partisan	0.2831	1.4660	0.849	−0.8826	2.0211	0.668
Temporal controls						
2002	0.9640	1.4904	0.526	1.2528	1.6105	0.447
2004	5.2576	2.2861	0.034	5.5651	2.0809	0.015
2006	6.0247	2.5595	0.030	6.2885	2.1250	0.008
Constant	42.9571	3.2774	0.000	46.9512	4.2035	0.000

Dependent variable = Incumbent vote
Number of observations = 95
Model 1 R-squared = 0.7022; Model 2 R-squared = 0.7213

TABLE 4-3. Televised campaign advertising and the electoral performance of state supreme court incumbents, 2002–2008, with interaction terms for all ad types.

Variable	Model 1 Coefficient	Model 1 Robust standard error	Model 1 P > |t|	Model 2 Coefficient	Model 2 Robust standard error	Model 2 P > |t|
Campaign features						
Attack airings against incumbent	−1.0423	0.3931	0.016	−0.9426	0.4210	0.038
Attack airings against incumbent × partisan	1.9336	0.5538	0.003	2.0383	0.5229	0.001
Attack airings against challenger	−0.6240	0.8853	0.490	−0.5252	0.8817	0.559
Attack airings against challenger × partisan	−1.0591	0.8167	0.211	−1.5424	0.8248	0.078
Promote airings for incumbent	0.3881	0.2628	0.157	0.4327	0.2933	0.157
Promote airings for incumbent × partisan	0.1281	0.3326	0.705	0.6392	0.3975	0.125
Promote airings for challenger	−0.8972	0.5898	0.146	−0.8175	0.5673	0.167
Promote airings for challenger × partisan	0.4514	1.0437	0.671	0.9397	1.0285	0.373
Contrast airings for incumbent	0.1655	0.6741	0.809	0.3204	0.6310	0.618
Contrast airings for incumbent × partisan	0.3509	0.8796	0.695	−0.1516	0.8538	0.861
Contrast airings for challenger	0.0394	0.7099	0.956	−0.0311	0.7208	0.966
Contrast airings for challenger × partisan	−0.9247	0.7117	0.210	−1.0482	0.7139	0.159
Spending differences	1.1707	0.2363	0.000	—	—	—
Incumbent spending	—	—	—	0.1812	0.1864	0.344
Challenger spending	—	—	—	−1.3925	0.3934	0.002
Candidates						
Unsafe seat	−7.9234	0.9816	0.000	−7.2053	0.7967	0.000
New appointee	−4.3933	1.8467	0.029	−3.5432	1.9861	0.091
Quality challenger	−3.7110	0.9584	0.001	−3.2931	1.0903	0.007
Institutional context						
Competitive court	−3.4740	1.4097	0.024	−1.6390	1.9322	0.407
Professionalization	23.9868	5.6467	0.000	19.3044	7.1027	0.014
Primary	−3.4799	1.6565	0.050	−4.5093	2.0308	0.039
Partisan	−1.3478	2.1285	0.535	−5.5468	2.9287	0.074
Temporal controls						
2002	0.2931	1.3515	0.831	1.0124	1.5295	0.516
2004	5.5287	2.1898	0.021	6.4413	1.8525	0.003
2006	5.4867	2.4736	0.040	6.0196	1.8885	0.005
Constant	43.3369	4.1916	0.000	49.3855	5.2398	0.000

Dependent variable = Incumbent vote
Number of observations = 95
Model 1 R-squared = 0.7205; Model 2 R-squared = 0.7508

Immediately apparent in Table 4-2, which represents the most appropriate modeling strategy, is the excellent performance of these models. Based on the features of campaigns, characteristics of the candidates, and institutional arrangements, the models in Table 4-2 can explain up to 72 percent of the variation in incumbent vote shares. Additionally, the substantive results and conclusions about the impact of attack advertising are not affected by how campaign spending is measured. In Model 1 and Model 2, the effects of attack advertising targeting incumbents clearly are conditioned in the same way by the presence or absence of partisan ballots in the predicted theoretical direction. Also, the "usual suspects" typically used to predict support for incumbents generally perform as expected. Overall, these models present a striking challenge to some of the rhetoric driving the contemporary court reform movement and the wisdom of preferring nonpartisan elections to partisan elections, at least on the single criterion of the destructive power of attack advertising on the incumbency advantage.

Specifically, as Model 1 and Model 2 in Table 4-2 document, the effects of attack advertising on incumbent vote shares are contingent on the presence or absence of partisan ballots. In both models, the interaction term (*attack airings against incumbent × partisan*) is statistically significant.[23] Moreover, in looking at the substantive impact of attack airings on incumbent vote shares, the effects of attack airings targeting incumbents are positive in partisan elections (–0.8288 [*attack airings against incumbent*] + 1.5233 [*attack airings against incumbent × partisan*] = 0.6945 in Model 1 and 1.0067 in Model 2) but are negative and statistically significant in nonpartisan elections.[24] In short, the impact of attack advertising on the electoral performance of incumbents depends on the type of election in which these ads appear, and attacks targeting incumbents have adverse effects on the incumbency advantage only in nonpartisan elections.

Why might attack ads designed to unseat incumbents in partisan elections improve their vote shares, as Model 1 and Model 2 suggest? The most obvious and straightforward explanation is that, for whatever reasons, a few of the nastiest advertising campaigns were launched against popular, electorally secure incumbents who would perform well no matter what.[25] As studies have shown (e.g., Bonneau and M. G. Hall 2009; M. G. Hall 2007b), the state minority party often has incentives to field candidates even when the probability of winning is not high, especially if the state enjoys healthy two-party competition.

As Table 4-2 also indicates, attack airings targeting challengers do not seem to play much of a role in the electoral performance of incumbents in state supreme court elections. The variable *attack airings against challenger* is not statistically significant.

Advertising to promote incumbents and challengers in partisan and non-partisan elections also has a discernable electoral impact. In Models 1 and 2, promote airings for the incumbent increase their vote shares while promote airings for the challenger decrease them. Moreover, promote airings for challengers have a stronger substantive impact than promote airings for incumbents. However, the fact that the coefficient for *promote airings for challenger* fails to attain statistical significance at the 0.05 level in Model 2 ($p = 0.062$) suggests the need to exercise caution in drawing inferences about these ads at this point in the development of the literature.

Unlike televised attack and promote airings, contrast advertising (for incumbents or challengers) does not have an effect on the election returns in partisan or nonpartisan state supreme court elections, as evidenced in Model 1 and Model 2. Perhaps it is the case that these mixed messages do not translate as well with voters as the straightforward appeals in attack and promote ads. Alternatively, given the relatively infrequent use of contrast ads, especially contrast airings favoring incumbents, there may not be enough of these airings to detect an impact. More election cycles will provide better insight into this question. Without additional analysis and more extensive data, it is difficult to say with any certainty what explains this interesting result.

As Table 4-2 also indicates, campaign spending plays a significant role in the electoral performance of incumbents. Measured in Model 1 as disparities between incumbents and challengers, the coefficient for *spending differences* reveals that when incumbents outspend challengers (the typical scenario), their vote shares increase by about 1.2 percentage points for every unit increase (in the models, logarithmic increases) in this differential. And because incumbents are advantaged in raising money, big spending should favor incumbents (e.g., Bonneau 2007; Bonneau and Cann 2011). Of course, when challengers outspend incumbents, the incumbency advantage is attenuated accordingly. Thus, incumbents can offset the adverse effects of other aspects of the campaign environment by increasing their spending. In fact, effective campaign financing seems imperative to counterbalance challengers, as common sense would suggest.

Model 2 in Table 4-2, which measures campaign expenditures separately for incumbents and challengers, supports this same story. Overall, spending by incumbents improves their electoral fates (by about a 0.46 percentage point per unit increase in spending logged, albeit only at the 0.066 level of confidence) while spending by challengers reduces incumbent vote shares (by 1.3 percentage points). These differential impacts in incumbent and challenger spending are entirely consistent with previous research (e.g., Bonneau 2007; Bonneau and Cann 2011). Generally, incumbents must spend more to influence their electoral fates, but many factors (including fundraising) favor incumbents in the first place.

Regarding the candidates, incumbents perform less well when they already hold unsafe seats, are newly appointed, or are facing quality challengers. Models 1 and 2 show that incumbents in unsafe seats earn about 7.0 to 7.5 percentage points less in vote shares, while appointees earn about 3.8 to 4.3 percentage points less. Similarly, quality challengers reduce incumbent votes by 2.8 to 3.4 percentage points. Taken together, a vulnerable incumbent (veteran or novice) facing a quality challenger can expect to earn about 13.7 to 15.2 percentage points less than popular incumbents facing inexperienced challengers.

These results illustrate well the capacity of the electorate in state supreme court elections to draw meaningful distinctions among challengers based on their job experience in the lower courts, even with attack advertising in play. The negative stereotypes of voters prevalent in legal scholarship and the advocacy literature (e.g., American Bar Association Commission on the 21st Century Judiciary 2003; Geyh 2003; Rottman and Schotland 2001; Schotland 1985) are overdrawn, as earlier studies have shown (e.g., M. G. Hall 2001a, 2014b; M. G. Hall and Bonneau 2006). If anything, effective campaigns and open public dialogue about candidates should improve the information available to voters and facilitate candidate-based choices.

Finally, institutions are paramount. In legislatures and courts, the impact of professionalism on the electoral security of individual members is substantively and statistically powerful. Likewise, *competitive court* is an excellent predictor of votes in Model 1. On balance, a tight race in the previous election cycle predicts a loss in votes for the next incumbents seeking reelection of about 3.5 percentage points.

Contrary to expectations, Models 1 and 2 do not produce convincing evidence that the timing of an election within the annual election cycle is

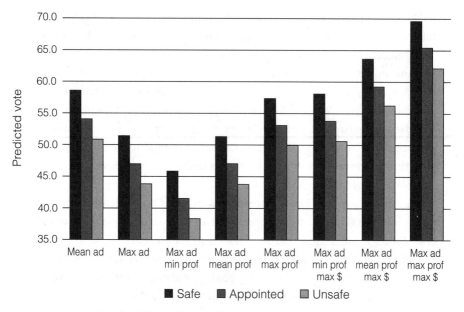

FIGURE 4-1. Predicted vote shares of state supreme court incumbents in nonpartisan elections at various levels of televised attack airings, professionalization, and campaign spending (using Model 1 in Table 4-2).

significantly related to the electoral performance of incumbents. Although there is better evidence in Model 1 that election outcomes settled in the primaries result in lower vote shares for incumbents, the variable *primary* is not significant at or below the 0.05 level in either specification. Likewise, partisan elections no longer differ from nonpartisan elections once the effects of advertising and other important campaign features are controlled.

Regarding the temporal controls in the model, the election results in 2004 and 2006 are statistically different from the omitted baseline year 2008. In both 2004 and 2006, incumbent vote shares were higher than in 2008. However, 2002 is not statistically different from 2008.

Predicted values of incumbent vote shares based on Model 1 in Table 4-2 place in stark relief these intriguing results.[26] Figure 4-1 displays these values graphically, illustrating clearly and concisely the power of attack advertising in nonpartisan elections, as well as the capacity for other factors to offset these effects. Although many might dispute the value of the incumbency advantage, professionalization and campaign spending seem to hold considerable promise for protecting supreme court justices seeking reelection against the adverse effects of televised attack advertising.

Consider first a scenario in which incumbents in nonpartisan elections are facing quality challengers in competitive states. Under these conditions, with all variables at their means including attack airings, predicted vote is 58.6 percent for incumbents in safe seats, 54.2 percent for appointees, and 51.1 percent for incumbents in unsafe seats. However, increasing attack airings against incumbents to their maximum value reduces vote shares to, respectively, 51.4 percent, 47.1 percent, and 43.9 percent. Thus, other things being equal, an average attack campaign can result in marginal wins for all but popular experienced incumbents. At their highest levels, these campaigns can produce marginal wins even for popular incumbents and losses for the newly appointed and less popular.

Professionalization can help to counteract the destructive power of attack advertising in nonpartisan elections for all types of incumbents seeking reelection. In the least professionalized courts with competitive seats and quality challengers, predicted votes in the most prolific attack campaigns against incumbents show that all types of incumbents would be expected to lose. Predicted votes under these conditions are 45.9 percent for justices in safe seats, 41.6 percent for the newly appointed, and 38.4 percent for justices in unsafe seats. However, as just shown, when attack airings are their worst and professionalism is average, predicted vote shares, respectively, are 51.4 percent, 47.1 percent, and 43.9 percent. Thus, average levels of professionalization help incumbents in safe seats to win when attack campaigns are the most severe but do not provide the same electoral boost to other incumbents. Even so, average professionalism increases the predicted vote shares of the newly appointed and justices in marginal seats substantially. Highly professionalized courts help all incumbents to weather the most vociferous attack campaigns and predict wins for all three sets of incumbents, ceteris paribus. When professionalism is set at the maximum value, predicted votes rise to 57.5 percent for popular incumbents, 53.1 percent for appointees, and 50.0 percent for marginal justices in nonpartisan elections.

Of course, other factors shape the net effects of campaign advertising, including spending by the incumbents. As with campaigns for other offices, some factors influencing the incumbency advantage are within the control of the candidates while others are set into motion long before campaigns begin by the fundamental choices states make about how elections are conducted and institutions are structured.

Figure 4-1 illustrates well the power of campaign spending in highly competitive nonpartisan elections with extremely negative campaigns and varying conditions of professionalization. In fact, predicted vote share is 58.2 percent for justices in safe seats, 53.9 percent for the newly appointed, and 50.7 percent for justices in unsafe seats when attack airings are at their worst and professionalism is at its least but spending favors incumbents at the maximum value of this differential. Under these extreme conditions, all types of incumbents would be predicted to receive a majority of the vote. When professionalism is average, predicted vote shares rise considerably, producing safe wins for even the most vulnerable incumbents. Predicted vote shares in this scenario are 63.8 percent for safe incumbents, 59.4 percent for the newly appointed, and 56.3 percent for marginal justices. When attack airings against incumbents are at their maximum, and professionalism and spending differences also are at their highest levels, incumbents of all types should enjoy huge victories. For justices in safe seats, the newly appointed, and justices in unsafe seats, predicted votes under this scenario are, respectively, 69.8 percent, 65.5 percent, and 62.3 percent in otherwise highly competitive nonpartisan elections. Overall, big spending can be an essential tool for securing not only electoral wins for incumbents in bruising contests but also can produce safe seats for justices seeking reelection.

An alternative conceptualization of state supreme court campaigns supports these same conclusions. Table 4-4 reports the results of measuring campaigns as the relative effects of the three types of campaign ads between incumbents and challengers.[27] As the models indicate, the differences in the impact of attacks targeting incumbents are statistically significant in nonpartisan elections compared with partisan elections. Likewise, as attack airings against incumbents increase in nonpartisan elections relative to attack airings against challengers, the electoral success of incumbents substantially declines. However, the opposite occurs in partisan elections.

Higher levels of promote airings from incumbents relative to challengers also improve incumbent vote shares. Positivity in volumes from incumbents relative to challengers may be another effective way to help offset the harmful effects of attack politics in nonpartisan elections.

Interestingly, contrast ads when considered separately as strategies for incumbents and challengers were not important influences on incumbent vote

TABLE 4-4. Televised campaign advertising as net effects and the electoral performance of state supreme court incumbents, 2002–2008.

	Model 1			Model 2		
Variable	Coefficient	Robust standard error	P > |t|	Coefficient	Robust standard error	P > |t|
Campaign features						
Net attack airings against incumbent	−1.1540	0.3473	0.004	−0.9712	0.3810	0.020
Net attack airings against incumbent × partisan	1.9833	0.3477	0.000	2.7823	0.6568	0.000
Net promote airings for incumbent	0.5742	0.2717	0.049	0.6801	0.2578	0.017
Net contrast airings for incumbent	0.6678	0.2764	0.027	0.6765	0.2407	0.012
Spending differences	1.3972	0.1795	0.000	—	—	—
Incumbent spending	—	—	—	0.2231	0.3037	0.472
Challenger spending	—	—	—	−1.5184	0.2802	0.000
Candidates						
Unsafe seat	−8.0903	1.2303	0.000	−7.3578	1.1917	0.000
New appointee	−4.4166	1.8667	0.029	−3.4067	1.9378	0.096
Quality challenger	−4.1882	1.3745	0.007	−2.8460	1.4278	0.062
Institutional context						
Competitive court	−3.6796	1.5077	0.025	−1.1636	1.5671	0.467
Professionalization	24.4709	4.3872	0.000	17.9160	5.4693	0.004
Primary	−3.0061	1.7424	0.102	−3.3891	2.0253	0.112
Partisan	−2.2209	1.1854	0.077	−4.8002	1.4729	0.004
Temporal controls						
2002	0.8430	2.0619	0.687	0.8541	2.1373	0.694
2004	5.3395	2.1398	0.023	5.6139	1.7239	0.004
2006	3.9612	2.4051	0.117	4.4212	1.8838	0.031
Constant	45.3976	3.4676	0.000	51.7584	4.3894	0.000

Dependent variable = Incumbent vote
Number of observations = 95
Model 1 R-squared = 0.6356; Model 2 R-squared = 0.6906

shares. However, contrast airings in relative terms do emerge as significant. As with promote ads, higher airings of contrast ads by incumbents relative to challengers improve their electoral fortunes and may be a useful tool for counteracting the deleterious impact of attack campaigns.

A comparison of Model 1 and Model 2 in Table 4-4 shows that these intriguing results about the significance of different types of campaign messages on the incumbency advantage are not biased by how campaign spending is measured, as with the models in Table 4-2 and Table 4-3. While a few of the coefficients change somewhat from Model 1 to Model 2, this is likely due to the increased multicollinearity in the models when spending is measured separately for incumbents and challengers.

Robustness Checks for Third-Party Challengers and Hybrid Election States

Two other aspects of state supreme court elections merit attention: (1) partisan elections in which the only challengers are third-party candidates and (2) the mixed-elections systems in Michigan and Ohio. First, although rather unusual, some partisan supreme court elections draw only minor-party candidates who pose no real threat to the incumbents. In the elections analyzed in this chapter, the only cases in which this occurs are nine of the twenty-six elections for the Texas Supreme Court (the civil court of last resort) and Court of Criminal Appeals (the criminal court of last resort). In these races, libertarian candidates were the only challengers to major-party incumbents in the general elections. Failing to control for this circumstance may bias the results in partisan elections by unduly inflating the vote shares of incumbents.

In the models, the primary tools for distinguishing between weak and strong challengers drawn from both major and minor parties in partisan and nonpartisan elections are the variables for quality challengers, spending, and advertising. In fact, weak challengers can be present in nonpartisan elections as well as partisan elections but are much more difficult to identify a priori given the absence of partisan labels and the difficulty of assigning partisanship in some states from biographical data about the candidates.

However, for additional confidence in the central inferences drawn in this chapter, I reestimated Model 1 in Table 4-2 with a dummy variable, *third-party challenger*, coded 1 for all races in which the only challenger is a third-party candidate and 0 otherwise. Interaction terms specific to these third-party races are not necessary because none of the Texas elections with libertarian challengers resulted in attack advertising. In fact, none of the campaigns for the twenty-six elections in Texas from 2002 through 2008 involved attack advertising for or against any candidate.[28]

Second, I address a serious contention proffered by some of the most vociferous critics of empirical judicial elections scholarship and partisan judicial elections (e.g., Brandenburg and Caufield 2009). The claim is that classifying supreme court elections as nonpartisan in Michigan and Ohio biases any consequent statistical analyses.[29] In particular, unlike other nonpartisan states, Michigan and Ohio use partisan processes to nominate candidates for the state court bench (i.e., party conventions in Michigan and partisan primaries in Ohio).[30] However, entirely consistent with other nonpartisan states, both Michigan and Ohio omit the partisan affiliations of judicial candidates on general elections ballots. Of course, this difference in nomination processes is mitigated somewhat in the post-*White* era given that no state is permitted to restrict judicial candidates from announcing their views on issues, just as many states have liberalized their speech codes in the wake of *White* (Caufield 2005, 2007). Nonetheless, as a robustness check, I recoded Michigan and Ohio as hybrid election systems (a combination of partisan and nonpartisan) and then reestimated the models.[31]

Specifically, to test whether the results about the impact of attack advertising are robust with regard to how state judicial elections systems are classified, I reestimated Model 1 in Table 4-2 with a variable *hybrid*, coded 1 for Michigan and Ohio and 0 otherwise, and then again with an interaction term for *hybrid × attack airings against incumbent*. Although it would be obviously incorrect to classify supreme court elections in Michigan and Ohio as partisan given the absence of partisan labels on the ballots in general elections,[32] classifying them into a third category is appropriate given the vigorous assertions from legal interest groups that empirical research failing to distinguish these races produces fatally flawed inferences (e.g., Brandenburg and Caufield 2009).[33] These results are reported as Models 1 and 2 in Table 4-5, along with the test for third-party challengers.[34]

As the results in Table 4-5 indicate, although *third-party challenger* is statistically significant, the inclusion of this control variable does not change the substantive inferences about the impact of negative advertising in partisan elections. The same is true when a dummy variable for Texas (not shown) is substituted for *third-party challenger*, although the Texas dummy variable is not statistically significant. In short, the results in this chapter are robust with regard to the treatment of third-party challengers. Substantively, incumbents

TABLE 4-5. Televised campaign advertising and the electoral performance of state supreme court incumbents, 2002–2008, with robustness checks for third-party challengers and hybrid election systems (Michigan and Ohio).

Variable	Model 1 Coefficient	Model 1 Robust standard error	Model 1 $P > |t|$	Model 2 Coefficient	Model 2 Robust standard error	Model 2 $P > |t|$
Control variables						
Third-party challenger	15.6065	3.2415	0.000	15.5631	3.3086	0.000
Hybrid	1.8433	2.7397	0.510	1.9489	2.5766	0.459
Hybrid × attack airings against incumbent	—	—	—	−0.4275	0.3844	0.281
Campaign features						
Attack airings against incumbent	−0.9268	0.3248	0.011	−0.7246	0.2925	0.023
Attack airings against incumbent × partisan	1.8040	0.6259	0.010	1.6476	0.6851	0.027
Attack airings against challenger	−0.8161	0.5449	0.152	−0.8925	0.5084	0.096
Promote airings for incumbent	0.5347	0.2652	0.059	0.5424	0.2596	0.051
Promote airings for challenger	−1.0396	0.4615	0.037	−1.0371	0.4469	0.032
Contrast airings for incumbent	0.2824	0.4255	0.515	0.2666	0.4210	0.534
Contrast airings for challenger	−0.3223	0.3495	0.369	−0.2931	0.3502	0.414
Spending differences	0.3761	0.1242	0.007	0.3947	0.1305	0.007
Candidates						
Unsafe seat	−6.3464	1.9826	0.005	−6.3982	2.0576	0.006
New appointee	−3.5402	1.7021	0.052	−3.2861	1.6231	0.058
Quality challenger	−2.5238	1.3765	0.083	−2.4859	1.3729	0.087
Institutional context						
Competitive court	−3.4423	1.5180	0.036	−3.6146	1.6276	0.039
Professionalization	19.4508	6.4829	0.008	19.3832	6.5628	0.009
Primary	−1.9137	1.5075	0.220	−1.8552	1.5242	0.239
Partisan	−1.5092	1.9430	0.447	−1.6716	2.0028	0.415
Temporal controls						
2002	2.7662	1.6442	0.110	2.6714	1.7729	0.149
2004	5.7474	2.1713	0.016	5.8763	2.1630	0.014
2006	5.6576	2.4085	0.030	5.5585	2.3567	0.030
Constant	43.8687	4.8012	0.000	43.9997	4.9312	0.000

Dependent variable = Incumbent vote
Number of observations = 95
Model 1 R-squared = 0.7647; Model 2 R-squared = 0.7667

in races with minor-party challengers can expect to do about fifteen percentage points better than their colleagues facing Democratic or Republican challengers.[35]

Regarding Michigan and Ohio, the coefficient for *hybrid* in Model 1 is not statistically significant and has no impact on the performance of the other coefficients or the overall performance of model itself.[36] In Model 2, *hybrid ×attack airings against incumbent* is not statistically significant either. There do not appear to be any statistically significant differences in the impact of attack airings in hybrid elections compared with nonpartisan elections. Additionally, the coefficients measuring the impact of attacks targeting incumbents on vote shares in both hybrid elections and nonpartisan elections are negative, while the coefficient for partisan elections is positive. In short, the models in this chapter are robust with regard to the treatment of third-party challengers and the elections in Michigan and Ohio.

The results for Michigan and Ohio are not surprising. All of the Michigan and Ohio races were decided in general elections and not in primaries, and in these general elections the most important ballot cue—partisan labels for each of the candidates—was missing for voters. Although some voters may have knowledge of the partisanship of the candidates from earlier in the process or from advertising and other sources of political information, this is true in any nonpartisan race, including those not using partisan nomination processes. Thus, when the focus is on formal ballot provisions and what voters know simply by looking at the ballot, Michigan and Ohio are not substantially distinct with regard to the impact of this structural feature on the incumbency advantage in state supreme court elections.

Overall, a comparison of all of the models in Table 4-2, Table 4-3, Table 4-4, and Table 4-5 shows a rather impressive level of stability across a variety of alternative specifications and measurement strategies. Collectively, these results provide considerable confidence in the robustness of the results and central inferences in this chapter.

Conclusion

This examination of state supreme court elections in an era of unprecedented television advertising and new rules of the game for candidates in some states represents an exciting dynamic synergy between theoretically driven empirical scholarship and practical concerns dominating the American political agenda. On the practical side, this study documents that concerns from judicial reform advocates about the potentially destructive consequences of rough-and-tumble campaigns are partially well founded. Attack advertising in state supreme court elections takes a toll on incumbents but only in nonpartisan elections. As Schaffner, Streb, and Wright (2001: 26) observed about mayoral and state legislative elections, nonpartisan elections may be situations in which "even a modestly effective campaign might have substantial effects." In sum, campaigns do matter but exactly how depends on the nature of the ballot. The states' decisions about nonpartisan versus partisan ballots in state supreme court elections play a vital role in determining how various types of campaign messages translate into citizens' candidate choices.

On balance, these fascinating findings call into question the wisdom of advocating nonpartisan elections by those whose overriding concerns are with maximizing the incumbency advantage while minimizing the adverse effects of caustic campaigns and the impact of electoral politics on the judiciary. As these results demonstrate, nonpartisan elections appear not to promote these goals.

Ironically, nonpartisan elections may enhance the linkage between citizens and the bench, a result wholly inconsistent with the reform advocates' goals for these elections. This study shows that incumbents targeted by televised attacks in nonpartisan elections can expect tighter margins of victory, which in extreme circumstances may mean electoral defeat. However, even without formal electoral censure, reduced vote shares have other tangible consequences. Among other things, justices in unsafe seats are more likely to defer to their constituencies when deciding controversial issues, thereby engaging in representational behavior characteristic of legislative and executive actors (e.g., Brace and M. G. Hall 2001; M. G. Hall 1987, 1992, 1995, 2014a). Moreover, competitive seats are likely to inspire future electoral challenge (e.g., Bonneau and M. G. Hall 2003; M. G. Hall and Bonneau 2006), setting into motion another cycle of electoral marginality and constituency responsiveness.[37]

In this regard, professionalizing state supreme courts holds promise for partially reconciling the interests of the judicial reform movement with the practice of electing judges. States can offset highly contentious electoral climates to some extent by increasing the salaries and staff of state supreme courts and removing the burdens of high-volume routine appeals from their dockets. These kinds of changes designed to improve the status and function of the judiciary are far less controversial than attempts to alter the means through which the justices are selected and retained and thus may be easier to implement in the political sphere.

Of course, enhanced campaign spending by incumbents relative to challengers also can help to shield incumbents in nonpartisan elections from the pernicious effects of televised attacks. In this regard, money is an effective tool for informing voters and retaining office. Televised campaign promotions also bolster the electoral performance of incumbents in both nonpartisan and partisan elections.

From a different perspective, this study documents that even in the era of televised attacks and well-financed campaigns, the electorate continues to prefer challengers who have successfully attained judicial office to challengers who would be novices as judges. Although this finding also reflects the name recognition and campaign experience that elected officials obtain from successfully seeking and holding office, the electorate's preference for quality challengers suggests that voting in judicial elections is more candidate centered than is widely appreciated.

Indeed, voters in state supreme court elections appear to be more capable of distinguishing among candidates than legal accounts suggest. The electorate's preference for quality challengers over novices for state supreme court seats represents, at least in part, a discerning choice to favor candidates for the state high court bench who have the professional experience appropriate for the job.[38] Similarly, state electorates systematically differentiate among various types of incumbents. As this study has shown, consistently with previous work (e.g., Bonneau and M. G. Hall 2009; M. G. Hall and Bonneau 2006, 2013; M.G. Hall 2014b), justices who initially were appointed and are seeking their first electoral victories on the state high court, along with justices who narrowly won their last elections, perform less well with voters. In other words, state electorates tend to disfavor state supreme court justices who never were approved by voters in the first place or have been electorally unpopular. Moreover, extant research has documented that state supreme court electorates cast issue-based votes, including retrospective evaluations, when enough information is available, even in nonpartisan elections (e.g., Baum and Klein 2007; M. G. Hall 2001a; Hojnacki and Baum 1992). In short, the long-standing stereotype of state electorates as obdurately ignorant or incapable of choosing the most qualified and experienced candidates in state supreme court elections is incorrect and should be discarded.

These findings also add to a rapidly developing body of evidence showing remarkable similarities between state supreme court elections and elections to other important offices in the United States. Previous work has demonstrated, among other things, that supreme court elections (partisan and nonpartisan) resemble legislative and executive elections in the strategies of challengers (Bonneau and M. G. Hall 2003; M. G. Hall and Bonneau 2006, 2008), strategic retirements by electorally vulnerable incumbents (M. G. Hall 2001b), and citizen mobilization (e.g., M. G. Hall 2007b; M. G. Hall and Bonneau 2006, 2013; Hojnacki and Baum 1992; Klein and Baum 2001). This study now documents that even in courts, which are steeped in normative expectations of apolitical behavior by judges and lack an explicit representative function, attack advertising does not have an adverse impact on the electoral performance of incumbents except when partisan labels are absent from the ballot.

This point is essential, not only for understanding the impact of attack advertising but also for thinking about cross-institutional comparisons in the scientific literature. Although studies of legislative and executive institutions provide important insights into the operations of state supreme courts and vice versa, cross-institutional generalizations become more tenuous when partisan labels are removed from ballots. In this regard, some of the most significant dissimilarities between state judiciaries and the political branches are not due to intrinsic differences in institutional functions but instead reflect the fact that nonpartisan elections fundamentally change the rules of the political game.

In the discipline of political science and studies of campaigns and elections, state supreme courts represent an outstanding analytical opportunity for addressing questions about how context shapes democratic politics, particularly in low-information settings and elections lacking the partisan cue. From this project, we now have evidence that certain institutional arrangements shape the power of campaigns, including the effectiveness of attack advertising. We also have new information about elections conducted in a nonpartisan context, which may have potential implications for the wide variety of offices in the United States selected in the same manner. Taken together, these results suggest that studies of state supreme court elections hold considerable promise for developing general theories of voter choice and campaign politics that better delineate the impact of institutions and other contextual contingencies on American politics. In sum, institutions matter, and this fundamental precept is visibly evidenced in state supreme court elections.

5   Attack Advertising and Citizen Participation in State Supreme Court Elections

DESPITE THE VIBRANCY AND ENDURANCE OF DEMOCRATIC government in the United States, the American electorate's ambivalence toward elections is pronounced. For offices at all levels of government, large proportions of the eligible electorate do not bother to vote,[1] causing scholars and politicians to ponder the likely effects of such behavior on the operations and legitimacy of the popularly elected institutions and to devise solutions to enhance citizen participation. As even the most casual observer of politics understands, the foundations of representative democracy rest squarely on the willingness of citizens to go to the polls. Stated succinctly by Hajnal and Trounstine (2005: 515), "At its core, democracy rests on the vote."

Given the inextricable linkage between voting and representative democracy, caustic campaigns and their potentially damaging effects on the electorate become a vital concern, especially in light of the fact that the rise of attack advertising largely has coincided with significant declines in voter turnout in the nation's most visible elections. In this regard, Ansolabehere et al. (1994; Ansolabehere and Iyengar 1995) ignited a firestorm by asserting that televised attack advertising in campaigns constitutes "a serious antidemocratic threat" (Ansolabehere and Iyengar 1995: 9) that alienates and demobilizes the electorate.[2] In these studies, the explanation for vote suppression was as disturbing as the effect itself. Ansolabehere and Iyengar (1995) argued that cynicism from viewing disparaging advertising was not simply directed toward the candidates being attacked or the candidates in the race but toward the electoral process and political institutions themselves.

In response to these and other arguments about the effects of harsh negativity in American politics, political scientists have produced a significant body of work assessing whether nasty below-the-belt campaigns demobilize the electorate and undermine the civic culture essential to an effective democracy.[3] Conspicuously absent from these critical discussions are judicial elections, including elections to the states' highest courts.[4] This is regrettable given the extraordinary efforts currently underway to end the practice of electing judges based largely on unverified assumptions and the distinct possibility that negative advertising may pack much more of a punch in judicial elections than other types of elections. In state judiciaries, deeply engrained normative expectations of judicial impartiality (e.g., Gibson 2008, 2009; Gibson et al. 2011) and the absence of a direct representative role may mean that derisive attacks on judges, their beliefs, and their choices will be particularly harmful to the mobilization of the electorate. Likewise, recent changes in campaign discourse in some states, including the rise of televised attack advertising and the U.S. Supreme Court's decision in *Republican Party of Minnesota* v. *White* (2002) to lessen speech restrictions on judicial candidates, may exacerbate these effects.

To address these issues, this chapter evaluates the impact of negative advertising and other types of campaign messages on citizen participation in state supreme court elections. Specifically, I assess whether attack ads depress voter mobilization and whether nonpartisan and partisan elections differ on this dimension. In doing so, I examine the ninety-six contested supreme court elections held contemporaneously with presidential, senatorial, or gubernatorial contests from 2002 through 2008 in states using partisan or nonpartisan elections to staff their highest courts. Comparing state supreme court elections systematically over time and across states will provide considerable insight into the effects of election-specific and state-level contextual forces on the propensity of the American electorate to vote. More specifically, the analysis will determine quite readily whether, and to what degree, voters respond to the various tones of campaign messages and other incentives believed to facilitate or inhibit voting. This research also will reveal whether and how any effects of campaign broadcasts are conditioned by partisan ballots.

Campaign Negativity in Political Science

In the past several decades, political scientists have devoted considerable attention to the question of whether negative campaign advertising, including harsh or scurrilous assaults on candidates and their records, has adverse consequences for the electorate and the American political system.[5] Perhaps the most damning assertions, and certainly the most influential, came from Ansolabehere et al. (1994) and Ansolabehere and Iyengar (1995). These two landmark studies produced plausible empirical evidence, generated largely through experiments, that negative campaigns decrease voter turnout and result in the diminution of fundamental individual attitudes essential for a robust civic society, including efficacy and confidence in political institutions.[6]

The Ansolabehere et al. (1994) and Ansolabehere and Iyengar (1995) studies inspired a wealth of research testing these and other hypotheses about the effects of campaign negativity on American voters. These subsequent works— all theoretically rich and methodologically rigorous—nonetheless constitute a diverse body of scholarship. Scientific studies assessing the effects of campaign negativity have used experiments (e.g., Brooks and Geer 2007; Clinton and Lapinski 2004), statistical analyses of various aggregate-level election results (e.g., Finkel and Geer 1998; Jackson and Carsey 2007; Lau and Pomper 2001), empirical analyses of individual-level survey data (e.g., Goldstein and Freedman 2002; Jackson and Carsey 2007; Lau and Pomper 2001), and meta analyses of extant research (e.g., Lau et al. 1999; Lau, Sigelman, and Rovner 2007). In doing so, scholars have assessed self-reported voting (e.g., Finkel and Geer 1998; Goldstein and Freedman 2002; Jackson and Carsey 2007; Jackson and Sides 2006; Lau and Pomper 2001); individual attitudes promoting civic engagement, such as efficacy, trust, and support for political institutions (e.g., Brooks and Geer 2007; Jackson, Mondak, and Huckfeldt 2009); and turnout rates (e.g., Finkel and Geer 1998; Lau and Pomper 2001).

In these works, data sources about campaign advertising have been varied. Some researchers have collected and coded television commercials and newspaper stories on their own (e.g., Brooks 2006; Jackson and Sides 2006; Lau and Pomper 2001). Others have employed the collections organized by the Campaign Media Analysis Group and the Wisconsin Ads Project (e.g., Goldstein and Freedman 2002; Jackson and Carsey 2007; Jackson, Mondak, and Huckfeldt 2009).

In defining negativity, studies have examined not only the overall tone of campaigns (negative or positive) but also various intensities of negativity, including "mudslinging" (Jackson and Sides 2006: 209) and "incivility" consisting of "attacks that go far beyond facts and differences, and move instead towards name-calling, contempt, and derision of the opposition" (Brooks and Geer 2007: 1).

Finally, scholars have examined negativity in a variety of elections to the nation's most visible offices, including presidential (e.g., Finkel and Geer 1998; Clinton and Lapinski 2004; Goldstein and Freedman 2002), congressional (e.g., Jackson and Carsey 2007; Jackson, Mondak, and Huckfeldt 2009; Jackson and Sides 2006; Lau and Pomper 2001) and gubernatorial races (e.g., Jackson, Mondak, and Huckfeldt 2009).

Overall, despite the variations in research methodology in this extensive body of work and some important variations in the specific conclusions offered by each study, the bottom line essentially is the same. Negative campaigns do not demobilize the electorate or threaten individual political attitudes essential for a healthy democracy, even when attacks "cross a proverbial line" by being "excessively harsh" (Brooks and Geer 2007: 1).[7] In fact, some evidence supports the contention that negative ads *enhance* citizen participation rather than diminish it (e.g., Finkel and Geer 1998; Goldstein and Freedman 2002; Jackson and Carsey 2007; Jackson and Sides 2006; Lau and Pomper 2001).[8]

These findings and their explanations form much of the theoretical basis underlying this research about campaign negativity in state supreme court elections. As numerous scholars have argued (e.g., Finkel and Geer 1998; Geer 2006; Jackson and Carsey 2007; West 2010), negative advertising improves the quantity and quality of information available to voters while better highlighting the differences between candidates. Negativity also enhances the degree to which citizens become interested and invested in election outcomes and heightens the ties between voters and their party's nominees (e.g., Finkel and Geer 1998). Stated succinctly by Geer (2006: 13) from the perspective of democratic theory:

> Negativity (and the threat of it) makes accountability possible. Without accountability, democracy falters. If an incumbent does a poor job, it is very unlikely that that person will be (publicly) self-critical . . . Of course, challengers are likely to raise more problems than may actually exist. Hence, the incumbent needs to respond . . . Negativity, therefore, creates a competitive dynamic that

should yield a richer information environment than if candidates just talked about their own plans for government.

Whether these intriguing precepts are applicable to state supreme courts is tested in the sections below.

Campaign Advertising in Judicial Elections

As with observers of American politics generally, many law school academicians, legal practitioners, and judicial reform advocacy organizations have expressed serious concerns about the consequences of expensive, hard-fought judicial campaigns. The principal charge is that costly campaigns that include televised attacks and other issue-based discourse will undermine public confidence in courts and create crises of legitimacy for state judiciaries. Recall the American Bar Association's (2003: viii) declaration:

> Whatever its historic rationale there can no longer be justification for contested judicial elections accompanied by "attack" media advertising that require infusions of substantial sums of money. These contested elections threaten to poison public trust and confidence in the courts by fostering the perception that judges are less than independent and impartial, that justice is for sale, and that justice is available only to the wealthy, the powerful, or those with partisan influence.

The National Center for State Courts (2002: 7), one of the nation's most highly regarded advocacy groups for state judiciaries, likewise suggests that "judicial election campaigns pose a substantial threat to judicial independence and impartiality, and undermine public trust in the judicial system." The National Center for State Courts (2002: 7) specifically charges that "unregulated issue advertisements . . . present a particularly grave and immediate threat." To correct these problems, the National Center suggests eliminating partisan elections in favor of nonpartisan elections or the Missouri Plan.

As a final example, the Justice at Stake Campaign (Goldberg et al. 2005: vi), which has played a particularly influential role in the judicial selection debate by disseminating for every two-year election cycle *New Politics of Judicial Elections* reports about various trends in modern judicial election campaigns, likewise observes:

> A perfect storm of hardball TV ads, millions in campaign contributions and bare-knuckled special interest politics is descending on a growing number of

Supreme Court campaigns. The stakes involve nothing less than the fairness and independence of courts in the 38 states that elect their high court judges.

Underlying all of these arguments is a fundamental assumption derived from normative theories of judging: that judges and courts should remain well above ordinary politics and quite distinct from the political branches of government to retain the respect and good will of the American people. A corollary to this principle is that citizens are incapable of viewing judges and courts as both political and impartial.

Indeed, the primary arguments offered by the legal academy and judicial reform advocates against the practice of electing judges and partisan elections in particular begin with the proposition that judges must be understood to be different than other political actors. In this regard, any form of politicking, including aggressive campaigning replete with television advertising and issue-based appeals to voters, is perceived as intrinsically damaging to judges and courts. Slogans that judges are being reduced to "mere politicians" or "politicians in robes" have become the battle cries used to criticize judicial elections and to denounce televised attack advertising and other aspects of contemporary judicial selection processes because of their presumed destructive impact on citizen support for courts. As Gibson (2012: 3) summarizes, "Alarm bells are being sounded throughout the United States, announcing the imminent demise of legitimacy in the country's elected state courts."

This thesis among legal scholars and judicial reform advocates about the far-reaching effects of scathing ads and other pernicious aspects of campaigning is entirely consistent with the primary arguments of Ansolabehere et al. (1994) and Ansolabehere and Iyengar (1995: 110), who asserted that negativity "undermines the legitimacy of the entire political process" and "leaves voters embittered towards the candidates and the rules of the game."[9] Judicial reform advocates likewise point to deep systemic threats stemming from these controversial messages.[10]

Empirical studies of state judicial legitimacy are rare.[11] Even so, one of the first published works on the topic using national survey data provided evidence favoring some aspects of the reformers' arguments (Benesh 2006). Although campaign advertising and other election-specific considerations were not part of these initial investigations, partisan elections and the concept of the "politicization" of judicial selection were central. The basic assumption was that partisan elections are more political in tone than other election or appointment plans and thus have the greatest capacity to delegitimize state judiciaries.

Specifically, using a 1999 national survey commissioned by the National Center for State Courts, Benesh (2006) detected a negative relationship between partisan elections and public confidence in "courts in the community," which were the undefined referent in the survey.[12] To explain this relationship, Benesh (2006) forwarded the argument that because voters prefer independence to accountability, courts staffed using partisan ballots are held in lower esteem than courts selected by other methods, even in states that expressly have chosen partisan elections as their preferred option for judicial recruitment and retention.

Other scholars using exactly the same survey quickly came to different conclusions. In an analysis that also evaluated citizen support for state legislatures and governors, Kelleher and Wolak (2007) failed to detect any relationship between partisan elections and public confidence in courts. Likewise, using a 2001 national survey commissioned by the Justice at Stake Campaign, Cann and Yates (2008) identified a negative relationship between public confidence and partisan and nonpartisan elections (considered separately) but only among the least politically knowledgeable. This intriguing finding suggests that information is a powerful antidote to diminished levels of public confidence and points to other causes of voter disaffection than the formal structure of elections.[13]

These findings at the national level about the significance of knowledge in enhancing judicial legitimacy are supported by recent evidence from the Texas Supreme Court, which operates in the nation's largest partisan judicial election state. Using survey experiments designed to capture the impact of various types of campaign messages on citizen support, McKenzie and Unger (2011) established that information about government and politics enhances institutional legitimacy, even after highly partisan and churlish campaign rhetoric. Overall, the scientific literature shows as "a recurring finding . . . that those who hold more information about the judiciary tend to support it more" (Gibson 2012: 81).

The most recent works on judicial legitimacy have directly evaluated the impact of campaign politics, including negativity, on the public's perceptions of state courts, and this new evidence sharply contradicts both Benesh's (2006) findings and the normative assumptions underlying the reform community's concerns about rough-and-tumble elections and attack advertising in particular. In a single-state study, McKenzie and Unger (2011) show that issue-based campaigning, including promises about how to treat future cases, does not detract from the support of citizens for the Texas Supreme Court.

Likewise, Gibson (2009) found using survey experiments that neither issue-based discourse from candidates for judgeships nor outright attacks on judicial candidates have harmful effects on judicial legitimacy in states that elect judges. Similarly, Gibson et al. (2011) show that although some campaign activities and types of messages in judicial elections can dampen citizen support for courts, the strongly legitimizing effects of the elections themselves outweigh any adverse effects of caustic ads. Even when the harshest attacks on judicial candidates are presented to voters, judicial elections continue to serve as powerful agents of judicial legitimacy.

Gibson's latest and most comprehensive work on the topic, *Electing Judges* (2012), provides additional evidence to bolster these intriguing earlier findings while questioning some of Benesh's (2006) central assumptions. Among other things, Gibson (2012) documents that Americans do not uniformly value judicial independence over accountability and that, in reality, citizens' views about what courts should provide are quite varied.[14] But the most critical evidence in *Electing Judges* is that citizens do not perceive electioneering by judicial candidates unfavorably to the detriment of judicial legitimacy. Instead, the practice of electing judges is a powerful legitimizing force that eclipses the adverse effects of campaigning, including any harms stemming from judges accepting campaign contributions from attorneys, law firms, and organized interests who later may have business before the courts.

The significance of this evidence cannot be overstated. Though certainly not the last word about a topic of scientific inquiry that still is in the nascent stages, Gibson (2012) essentially has shaken the bedrock underlying the claims of the legal and advocacy communities about the deleterious effects of judicial campaign politics on public support for courts. At the level of individual attitudes essential to judicial legitimacy, electioneering by judges and attack ads in judicial campaigns do not appear to damage state court judges or state judiciaries.

These findings are entirely consistent with one of the most fundamental precepts of political science, which deems as axiomatic the principle that elections are powerful agents of political legitimacy. Gibson's (2012) conclusions also are manifestly similar to research on campaign negativity in legislative and executive elections. As just discussed, in studies evaluating the effects of attacks on institutional approval and political efficacy in presidential and congressional campaigns, "The search for evidence against negative advertisements has yielded nothing" (Jackson, Mondak, and Huckfeldt 2009: 63).

Finally, extant empirical scholarship on voting behavior in state supreme court elections, measured at the aggregate level as ballot roll-off, has demonstrated that rather than being alienated by aggressive campaigns, the electorate is mobilized to vote by a variety of factors that increase the salience of the races and improve the volume and quality of information available to voters (e.g., Baum and Klein 2007; Bonneau and M. G. Hall 2009; Dubois 1980; M. G. Hall 2007b; M. G. Hall and Bonneau 2008; Hojnacki and Baum 1992; Klein and Baum 2001). Partisan elections, hotly contested seats, and substantial spending (Baum and Klein 2007; Bonneau and M. G. Hall 2009; M. G. Hall 2007b; M. G. Hall and Bonneau 2008) mobilize rather than demobilize voters. These well-documented patterns are manifestly inconsistent with an alienated, disaffected electorate.

Although these intriguing studies are informative, none has yet to evaluate the effects of campaign messages, including attack advertising, on the propensity of citizens to vote in state supreme court elections (but see M. G. Hall and Bonneau 2013). As such, these models are incomplete. Likewise, Gibson's (2012) work addresses only part of the campaign advertising equation—the impact of electioneering on citizens' individual attitudes toward judges and courts. It now seems essential to examine the actual behavior of state electorates in judicial elections using fully specified models that introduce election-specific variables into the equations, especially the tone of the messages broadcast to voters. Demobilization, though dependent on citizen attitudes, is in its essence a behavioral trait.

Campaign Models of Voter Participation in State Supreme Court Elections

This research evaluates whether televised attack advertising in state supreme court elections has adverse effects on citizen participation in these races and whether any effects are conditioned by the presence or absence of partisan ballots. In doing so, this project tests the two competing theories just discussed about campaign negativity in American politics. The first, derived from normative legal theory and arguments posited by Ansolabehere et al. (1994; Ansolabehere and Iyengar 1995), predicts that attack advertising will demobilize state electorates. The second, consistent with most empirical studies of campaign advertising, suggests that negativity will have either neutral consequences for citizen participation or will mobilize the electorate.

With regard to differences between partisan and nonpartisan elections, both theoretical perspectives reasonably can be inferred to predict conditional effects with attack advertising but in opposite directions. From the legal perspective, aggressive campaigns brought about by *Republican Party of Minnesota* v. *White* (2002) and other changes in the campaign context should be particularly damaging in nonpartisan elections, which until recently were low-information, issue-free elections in some states. From this perspective, campaign attack advertising should have greater shock value and thus stronger demobilizing effects in nonpartisan elections than in partisan elections. Alternatively, as most empirical studies have shown, negativity is an important device for energizing and informing voters, which in turn motivates citizens to vote. In nonpartisan elections, which remove the most important heuristic (i.e., the partisan affiliations of the candidates) from the ballot, the mobilizing effects of heated campaigns should be especially pronounced.

Given the larger body of empirical evidence generated to date from legislative and executive elections (which use partisan ballots) and the compelling theoretical story about why attack advertising does not have the damaging effects initially predicted, this study hypothesizes that negativity in state supreme court elections will have neutral or positive effects on voting in partisan elections but will have distinctly mobilizing effects in nonpartisan elections. In other words, the positive effects of attack advertising on citizen participation will be magnified in nonpartisan elections.

In testing these propositions, my specific empirical focus is on the fifty-one nonpartisan supreme court elections[15] and forty-five partisan supreme court elections held contemporaneously with a presidential, gubernatorial, or U.S. Senate election from 2002 through 2008. Overall, eighteen states are included in the analysis.[16] As with the empirical models in Chapter 4, these models are restricted to contested races only (e.g., Bonneau 2007; Bonneau and Cann 2011; M. G. Hall and Bonneau 2008) and rely on television advertising data collected by the Campaign Media Analysis Group (CMAG) and coded by researchers at the Brennan Center for Justice.[17] As is standard practice, the ads are classified by tone as "promotion of one candidate," "attack on the opponent," or "contrasting two or more candidates," which collectively constitute mutually exclusive and exhaustive categories.

Defining Citizen Participation in State Supreme Court Elections

In testing hypotheses about televised attack advertising in state supreme court elections, this chapter essentially replicates extant models of voter mobilization generated in studies of other national and state elections. However, a discussion of model specification for state supreme court elections must begin with obvious differences between judicial elections and the most visible elections in the United States and particularly the issue of how to operationalize the electorate's propensity to vote.

Heretofore, studies of negative campaigning in American elections have focused primarily on elections to the nation's most visible offices, especially presidential and U.S. Senate elections. In other words, the scientific literature on the impact of attack advertising and other forms of political messages is based largely on high-salience elections placed at the very top of the ballot. For these elections, voter turnout is an appropriate measure of citizen participation because top-ballot elections will play a powerful, if not determinative, role in how many voters actually go to the polls.

Elections occurring farther down the ballot are different. Studies of judicial elections (e.g., Bonneau and M. G. Hall 2009; Dubois 1980; M. G. Hall 2007b; M. G. Hall and Bonneau 2008, 2013; W. K. Hall and Aspin 1987), elections to the U.S. House of Representatives (e.g., Wattenberg, McAllister, and Salvanto 2000), and subgubernatorial elections (e.g., Bullock and Dunn 1996; Nichols and Strizek 1995; Vanderleeuw and Engstrom 1987) have recognized that it is unlikely that turnout is determined by lower-level races when a presidential, senatorial, or gubernatorial contest is on the ballot. Thus, generating single models that maintain parsimony while controlling for the variety of factors affecting the electoral climate in general, and turnout for the most salient races in particular, is daunting.

To address this issue, studies of less visible contests typically have used ballot roll-off rather than voter turnout as the measure of electoral participation. Substantively, roll-off is a fascinating form of political behavior in its own right (e.g., Wattenberg, McAllister, and Salvanto 2000). However, the primary advantage of examining ballot roll-off is analytical. Measuring voter participation as roll-off provides an efficient and practical means to address the complicated set of specification issues that arise when modeling a process affected by elections not being evaluated and not easily included.

Therefore, this study follows the well-beaten path established in earlier elections studies by defining the dependent variable as ballot roll-off rather than voter turnout. Examining roll-off, though not a perfect solution, helps to alleviate serious specification problems by treating turnout for the most important offices as a baseline and then gauging interest in other elections relative to the top draw on the ballot.

Specifically, ballot roll-off is measured in this context as the percentage of the electorate casting votes for the major office on the ballot who do *not* vote in each supreme court race. Also consistent with previous work, this study defines the major office as "the presidential, gubernatorial, or U.S. senatorial contest attracting the most voters in each election" (Dubois 1980: 66).[18] Thus, higher values of roll-off indicate lower levels of participation in supreme court races.[19]

Theoretically, the problem of voter apathy seems particularly acute when those who actually do make it to the polls fail to complete their ballots.[20] In fact, ballot roll-off, whereby voters cast votes only for a selective set of offices, raises serious issues about legitimacy and accountability in the same manner as low voter turnout and thus has received considerable attention from scholars of electoral politics. By examining ballot roll-off in elections to the U.S. Senate (e.g., Ansolabehere and Iyengar 1995), House of Representatives (e.g., Wattenberg, McAllister, and Salvanto 2000), state legislatures (e.g., Schaffner, Streb, and Wright 2001), a variety of local offices (e.g., Bullock and Dunn 1996; Schaffner, Streb, and Wright 2001), and on ballot propositions (e.g., Bowler, Donovan, and Happ 1992; Magleby 1984), scholars have determined that ballot roll-off, like voter turnout, largely is the product of factors specific to each election and the external political environment, including institutional arrangements governing the conduct of elections. These studies provide an excellent basis for the model specification required by this inquiry.

As with voter turnout in American elections generally, ballot roll-off in state supreme court elections varies considerably across both elections and states. In this regard, it is somewhat understandable that many would criticize voters in state supreme court elections. Overall, the contested elections analyzed in this chapter have a roll-off rate that averages 14.5 percent.[21] However, the states, and elections within states, differ markedly, and there are reasons to criticize judicial elections while viewing them as an excellent means for assessing the factors that promote mass political participation. Specifically, average ballot roll-off ranges from –3.5 percent (Mississippi)[22] to 36.8 percent

(Michigan) across elections, and averages from 4.4 percent (Alabama, Illinois) to 32.6 percent (Michigan) across states. These differences of twenty-eight to forty percentage points across elections and states are dramatic reflections of the extent to which voters can, and cannot, be motivated to participate in supreme court elections. In sum, the extraordinary variations that occur in citizen participation both across and within states do not speak to a consistently apathetic or cynical electorate and beg scientific explanation.

Modeling Voter Participation in State Supreme Court Elections

The extensive literature on voter turnout and ballot roll-off provides an excellent theoretical basis for understanding the politics of judicial elections and for correctly specifying models of ballot roll-off. Although reducing a complex body of research to a few basic theoretical propositions necessarily results in oversimplification, studies at both individual and aggregate levels suggest that: (1) various aspects of intense electoral competition, including campaign advertising and substantial spending, enhance the salience of elections and provide information to voters; (2) partisanship is a critical force in elections, with partisan labels on ballots serving as vital voting cues; (3) incumbency serves as a low-cost informational cue when partisan labels are absent; and (4) institutional arrangements create incentives or disincentives to vote and thus structure the manner in which voters are willing and able to participate.[23]

Stated somewhat differently, voter turnout and ballot roll-off are a function of a variety of institutional arrangements (e.g., Dubois 1980; Francia and Herrnson 2004; W. K. Hall and Aspin 1987; Kim, Petrocik, and Enokson 1975; Schaffner, Streb, and Wright 2001) and other contextual forces (e.g., Bowler, Donovan, and Happ 1992; Bullock and Dunn 1996; Hogan 1999; Magleby 1984; Milton 1983; Patterson and Caldeira 1983; Tucker 1986) that make elections interesting and important while providing easily accessible information to voters. Reduced to the most basic element, voters vote when they have interest, readily available information, and choice.[24]

Generally speaking with respect to context, factors related to each particular electoral contest—including campaign advertising, campaign spending, and the candidates themselves—as well as forces that characterize the overall context of each election should influence the willingness of voters to complete their ballots in judicial races. Especially important are the formal means by which elections are organized. These institutional arrangements have a direct impact on voting but also interact with other forces influencing citizen participation (e.g., Bonneau and M. G. Hall 2003, 2009; Brace and M. G. Hall 1997; M. G. Hall 2001a).

State Supreme Court Campaigns

The primary hypothesis to be tested in this chapter is that the content of political campaigns influences ballot roll-off in state supreme court elections. In the models, I measure content by taking into account the volume of the campaign messages broadcast to voters categorized by tone: attack airings, promote airings, and contrast airings.

Starting with attack advertising, the focal point of the empirical tests, I first count the total number of attack airings for all candidates in each race (*attack airings*). Consistent with common practice, I then transform the airings figures into their natural logarithms because of an expected diminishing marginal impact on ballot roll-off at higher levels of airings. I follow this same practice with promote airings and contrast airings. This measurement strategy will facilitate a determination of whether messages other than outright attacks influence citizen behavior in state supreme court elections.[25]

These count variables include all advertising aired in each race, regardless of sponsor. Thus, the variables take into account the advertising behavior of the candidates, political parties, interest groups, and all others involved in these elections. Likewise, because the primary empirical concern is with the overall impact of a campaign in its entirety on the electorate, in contrast to models focused on the activities of each candidate in influencing his or her electoral performance, the advertising and spending variables in this chapter are not disaggregated by candidate type as in the models in Chapter 4.

Although the scientific literature is not clear about what to expect regarding the effects of promote or contrast ads, it may be the case that positive messages in promote ads will not have the same impact as outright attacks, even in nonpartisan elections. Although Ansolabehere and Iyengar (1995: 101) argued that advertising can stimulate voters "only through positive campaign messages," other studies failed to find any consistent impact of positive ads on voting (e.g., Jackson and Carsey 2007) or have shown that positive messages are the least likely to promote participation (e.g., Brooks and Geer 2007). Interestingly, Jackson and Carsey (2007) found that positive advertising *reduces* voter turnout in some races.

In reality, positive messages may not be as interesting or informative as attack ads and are far less likely to mention specific issues. As reported in Chapter 3, promote ads in state supreme court elections tend to emphasize candidate traits and values, compared with attack ads focused on issues. However, because contrast ads directly compare candidates and also have fairly high issue content, these messages may have more of an impact than previously suggested.

Beyond advertising, another key component of campaigning is spending by the candidates, which is the principal indicator of overall campaign activity in American election studies and is an excellent gauge of the competitiveness and intensity of any race. Well-financed campaigns should significantly reduce ballot roll-off in state supreme court elections as in elections to other important offices in the United States. Summarized well by Bonneau and M. G. Hall (2009: 38), "The more money candidates spend, the more information they can provide to the voters; and the more information voters have, the more likely they are to participate."

Please note that campaign advertising and campaign spending are conceptually distinct. Campaign expenditures capture the overall scope and intensity of campaigning while attack, promote, and contrast airings reflect the content and saturation of messages broadcast to voters. Also, campaign advertising is only a part of overall spending in any race and is not used in every contested state supreme court election. Even so, campaign spending does interject mild collinearity into models that also include volumes of advertising. Thus, as a robustness check, I estimate the models with and without spending by the candidates.

To measure campaign spending, I add the dollars spent by all candidates in each race and then transform these sums into 2002 dollars to control for inflation. To take into account differences across states in population and to render the figures comparable across states, I divide total spending by the voting age population of the state (or electoral district if the constituency is not statewide). Finally, consistent with standard practice and the airings measures, I log the values of per capita spending because of expected diminishing marginal returns (*per capita spending*).

Candidate-Specific Variables

Another set of election-specific variables that should enhance the electorate's propensity to vote in state supreme court elections relates to the candidates themselves and their status and experience with voters. Consistent with the sophomore surge phenomenon in legislative elections (e.g., Cover and Mayhew 1981; Holbrook and Tidmarch 1991) and earlier state supreme court elections (M. G. Hall 2001a, 2007a, 2007b), one reasonably might expect that incumbents will establish stable and secure electoral coalitions over time, especially after the first successful election bid. In state supreme court elections, this aspect of the incumbency advantage should increase ballot roll-off.

Alternatively, some types of candidates are electorally vulnerable and thus should attract greater interest from challengers, the media, and voters, which in turn should stimulate higher levels of participation. Three specific types of candidates, who are quite distinct from successful incumbents in safe seats, are the following: (1) incumbents who narrowly won their last reelection bids (*unsafe seat*), (2) justices who are newly appointed to the state high court bench and are seeking their first electoral wins (*new appointee*), and (3) candidates vying for open seats (*open seat*). In fact, studies (e.g., Bonneau 2004, 2005; Bonneau and M. G. Hall 2003, 2009; M. G. Hall 2001, 2007a; M. G. Hall and Bonneau 2006) show that races involving these types of candidates are more competitive and expensive than elections with well-established incumbents. However, even with competition and spending controlled, these three types of candidates tend to perform worse than popular incumbents and are more likely to decrease ballot roll-off.

To take these various aspects of incumbency into account, this study includes the variables *unsafe seat, new appointee, and open seat*, each coded 1 for elections involving the specified type of candidate and 0 otherwise. These variables distinguish incumbents who have had at least one successful campaign and hold safe seats (the omitted baseline category) from other marginal or less well-known candidates. To state the matter differently, these variables identify what are likely to be interesting and vigorous contests because challengers actually have a higher probability of winning (e.g., Bonneau and M. G. Hall 2009; M. G. Hall 2007b; M. G. Hall and Bonneau 2006, 2008). In turn, voters should respond to this intensity.

Institutional Context

Various aspects of context beyond the specific features of each election should influence the willingness of the electorate not to defect in state supreme court elections after having already gone to the polls for other offices. The first is the presence of a presidential election. Studies clearly have established that turnout (e.g., Dubois 1980; Hill and Leighley 1993; Patterson and Caldeira 1983) and ballot roll-off (e.g., Bonneau and M. G. Hall 2009; Dubois 1980; M. G. Hall 2007b; M. G. Hall and Bonneau 2008, 2013; Nichols and Strizek 1995; Streb, Frederick, and LaFrance 2009) are higher when presidential elections are on the ballot. In essence, presidential elections, which always are highly salient, entice voters to the polls, but a significant number of these voters have no information about, or interest in, other races. Therefore, this study includes the variable *presidential election* to capture these effects.

As a robustness check for the impact of top-ballot races on state supreme court electoral participation, especially given the use of ballot roll-off as the dependent variable rather than voter turnout, the models include an alternative measure of the intensity of the stimulus from the most important elections on the ballot in each election cycle. Specifically, the models include a weighted measure of election salience that assumes, consistent with extant election studies and turnout rates, that presidential elections are of greatest salience to voters, followed by gubernatorial elections, and then U.S. Senate elections.[26] Thus, I generate a variable (*election salience*) ranging from 1 to 6 that assigns the value of 3 for presidential elections, 2 for gubernatorial elections, and 1 for senatorial races (M. G. Hall and Bonneau 2013). Any or all of these elections can be on the ballot with judicial races.

Another structural feature of state politics that should influence the extent to which citizens are motivated to participate in the judicial selection process is the professionalization of state supreme courts. Generally, studies have shown that highly professionalized legislatures enhance the incumbency advantage, leaving challengers with a difficult job when trying to unseat incumbents (e.g., Berry, Berkman, and Schneiderman 2000; Hogan 2004). In fact, the incumbency advantage is greatest in professionalized legislatures, where incumbents garner larger percentages of the vote and are much more likely to win (Carey, Niemi, and Powell 2000). These same patterns are evidenced in state supreme court elections, as shown in Chapter 4. Theoretically speaking, professionalism insulates institutions from their external environments and shields incumbents from exogenous shocks (Berry, Berkman, and Schneiderman 2000). Under these conditions, voters have fewer incentives to vote.

Therefore, higher levels of ballot roll-off should be observed in states where the high court bench is professionalized. The models in this chapter capture this effect using Squire's (2008) state supreme court professionalization measure (*professionalization*), which largely reflects the salary, staff support, and docket control available to state supreme courts, standardized against the U.S. Supreme Court.[27] The Squire index ranges from 0 (least professionalized) to 1 (most professionalized) and should increase ballot roll-off.[28] Generally, professionalized courts have a greater capacity to attract quality members, decide cases more efficiently and effectively, and use dockets strategically to minimize political controversy by avoiding some controversial decisions or at least controlling their timing to minimize criticism from opponents. Overall, professionalization should lessen the need for monitoring by voters while providing fewer incentives and opportunities for challengers to seek to unseat incumbents or run high-cost negative campaigns.

The components of Squire's professionalism index "gauge a court's ability to generate and evaluate information" (Squire 2008: 223) and overall institutional capacity. As a critical matter, this measure does *not* include method of judicial selection, which has little to do with the information or performance capacity of courts.[29]

As a third contextual influence on voting, ballot type is central. Studies have established that voters participate in elections when they have readily accessible information, and there simply is no better informational cue in any election than the partisan affiliations of the candidates. At the individual level of analysis, some of the best evidence about the impact of partisan information in judicial elections was presented by Klein and Baum (2001), who determined through an experimental design that partisanship substantially improves participation. These findings are consistent with evidence generated in studies at the aggregate level, including Dubois's (1980) earlier observations and the more recent findings of M. G. Hall (2007b; Bonneau and M. G. Hall 2009; M. G. Hall and Bonneau 2008, 2013). Even studies of ballot roll-off in mayoral and state legislative elections (Schaffner, Streb, and Wright 2001) show that removing partisan labels from ballots increases roll-off. Thus, this study predicts that partisan elections will lessen roll-off in state supreme court elections. To measure these effects, the models in this chapter include a dummy variable for partisan elections (*partisan*), with nonpartisan elections omitted as the baseline category.

Equally important, partisan elections should condition the impact of attack ads on ballot roll-off and may have similar effects with other types of televised campaign messages in state supreme court elections. Thus, the variable *partisan* is included as a multiplicative term with each of the three tonal categories of campaign messages (*attack airings, promote airings, contrast air-*

ings). The impact of attack advertising should be more pronounced in nonpartisan than in partisan elections. Likewise, promote and contrast ads may also reflect these same patterns. As mentioned, there is little theoretical guidance in the scientific literature with regard to promote and contrast ads.

Finally with regard to institutional context, the type of geographic constituency represented by the seat may influence citizen participation in state supreme courts (e.g., M. G. Hall 2007b; M. G. Hall and Bonneau 2008, 2013). Although most supreme court justices are elected statewide, some are chosen from districts composed of select geographic subsets of voters within a state. These differences in constituencies may have significant electoral implications. Among other things, the minority party in district-based elections has a stronger incentive to field candidates, particularly when the minority party is concentrated geographically. Also, in smaller constituencies, voters have a higher probability of being contacted directly by a campaign or receiving campaign materials about the supreme court race in their district. Therefore, this study includes a dummy variable for district elections (*district*) and posits that roll-off will be lower in these types of constituencies.[30]

Temporal Controls

To control for any temporal effects, some of the models include dummy variables for each election cycle (2002, 2004, and 2006) except 2008, which serves as the omitted baseline category. This is an appropriate specification only when *election salience* is used to measure the effects of top ballot races rather than *presidential election*. Because there are only four election cycles in these data, two of which correspond with presidential elections, using temporal controls would introduce serious collinearity into the models when *presidential election* is also included. However, this problem is not as severe when *election salience* is used instead. From a theoretical perspective, modeling the effects of *presidential election* is more important than controlling for undefined temporal effects given a specific theoretical expectation for the former and not the latter.

Estimation Technique

Given the continuous nature of the dependent variable, the models are estimated using ordinary least squares regression (OLS). Further, because of the structure of the data and the potential for within-group (i.e., state) correlation, OLS standard errors are replaced with robust standard errors clustered by state, as is standard practice in state supreme court election studies (e.g., Bonneau and M. G. Hall 2009, 2013; M. G. Hall 2007b).

Descriptive Statistics on the Dependent and Independent Variables

To provide a substantive context for the hypothesis tests and to illustrate similarities and differences between nonpartisan and partisan elections in these types of supreme court races (contested elections held contemporaneously with other major elections), Table 5-1 shows the mean value of each variable included in the multivariate models. These means are displayed for all elections and, separately, for nonpartisan and partisan elections. Only those observations actually analyzed in the models are included, which requires the absence of any missing data on any of the variables.

TABLE 5-1. Variable means, overall and by election type, in campaign-based models of ballot roll-off.*

Variable	All elections	Nonpartisan elections	Partisan elections
Ballot roll-off	14.51	18.24	10.27
Attack airings	281.63	240.25	328.52
Promote airings	998.68	1006.22	990.14
Contrast airings	255.94	209.43	308.65
Spending per capita	490.84	448.54	538.79
Unsafe seat	.1979	.2157	.1778
New appointee	.1875	.1569	.2222
Open seat	.2604	.2353	.2889
Presidential election	.5729	.6863	.4444
Election salience	3.43	3.57	3.27
Professionalization	.6229	.5938	.6559
Partisan	.4688	0	1
District	.1458	.2157	.0667
2002	.2188	.1569	.2889
2004	.3229	.4118	.2222
2006	.2083	.1569	.2667
2008	.2500	.2745	.2222
N	96	51	45

* Means shown for the advertising and spending variables are actual values (airings or dollars) rather than natural logarithms.

As Table 5-1 indicates, ballot roll-off is higher on average in the nonpartisan elections evaluated in this chapter than in the partisan elections, by almost eight percentage points. Nonpartisan elections have an average roll-off rate of 18.2 percent, compared with partisan elections at 10.3 percent.[31] These statistics are consistent with other studies (e.g., Dubois 1980; M. G. Hall 2007a; M. G. Hall and Bonneau 2008) identifying substantial gaps in voter participation between nonpartisan and partisan state supreme court elections and with the data reported in Chapter 2.

Table 5-1 also shows that attack airings, contrast airings, and campaign spending per capita are higher on average in partisan elections, although promote airings are used more often in nonpartisan elections (but this difference is rather small). From the perspective of candidate factors, elections for incumbents holding unsafe seats are somewhat more common in the dataset in nonpartisan elections, while races involving newly appointed incumbents and open seats are more typical in partisan elections.

Looking at contextual variations, the nonpartisan elections included in the models are more likely to take place during presidential election years and in district constituencies, compared with partisan elections. Regarding election salience, partisan and nonpartisan elections look fairly similar. Interestingly, average professionalization is higher in partisan elections than nonpartisan elections but not by any significant measure.

Finally, there are some differences in the ways nonpartisan and partisan elections are distributed across the time series. Partisan elections occur relatively evenly across the four election cycles, while nonpartisan elections are clustered more in presidential election years, especially in 2004.

Results

The central purpose of the empirical analysis in this chapter is to assess the impact of attack advertising on ballot roll-off in state supreme court elections and to determine whether these effects are conditioned by the presence or absence of partisan ballots. To this end, I estimated a total of five sets of models (in Tables 5-2, 5-3, 5-4, 5-5, and 5-6) that address this vital question in a systematic way while providing essential robustness checks on the initial results.

Collectively, these results reveal the powerful extent to which highly contentious campaigns and basic institutional arrangements can influence citizen participation in state supreme court elections, in ways that directly contradict

TABLE 5-2. Televised campaign advertising and ballot roll-off in state supreme court elections, 2002–2008, with controls for presidential election years.

Variable	Model 1 Coefficient	Model 1 Robust standard error	Model 1 $P > |t|$	Model 2 Coefficient	Model 2 Robust standard error	Model 2 $P > |t|$
Campaign features						
Attack airings	−0.3635	0.1515	0.028	−0.3401	0.1391	0.026
Attack airings × partisan	0.6054	0.5269	0.266	0.7559	0.5446	0.183
Promote airings	−0.0192	0.1531	0.902	0.1749	0.1260	0.183
Contrast airings	−0.7116	0.2421	0.009	−0.6873	0.2288	0.008
Spending per capita	—	—	—	−0.9143	0.3226	0.011
Candidates						
Unsafe seat	−2.1584	2.7661	0.446	−2.1999	2.8853	0.456
New appointee	−1.9016	1.6508	0.265	−1.0714	1.3948	0.453
Open seat	−1.8195	2.2996	0.440	−0.7371	2.0609	0.725
Institutional context						
Presidential election	2.9089	0.9211	0.006	2.5751	1.0946	0.031
Professionalization	39.2125	5.0349	0.000	36.7671	5.5793	0.000
Partisan	−9.6810	1.3014	0.000	−10.4453	1.4752	0.000
District	−3.6621	1.6162	0.037	−2.0999	1.4170	0.157
Constant	−5.3752	3.3524	0.127	−0.3158	4.5227	0.945

Dependent variable = Ballot roll-off
Number of observations = 96
Model 1 R-squared = 0.6162   Model 2 R-squared = 0.6273
Model 1 F = 23.31, Prob > F = 0.000   Model 2 F = 85.35, Prob > F = 0.000

the bold assertions of the judicial reform and legal communities and some political scientists.

The analysis starts with the most parsimonious models, reported in Table 5-2, which also are the most consistent with previous studies of ballot roll-off in the scientific literature (e.g., M. G. Hall 2007b; Bonneau and M. G. Hall 2008). These models use *presidential election* as the primary substantive variable of interest related to the timing of state supreme court elections. Table 5-3 presents the same models but with an alternative treatment of top-ballot campaign stimulation (*election salience*) and election cycle temporal

TABLE 5-3. Televised campaign advertising by tone and ballot roll-off in state supreme court elections, 2002–2008, with controls for the salience of top-ballot races and election year.

	Model 1			Model 2		
Variable	Coefficient	Robust standard error	$P > |t|$	Coefficient	Robust standard error	$P > |t|$
Campaign features						
Attack airings	−0.3057	0.1605	0.074	−0.2754	0.1373	0.061
Attack airings × partisan	0.5853	0.4869	0.246	0.7349	0.4909	0.153
Promote airings	−0.0966	0.1537	0.538	0.1078	0.1289	0.415
Contrast airings	−0.7226	0.2323	0.006	−0.6948	0.2229	0.006
Spending per capita	—	—	—	−0.9570	0.2792	0.003
Candidates						
Unsafe seat	−1.7746	2.2035	0.432	−1.8367	2.2338	0.422
New appointee	−1.5203	1.5048	0.327	−0.6371	1.2067	0.604
Open seat	−0.6108	1.7194	0.727	0.4540	1.4459	0.757
Institutional context						
Election salience	−0.3781	0.7059	0.599	−0.2522	0.7250	0.732
Professionalization	41.1597	4.8088	0.000	38.4091	5.3869	0.000
Partisan	−10.0127	1.2046	0.000	−10.8025	1.4130	0.000
District	−3.1710	1.6738	0.075	−1.5043	1.4790	0.323
Temporal controls						
2002	−7.5684	1.4584	0.000	−7.0727	1.5355	0.000
2004	−1.9901	2.4172	0.422	−2.0186	2.4358	0.419
2006	−1.2761	2.6547	0.637	−0.7339	2.9009	0.803
Constant	−1.1699	2.5335	0.650	3.4067	3.6100	0.359

Dependent variable = Ballot roll-off
Number of observations = 96
Model 1 R-squared = 0.6618   Model 2 R-squared = 0.6739
Model 1 F = 93.28, Prob > F = 0.000   Model 2 F = 97.45, Prob > F = 0.000

variation (*2002, 2004,* and *2006*). Both sets of models in Table 5-2 and Table 5-3 are estimated with, and without, campaign spending, which interjects mild collinearity.[32] In both tables, Model 1 shows the results without campaign spending, while Model 2 presents results with campaign spending.

TABLE 5-4. Televised campaign advertising and ballot roll-off in state supreme court elections, 2002–2008, with interaction terms for all ad types.

Variable	Model 1 Coefficient	Model 1 Robust standard error	Model 1 $P > |t|$	Model 2 Coefficient	Model 2 Robust standard error	Model 2 $P > |t|$
Campaign features						
Attack airings	0.5125	0.1396	0.002	−0.4301	0.2140	0.061
Attack airings × partisan	0.8877	0.6783	0.208	0.8187	0.5794	0.176
Promote airings	−0.1292	0.1569	0.422	−0.1918	0.1563	0.236
Promote airings × partisan	0.2789	0.3637	0.454	0.2461	0.3060	0.432
Contrast airings	−0.3938	0.1966	0.061	−0.4508	0.2643	0.106
Contrast airings × partisan	−0.6717	0.4159	0.125	−0.5727	0.4649	0.235
Candidates						
Unsafe seat	−2.1779	2.8600	0.457	−1.8101	2.2571	0.434
New appointee	−1.9812	1.8069	0.288	−1.5918	1.6344	0.344
Open seat	−2.4382	2.4868	0.341	−1.2011	1.9410	0.544
Institutional context						
Presidential election	3.2919	0.9173	0.002	—	—	—
Election salience	—	—	—	−0.3073	0.6772	0.656
Professionalization	40.5832	5.1193	0.000	42.2095	4.9687	0.000
Partisan	−10.4704	1.8426	0.000	−10.7030	1.6972	0.000
District	−3.2020	1.6958	0.076	−2.7746	1.8270	0.147
Temporal controls						
2002	—	—	—	−7.7017	1.5996	0.000
2004	—	—	—	−1.9550	2.3215	0.411
2006	—	—	—	−1.5471	2.6285	0.564
Constant	−5.8144	3.2248	0.089	−1.4280	2.5620	0.585

Dependent variable = Ballot roll-off
Number of observations = 96
Model 1 R-squared = 0.6235   Model 2 R-squared = 0.6672
Model 1 F = 15.66, Prob > F = 0.000   Model 2 F = 953.20, Prob > F = 0.000

Additionally, the models in Tables 5-2 and 5-3 are estimated with the only interaction term absolutely essential to the hypothesis tests: the interaction between attack advertising and partisan elections. Models with all interaction terms—which are not statistically significant for promote airings or contrast airings—are reported in Table 5-4 as a robustness check and demonstrate that the central inferences about attack advertising are not biased by choices about whether to include or exclude all possible conditional relationships for advertising tone in the equations even if these relationships are not statistically significant. As the results in Table 5-4 clearly illustrate, when all interaction terms are included in the models, the central inferences about attack advertising do not change.[33]

But first consider the fascinating results reported in Table 5-2. Overall, the performance of the two models in Table 5-2 is excellent. The models account for 62 percent to 63 percent of the variation in ballot roll-off, and most of the variables perform as theoretically predicted. In essence, the electorate's tendency to vote in state supreme court elections is neither random nor impervious to democratic incentives and is, in part, a consequence of campaign negativity conditioned by the presence or absence of partisan ballots.

Specifically from a substantive perspective, attack airings in nonpartisan elections (*attack airings*) reduce ballot roll-off significantly, in contrast to attack airings in partisan elections (*attack airings* × *partisan*), which have positive coefficients (–0.3635 [*attack airings*] + 0.6054 [*attack airings* × *partisan*] = 0.2419 in Model 1, and 0.4158 in Model 2) but are not statistically different from zero. These findings about the absence of a demobilizing effect of attack airings in nonpartisan and partisan elections are precisely the opposite of what normative legal theory and the advocacy literature would predict, as well as the work of Ansolabehere et al. (1994) and Ansolabehere and Iyengar (1995).

Likewise, other forms of campaign negativity reduce ballot roll-off. Contrast airings, which also contain attack themes framed within the context of direct candidate comparisons, reduce ballot roll-off in partisan and nonpartisan elections. Campaign spending has the same effect. In short, if there are adverse effects on the electorate of vigorous campaigning, either in the form of negative messages broadcast to voters or substantial spending, these effects are not evidenced in these models. Moreover, adding campaign spending to the equations does not alter the intriguing inferences about attack or contrast airings.[34] There simply is no evidence in these models of a disaffected electorate stemming from high campaign costs or derisive campaign advertising.

Because of the interaction term, ascertaining the exact effects of the negative advertising variables in nonpartisan elections is complicated. To provide substantive meaning to the statistical results, I take the most straightforward approach by using Model 2 in Table 5-2 (which includes campaign spending) to estimate predicted values of ballot roll-off in nonpartisan elections.

First consider a scenario in nonpartisan elections when attack and contrast airings are set at their minimum values (i.e., none of these types of messages aired) but all other factors are held at their means.[35] Under these conditions, predicted roll-off is 21.7 percent, or a situation in which one in every five voters already at the polls would fail to vote in the supreme court race. However, when attack and contrast airings are raised to their maximum values, predicted roll-off declines to 10.9 percent, for a notable reduction of almost 50 percent.

For a perspective on attack airings alone, when all variables in the model are set at their means, including contrast airings, and attack airings are at their minimum, predicted roll-off in nonpartisan elections is 20.3 percent. However, raising attack airings to the maximum value reduces predicted rolloff to 16.6 percent. When this same procedure is used with contrast ads, predicted ballot roll-off declines from 21.0 percent to 13.9 percent. Thus, as Table 5-2 also indicates, contrast ads actually pack a stronger punch than attack airings in improving citizen participation in nonpartisan elections, but both types of airings translate into civic engagement.[36]

Unlike campaign messages, none of the candidate-specific variables is statistically significant in Model 1 or Model 2, although each coefficient is in the theoretically predicted direction. In state supreme court elections, these candidate-specific factors related to various conditions of incumbency appear to be eclipsed by specifically measurable aspects of the campaigns and institutional contexts. M. G. Hall and Bonneau (2013) obtained similar results for open-seat races and newly appointed justices when advertising content was introduced into supreme court ballot roll-off models.

Contextual factors are vitally important in promoting citizen participation in state supreme court elections. As Model 1 and Model 2 in Table 5-2 show, ballot roll-off is higher in presidential election years, as predicted. The estimated impact is an increase in ballot roll-off of about 2.6 to 2.9 percentage points when a presidential race is on the ballot.

Likewise, partisan ballots are important influences on citizen participation. Partisan elections without attack advertising (*partisan*) reduce ballot roll-off relative to nonpartisan elections without attack advertising (the omitted baseline category) by approximately ten percentage points.

Similarly, ballot roll-off in district-based constituencies is lower than in statewide races by about 3.7 percent, as evidenced in Model 1. However, this effect disappears when spending is introduced into the equations, almost certainly because *district* and *spending per capita* are moderately correlated.[37] Although the spending variable has already been adjusted by the voting-age population of the constituency, many district elections have been extremely expensive and highly competitive relative to statewide races, as previous research has shown (e.g., Bonneau 2004; M. G. Hall and Bonneau 2008). Overall, the only significant inconsistency between Model 1 and Model 2 is with the *district* variable.

Aside from the findings about negativity, one of the most intriguing findings in Table 5-2 concerns the impact of professionalization on citizen participation in state supreme court elections. As predicted, by increasing the justices' salaries, providing substantial support staff, and enhancing discretionary docket control, the professionalization of state supreme courts increases ballot roll-off in state supreme court elections. Why would this seemingly enigmatic effect occur? As other studies have determined, professionalization decreases the effectiveness of challengers and improves the incumbency advantage, both of which make elections less interesting to voters while reducing the need for monitoring (e.g., Berry, Berkman, and Schneiderman 2000; Carey, Niemi, and Powell 2000). From the perspective of state judiciaries, professionalism also enhances the ability of the justices to use their dockets strategically to avoid contentious decisions or to control the timing of these cases to maximize reelection prospects.

Recall from Chapter 4 the substantively powerful impact of professionalization on improving the incumbency advantage in state supreme court elections. Thus, professionalization reduces the civic responsibilities of voters while protecting incumbents from those who actually do vote.

To illustrate the substantive impact of supreme court professionalization on ballot roll-off, I estimated predicted values of roll-off for nonpartisan and partisan elections separately using the results in Model 2 of Table 5-2. With all other variables set at their means, predicted roll-off in nonpartisan elections with professionalization at its minimum is 11.5 percent. Increasing professionalization to its maximum value increases ballot roll-off to 29.8 percent. Similar effects are evidenced in partisan elections, with a shift from the minimum to maximum value of professionalism changing predicted roll-off from

0.81 percent to 19.2 percent. Model 1 in Table 5-2 produces very similar results (not shown).

In short, the professionalization of state supreme courts is a statistically and substantively powerful influence on voter participation in these races. Exactly why this is the case will be an important avenue for future research, although there already is excellent theoretical guidance in the scientific literature (e.g., Berry, Berkman, and Schneiderman 2000) for beginning this exploration.

Of course, it is important to note that other forces in state supreme court elections can offset these effects, including substantial campaign spending and televised airings of attack and contrast ads. Although professionalization is a demobilizing force, other aspects of the campaigns and other contextual forces surrounding the election can counterbalance this adverse influence on citizen participation.

For example, based on estimates derived from Model 2 in Table 5-2, predicted ballot roll-off in nonpartisan elections is 19.6 percent when all variables are at their means, including supreme court professionalization. However, increasing per capita spending (logged) to the maximum reduces roll-off to 15.5 percent, which is below average for the nonpartisan elections analyzed in this chapter. In partisan elections, predicted roll-off is 9.0 percent when all variables are at their means but decreases to 4.9 percent when spending is increased to the maximum.

The two models in Table 5-3, shown for validation purposes, tell essentially the same story using a different specification and measurement strategy. In Table 5-3, a detailed measure of the number and salience of top ballot races is included (*election salience*), along with election cycle variables that control for any other temporal effects in the data. As with the models in Table 5-2, the statistical performance of these models is excellent, accounting for about 66 percent to 67 percent of the variation in ballot roll-off. These models provide an alternative way of thinking about upper-ballot races and cycle-specific election effects.

In essence, as both models in Table 5-3 illustrate, the electorate's tendency to vote in state supreme court elections is, in part, a consequence of campaign negativity conditioned by the presence or absence of partisan ballots. Although the coefficients for *attack airings* in Table 5-3 are less reliable ($p = 0.074$ in Model 1, $p = 0.061$ in Model 2) than the results in Table 5-2, they nonetheless are within reasonable bounds given the fact that there are only fifty-one nonpartisan elections in the models. In fact, when the election-cycle dummy variables responsible for mild collinearity are removed (not shown), the statistical performance of *attack airings* improves considerably, falling well within the 0.05 level of confidence.

Overall, in the more complex specifications in Table 5-3, the evidence about the mobilizing effects of attack airings in nonpartisan elections is less clear and convincing. Even so, there still is no evidence that attack advertising demobilizes voters in nonpartisan or partisan elections. In fact, there is no evidence of such an effect whatsoever in Table 5-2, Table 5-3, or Table 5-4.

Otherwise, the results in Table 5-3 are quite similar to those in Table 5-2, including the fact that contrast airings are shown to reduce ballot roll-off in both nonpartisan and partisan elections. However, unlike *presidential election*, which is statistically significant in Table 5-2, *election salience* is not significant in the models in Table 5-3, nor are the coefficients in the predicted direction. When the temporal controls, which introduce mild collinearity, are removed from the equations (not shown), *election salience* does not attain statistical significance, but the sign of the coefficient does change to the expected direction. Overall, the substantive inferences derived from Table 5-2 and Table 5-3 are reasonably consistent across specifications. And as just mentioned, the results in Table 5-2 and Table 5-3 are not biased by choices about whether to include or exclude all possible conditional relationships for advertising tone, as indicated in Table 5-4.

To explore the issue even further, consider the models in Table 5-5. Yet another way of looking at the issue of campaign negativity is to examine nonpartisan elections separately. This is a very tricky enterprise given that there are not that many observations ($n = 51$), but one way to minimize the degrees of freedom problem and other issues associated with relatively small ns is to drop all nonsignificant variables (i.e., *unsafe seat, new appointee, open seat*). These results are shown in Table 5-5 using all four specifications initially shown in Tables 5-2 and 5-3 but with the modifications just noted.

In each of the four models in Table 5-5, the coefficient for *attack airings* is statistically significant and in the predicted direction.[38] In all four models, attack advertising in nonpartisan elections is a mobilizing force in state supreme court elections rather than a demobilizing force. Additionally, when spending is not included in the models, promote airings emerge as important, but caution should be exercised with this result given that no other models show the same effect. The same is true of the finding that contrast airings are

TABLE 5-5. Televised campaign advertising and ballot roll-off in state supreme court elections, 2002–2008, in nonpartisan elections only.

Variable	Model 1 Coefficient	Robust standard error	$P > \|t\|$	Model 2 Coefficient	Robust standard error	$P > \|t\|$
Campaign features						
Attack airings	−0.5377	0.1298	0.002	−0.4669	0.1211	0.003
Promote airings	−0.2893	0.1329	0.052	−0.0581	0.0971	0.562
Contrast airings	−0.2611	0.2193	0.259	−0.1581	0.2725	0.573
Spending per capita	—	—	—	−1.8449	0.6269	0.013
Institutional context						
Presidential election	3.9506	1.2642	0.010	4.1240	1.1047	0.003
Professionalization	47.7334	2.9714	0.000	40.2220	5.5335	0.000
District	−1.5838	1.0595	0.163	0.5928	1.2475	0.644
Constant	−11.4762	1.9978	0.000	1.3690	5.4329	0.806
	Model 3			Model 4		
Campaign features						
Attack airings	−0.5011	0.1737	0.015	−0.4338	0.1524	0.016
Promote airings	−0.2880	0.1223	0.038	−0.0556	0.1077	0.616
Contrast airings	−0.3043	0.2373	0.226	−0.1857	0.2908	0.536
Spending per capita	—	—	—	−1.8743	0.7279	0.026
Institutional context						
Professionalization	47.6457	2.9283	0.000	40.0325	5.2616	0.000
District	−1.7778	1.1002	0.134	0.5240	1.4629	0.727
Temporal controls						
2002	−5.0514	1.3557	0.003	−5.4502	1.2229	0.001
2004	−1.4620	2.2855	0.535	−1.1905	1.9942	0.563
2006	−4.5356	1.2629	0.004	−4.1825	1.1722	0.004
Constant	−6.5809	2.4213	0.020	6.4710	5.3375	0.251

Dependent variable = Ballot roll-off
Number of observations = 51
Model 1 R-squared = 0.8041   Model 2 R-squared = 0.8225
Model 1 F = 107.20, Prob > F = 0.000   Model 2 F = 96.54, Prob > F = 0.000
Model 3 R-squared = 0.8084   Model 4 R-squared = 0.8267
Model 3 F = 408.85, Prob > F = 0.000   Model 4 F = 98.15, Prob > F = 0.000

unimportant though the coefficients are in the predicted direction. There may not be enough instances of contrast airings in nonpartisan elections to detect an effect in these models.

These results in Table 5-5 bolster the evidence in Table 5-2 and Table 5-3 (as well as Table 5-4) that attack airings enhance citizen participation in nonpartisan state supreme court elections. But regardless of whether one accepts the mobilizing effects of attack advertising in nonpartisan elections or not, the absence of a demobilizing effect is unambiguous and undeniable.

Robustness Checks for Third-Party Challengers and Hybrid Election States

As with the models of the incumbency advantage in Chapter 4, a final set of robustness checks is in order with the ballot roll-off models in this chapter. First, the models should test for the impact of partisan elections in which the only challengers in the general elections are third-party candidates. Second, the models should be evaluated for any bias resulting from coding decisions about the elections systems in Michigan and Ohio.

As mentioned in Chapter 4, some atypical supreme court elections draw only minor-party challengers who are not seriously viable candidates and thus do not render these elections much of a contest. In the elections analyzed in this chapter, the only cases in which this occurs are nine of the twenty-six elections for the Texas Supreme Court (the civil court of last resort) and Court of Criminal Appeals (the criminal court of last resort). In these races, libertarian candidates were the only challengers to major-party incumbents in the general elections. Failing to control for this circumstance may bias the results.[39]

In the models, the primary tools for identifying aggressive contestation are the spending and advertising variables. In fact, weak challengers can be present in nonpartisan elections as well as partisan elections but are much more difficult to identify a priori given the absence of partisan labels and the difficulty of identifying partisanship in some states. However, for additional confidence in the central inferences drawn in this chapter, I reestimated Model 1 in Table 5-2 with a dummy variable, *third-party challenger*, coded 1 for all races in which the only challenger is a third-party candidate and 0 otherwise. No attack ads were aired in any of these races.

Second, because critics of judicial elections and political science scholarship (e.g., Brandenburg and Caufield 2009) have asserted that coding Michigan and Ohio as nonpartisan elections biases empirical results, I recoded these states as hybrid systems. Specifically, I reestimated Model 1 in Table 5-2 with a variable *hybrid*, coded 1 for Michigan and Ohio and 0 otherwise. I also included a separate specification with an interaction term between *hybrid* and *attack airings* given that some of the Michigan and Ohio races included attack advertising. These results are reported in Table 5-6, which also includes the control *third-party challenger*.

As the results in Table 5-6 indicate, although *third-party challenger* is statistically significant in Model 1 and Model 2, the inclusion of this control variable does not change the substantive inferences about the impact of negative advertising. In short, the results in this chapter are robust with regard to the treatment of third-party challengers.[40] Substantively, supreme court elections with only minor-party challengers can expect to experience about a seventeen percentage point drop in citizen participation, even though all of the races are partisan.

Regarding Michigan and Ohio, adding the dummy variable *hybrid* to Model 1 does not change the substantive inferences in the model, including inferences about the mobilizing effects of attack advertising in nonpartisan elections. Model 2 with the interaction term tells a somewhat similar story, although the results are not as obviously interpretable. In Model 2, adding the interaction term for attack advertising in hybrid elections does little to improve the overall performance of Model 2 relative to Model 1 and indicates that the difference between the impact of hybrid and nonpartisan elections on ballot roll-off is not significant. However, adding the interaction term does cause the coefficient for attack airings in nonpartisan elections (*attack airings*) to lose significance. Why would this likely occur? The most obvious explanation relates to limits in the structure of the data. As Model 2 shows, there are no statistically significant differences in ballot roll-off between hybrid and nonpartisan elections, but substantial multicollinearity is introduced by the additional interaction term. The most cautious readers might prefer to interpret Model 2 as evidence against the mobilizing effects of attack advertising in nonpartisan elections. Others would attribute the performance of the *attack airings* variable to overspecification. But even the most cautious readers would not find evidence of voter demobilization in Model 1 or Model 2.

TABLE 5-6. Televised campaign advertising and ballot roll-off in state supreme court elections, 2002–2008, with robustness checks for third-party challengers and hybrid election systems (Michigan and Ohio).

Variable	Model 1			Model 2		
	Coefficient	Robust standard error	P > |t|	Coefficient	Robust standard error	P > |t|
Control variables						
Third-party challenger	17.2873	2.0337	0.000	17.3205	2.0382	0.000
Hybrid elections	1.0179	2.6601	0.707	1.1944	2.6692	0.660
Attack airings × hybrid elections	—	—	—	−0.2905	0.3281	0.388
Campaign features						
Attack airings	−0.4570	0.1161	0.001	−0.2966	0.2856	0.313
Attack airings × partisan	0.7324	0.4968	0.159	0.5658	0.6499	0.396
Promote airings	0.1917	0.1952	0.340	0.1887	0.1921	0.340
Contrast airings	−0.5912	0.1319	0.000	−0.5934	0.1289	0.000
Candidates						
Unsafe seat	0.3082	1.5343	0.843	0.2701	1.5711	0.866
New appointee	−0.1750	0.9602	0.858	0.0529	0.8729	0.952
Open seat	0.5522	1.6362	0.740	0.6920	1.6940	0.688
Institutional context						
Presidential election	3.1429	0.8351	0.002	3.3880	0.9844	0.003
Professionalization	36.0844	6.6913	0.000	35.7945	6.6699	0.000
Partisan	−12.2395	2.3639	0.000	−12.3745	2.3883	0.000
District	−3.4749	1.6577	0.051	−3.7154	1.4806	0.023
Constant	−6.2753	3.5564	0.096	−6.1311	3.5011	0.098

Dependent variable = Ballot roll-off
Number of observations = 96
Model 1 R-squared = 0.8046   Model 2 R-squared = 0.8058

In fact, looking carefully at the results in Model 1 and Model 2 in Table 5-6, the coefficient for *partisan* is negative and statistically significant while *hybrid* is positive though not significant relative to nonpartisan elections, the omitted baseline category. All things considered, state supreme court elections in Michigan and Ohio without attack advertising resemble other nonpartisan elections much more than they resemble partisan elections without attack advertising, as far as their impact on ballot roll-off is concerned.

Interestingly, contrast advertising reduces ballot roll-off in Model 1 and Model 2 in Table 5-6. Adding the interaction term for attack advertising in hybrid elections does not change the mobilizing effects of contrast airings in state supreme court elections.

These results about Michigan and Ohio are not unexpected. Voters in these states are not provided with the partisanship of the candidates on general election ballots (and in the case of Michigan, on any ballot), and thus citizens are deprived of the most important heuristic in American elections. Given a sharp theoretical focus in this project on institutional arrangements and what voters know simply from looking at the ballot, Michigan and Ohio are quite different from their partisan counterparts.[41]

In sum, despite multiple specifications and different measurement strategies for key variables, empirical analysis reveals that attack airings do not have the toxic impact on the behavior of state electorates posited by the judicial reform community, legal academy, and some political scientists. There simply is no evidence that televised attack advertising demobilizes voters in nonpartisan or partisan supreme court elections. In fact, considerable evidence supports the inference that attack advertising and other negative messages in the form of contrast ads enhance citizen participation. To wit, state supreme court elections look a lot like their executive and legislative counterparts, at least on the issue of how the electorate responds to heated campaigns that include harsh advertising and substantial candidate spending. Expensive campaigns replete with incumbent and challenger bashing in television advertising campaigns do not deter voters in the post-*White* era.

Conclusion

Overall, the results of this chapter are a powerful illustration of the extent to which expensive campaigns replete with televised attack advertising, as well as fundamental institutional arrangements governing the conduct of elections, influence citizen participation in state supreme court elections. Importantly, some of these effects are manifested in ways that directly contradict the bold assertions of many in the legal community and some political scientists.

The most striking conclusion derived from the empirical analyses just presented is that televised attack advertising in state supreme court elections does not demobilize the electorate in nonpartisan or partisan elections. This is the case despite the fact that state supreme court elections, and nonpartisan elections in particular, may represent some of the most ideal conditions under which the demobilization thesis of Ansolabehere et al. (1994; Ansolabehere and Iyengar 1995) and the arguments of the legal and advocacy communities might best apply. Indeed, scholars reasonably might surmise that if support for the demobilization hypothesis and the damaging consequences of attack advertising would be found anywhere, it would be found with institutions lacking a formal representative function, separated from the legislative and executive branches by design, and steeped in myths about the apolitical nature of their decisions.

The various results in this chapter reveal a different reality. Even under the conditions surrounding and defining state judiciaries and the electoral process, televised attack advertising and other negative campaign messages do not inhibit voting. In fact, the larger body of evidence shows that attack airings *mobilize* voters in nonpartisan state supreme court elections, just as contrast airings enhance voter participation in nonpartisan and partisan elections.

From the perspective of campaign politics, voters in state supreme court elections appear to respond to campaign stimuli in exactly the opposite manner posited by normative legal theory and critics of contestable judicial elections. Although substantial proportions of the electorate do not vote in supreme court elections in many contexts, sizeable numbers of voters already at the polls for other important elections can be retained when these elections are intensely competitive. Heated exchanges that include attack and contrast advertising, as well as big spending by the candidates, enhance the willingness to vote in supreme court elections. These findings are entirely consistent with previous studies of state supreme court elections and most political science scholarship on legislative and executive elections. In this regard, state supreme court elections are not unique, and the electorate does not reflect a universal indifference toward supreme court elections that cannot be influenced in significant ways. Campaign advertising, campaign spending, and other contextual factors such as the basic structure of elections are critical keys to an active and engaged electorate.

Indeed, institutional arrangements governing the conduct of elections are significant in promoting electoral participation. Through the lens of judicial reform, by adopting partisan elections and district-based constituencies, the American states could reduce the problem of voter defection considerably. As this study documents, consistently with previous studies, these structural factors substantially increase the willingness of voters to express their preferences in supreme court elections once these voters have already been mobilized in the first place, ceteris paribus. Alternatively, removing partisan labels effectively shrinks supreme court electorates, even when these races are contested. Thus, reform advocates have exacerbated the problem of civic engagement by replacing partisan elections with nonpartisan elections, as other studies have shown (e.g., Dubois 1980; M. G. Hall 2001a, 2007a, 2007b; M. G. Hall and Bonneau 2008, 2013).

Of course, improving voter participation would be meaningless or even undesirable if voters were incapable of making reasonably informed choices. However, studies of supreme court elections, as well as the results just presented in Chapter 4, have demonstrated that state electorates distinguish quality from nonquality challengers and also distinguish among different types of incumbents (e.g., Bonneau and Cann 2011; Bonneau and M. G. Hall 2009; M. G. Hall 2014b; M. G. Hall and Bonneau 2008). Likewise, the electorate votes retrospectively on issues relevant to judges, even when partisan labels are not on the ballot (e.g., Baum 1987; Bonneau and Cann 2011; M. G. Hall 2001a; Hojnacki and Baum 1992).

Beyond these studies, two fundamental tenets of American politics speak to this issue. First, partisanship is an effective heuristic; therefore, partisan cues are a rational basis on which to vote. Second, partisanship is an excellent predictor of supreme court justices' votes in the cases before their courts (e.g., Brace and M. G. Hall 1995, 1997; M. G. Hall and Brace 1992, 1994, 1996). Thus, in partisan elections, even if the electorate merely responds to partisan labels apart from candidate- or issue-based evaluations, these partisan-based choices still are meaningful by the standards of American politics. By effectively summarizing ideological orientations toward politics, partisanship allows voters to choose as if fully informed.

A recent affirmation of this principle in a nonjudicial context is *The American Voter Revisited* (Lewis-Beck et al. 2008), which assesses the 2000 and 2004 presidential elections. Even for the most powerful and politically visible office in the nation, most Americans vote largely on the basis of partisanship. In fact, Lewis-Beck et al. (2008: 415) reiterate that "the typical American voter . . . shows little political involvement, limited grasp of the issues, and not much ability to think in coherent, ideological terms." However, "American voters are far from fools" because of the power of the partisan choice (Lewis-Beck et al. 2008: 425).[42]

Intriguingly, the professionalization of state supreme courts has substantial consequences for citizen participation in state supreme court elections. Professionalism improves institutional capacity, enhances the incumbency advantage, and reduces the need for monitoring, which in turn decreases citizen participation in supreme court elections. Even so, much more work is needed to explain this fascinating result and to explore implications for the judicial function and supreme court elections.

From the perspective of empirical inquiry, this study reveals that scientific accounts of elections to representative institutions are highly relevant to courts. Obviously much remains to be explained about state supreme court elections, including the demographics of those who vote versus those who opt out. Similarly, scientific studies are needed of the consequences of roll-off on election outcomes and the types of linkages forged between citizens and the judiciary. Unfortunately, the rich resources for exploring voting behavior in legislative and executive elections at the individual level of analysis are rare for judicial elections, and vital infrastructure is needed to continue to move the boundaries of science. Even so, a wide array of questions can be addressed with aggregate data. The results of this analysis clearly demonstrate that aggregate-level studies can provide insights into judicial elections, as well as elections to other important offices in the United States.

In this regard, it appears that the factors promoting voter turnout in the most highly visible and publicly salient races also influence the willingness of citizens to vote in lower ballot races like state supreme courts, despite differences in the measurement of citizen participation (i.e., voter turnout versus ballot roll-off) and in the nature and function of the institutions. These results speak strongly to the importance of context in structuring electoral politics broadly considered, as well as the value of comparative state research designs for identifying these effects.

In fact, studies of judicial elections should be useful in informing our understanding of legislative and executive elections and should enhance opportunities for crafting general theories of electoral politics and democratic representation. For instance, this chapter provides additional evidence about the value of mobilization models and the important ways in which contextual forces stimulate citizen participation. But most critical is the additional evidence that attack advertising does not have the deleterious impact on civic engagement that some accounts suggest, even in low-salience settings and institutions shaped by norms sharply inconsistent with aggressive campaigning. This is good news indeed for those concerned with the potentially harmful effects of contemporary campaign politics but also for scholars interested in using comparative state research designs to explore important questions about politics. Studies of state supreme court elections appear to hold considerable promise in this regard.

6 State Supreme Court Elections Are Different—by Design

I N RECENT YEARS, TELEVISED ATTACK ADVERTISING HAS EMERGED as one of the most controversial and worrisome trends in American politics. Nasty hard-hitting exchanges broadcast to the electorate have raised serious concerns from a wide range of political observers, practitioners, and some political scientists that these types of messages may have dangerous consequences for representative democracy. In response to these damning criticisms, and particularly after some confirmatory evidence from Ansolabehere et al. (1994) and Ansolabehere and Iyengar (1995), political scientists have engaged in vigorous debate about the impact of campaign negativity in American politics, producing a wave of compelling empirical findings about whether and how attack advertising influences candidates, voters, and political institutions.

After several decades of rigorous analysis, and despite some contrary findings in the literature (e.g., Kahn and Kenney 1999), the larger body of empirical work on the nation's most visible legislative and executive elections generally has failed to identify any damaging effects of campaign negativity on candidate preference (e.g., Lau et al. 1999; Lau, Sigelman, and Rovner 2007), voter mobilization (e.g., Geer 2006; Jackson, Mondak, and Huckfeldt 2009; Krasno and Green 2008), or individual attitudes essential for a robust civic society (e.g., Brooks and Geer 2007; Jackson, Mondak, and Huckfeldt 2009). In fact, a select subset of studies (e.g., Goldstein and Freedman 2002; Jackson and Carsey 2007; Lau and Pomper 2001) has shown that campaign rancor has the observable benefit of mobilizing the electorate to vote in some races. These findings are a welcome relief given the gravity of the earliest predictions about the potential harms, including long-term systemic damage, of disparaging campaign advertising.

But do televised attack campaigns have different consequences in judicial elections, in which the integrity, impartiality, and wisdom of judges are being impugned? Many legal scholars, legal practitioners, and judicial reform advocates certainly think so and have offered the same sorts of alarming speculations as some political scientists about the potentially destructive effects of intense campaigns on judicial candidates, state electorates, and state judiciaries. Indeed, these worries are so endemic that the American Bar Association has condemned the practice of electing judges outright while others have revitalized their long-standing crusades against partisan elections and, in some camps, nonpartisan elections.

These serious trepidations about harsh campaign negativity in the judicial context, as in American politics generally, are not unreasonable. In fact, from the perspective of normative legal theory, there are several reasons to suspect that the impact of televised attack advertising might be worse in judicial elections than in elections to legislative and executive offices in the United States. First and foremost, judges do not serve as democratic representatives and traditionally have been shrouded in myths of politically neutral decision making and deeply instilled notions about the tightly constraining force of law. In the same manner, judges may depend on perceptions of impartiality to retain their high esteem with ordinary citizens. Thus, aggressive campaign politics, including vituperative assaults against judges, plausibly have portended ruinous consequences in the judicial context. The U.S. Supreme Court's decision in *Republican Party of Minnesota* v. *White* (2002) only heightened these fears as some states began to experience for the first time judicial campaigns that included televised attacks and other issue-based dialogue believed by many to be antithetical to citizens' positive perceptions of judges and state courts.

Alternatively, from the perspective of theories of institutions and electoral processes in political science, attack advertising might have different consequences for some judges, state electorates, and state courts because of systematic differences across the states in the basic rules of the electoral game. In an effort to depoliticize recruitment and retention processes for the state court bench, some states have removed partisan labels from ballots, thereby eliminating the most important heuristic in American elections. This reengineering of ballots should have tangible consequences for how well campaigns work by restructuring the manner in which voters receive and use information and the ways in which candidates and other political heavyweights engage in campaigns. Generally, with the power of the partisan ballot, attack advertising should not be very effective in swaying voters and shaping the participatory behavior of state electorates in partisan judicial elections, as is the case in legislative and executive elections (which use partisan ballots). However, in nonpartisan elections, the mobilizing effects of campaign negativity should be pronounced, just as incumbents should become more vulnerable to derisive attacks. In other words, differences between judicial elections and elections to other important offices may have less to do with dissimilarities in institutional function and more to do with the fundamental conditions under which campaigns are conducted and votes are cast.

The primary purpose of this project has been to test these competing conceptualizations of judicial elections within the context of state supreme courts. Specifically, I employed a wide array of systematic tests using supreme court election results from 2002 through 2008 to answer two pivotal questions about televised campaign advertising. First, do televised attacks reduce the vote shares of the justices seeking reelection? Second, do attack ads diminish the participatory propensities of state electorates? Central to this inquiry is an examination of institutional and other contextual features that help to determine the electoral performance of incumbents and the willingness of state electorates to vote.

To provide an essential framework for rigorous hypothesis tests, I also explored trends in the competitiveness of state supreme court elections and in the participatory proclivities of state electorates from 1980 through 2010. A particularly important concern was whether some of the most consequential features of these races have changed in the post-*White* era. Additionally, using data on every ad broadcast in state supreme court elections from 2002 through 2008, I delineated the exact nature of televised campaign broadcasting, particularly with regard to the extent of televised advertising, campaign negativity, and the sponsorship of ads and airings by tone and by substantive focus.

Evidence derived from the hypothesis tests, as well as much of the information presented throughout the chapters, contradicts many of the bold assertions of those in the legal and advocacy communities about how judicial elections actually work. Generally speaking, there is scant evidence of a degenerating electoral climate for justices seeking reelection, public disengagement from the process of electing judges, or substantial changes over time in the performance of the empirical models consistent with "epochal" (Brandenburg and Caufield 2009: 80) transformations in state supreme court elections in the twenty-first century.

Likewise, the evidence in this project challenges the notion that intense televised attacks and costly campaigns necessarily threaten incumbents or inhibit the willingness of the state electorates to vote. Generally speaking, partisan ballots and other institutional arrangements insulate supreme court justices and state citizenries from any adverse effects of short-lived events like televised attack ads. When partisan labels are on the ballot, attack advertising does not reduce the electoral performance of incumbents or reduce citizen participation in these races.

However, when partisan labels are removed from ballots, campaigns have pronounced consequences. Specifically, attack advertising attenuates the incumbency advantage in nonpartisan elections, creating a strategic contingency within which some of the most damaging consequences of negative advertising can manifest. In other words, the palliative engineered by judicial reform advocates to shield justices from external political forces has had exactly the opposite effect intended, at least where televised negativity is concerned. Similarly, attack advertising and other factors related to aggressive competition *increase* voter participation in nonpartisan elections, another consequence contrary to predictions derived from traditional legal theory and much of the rhetoric in the judicial reform literature.

Overall, the results generated in this project are much more consistent with political science accounts than with legal accounts of judicial elections. These findings also illustrate well the power of institutions in shaping American politics.

With regard to legal advocacy, court reform advocates and other pundits are partially right about the harmful effects of harsh negativity in state supreme court elections but for the wrong reasons. Nonpartisan elections are influenced to a greater extent by hard-fought campaigns not because judicial elections are intrinsically different but because nonpartisan elections alter some of the most fundamental rules governing the conduct of these races.

Through the lens of political science, those predicting the pernicious effects of negativity (e.g., Ansolabehere et al. 1994; Ansolabehere and Iyengar

1995) missed the institutions and the processes to which their arguments best apply. A sharper focus on nonpartisan elections and less visible contests produces interesting insights into the conditions under which campaigns do, or do not, matter in American politics.

The Politics of Contemporary State Supreme Court Elections

There is no doubt that some significant aspects of state supreme court elections have changed in recent decades. The costs of seeking office have risen appreciably since the early 1990s. The speech rights of judicial candidates have been redefined in some states by the U.S. Supreme Court's decision in *Republican Party of Minnesota v. White* (2002) and subsequent revisions in state codes of judicial conduct implemented in response to this landmark decision. States have spent considerable energy redesigning their selection and retention systems. Television advertising has become the norm in contested races. Interest group involvement in the form of independent spending has increased, especially in connection with the sponsorship of campaign advertising in nonpartisan elections. Political activists are paying greater attention to these races. And certainly political scientists are studying these races more now than ever before to discover the ways in which judicial elections work and their consequences for state judiciaries and the American people.

But the fact of the matter is that many misinterpreted the historical record about how competitive state supreme court elections actually have been. As numerous accounts (Dubois 1980; M. G. Hall 2001a, 2007a; Kritzer 2011, forthcoming), including the data in Chapter 2, document, state supreme court elections have been competitive by the standards of the most visible elections in the United States for decades. For instance, Chapter 2 shows that in state supreme court elections from 1980 through 2010, the defeat rate was 20.7 percent in partisan elections and 8.2 percent in nonpartisan elections, compared with the U.S. House of Representatives at 5.9 percent. Other studies describe intense competition and voter involvement in some races all the way back to the late nineteenth and early twentieth centuries (K. Hall 1984, 2005). Thus, voters have not been recently blindsided by vigorously contested state supreme court elections. Voters in numerous states experienced intense competition and electoral defeats long before the advent of televised campaigns or other recent trends in the contemporary era.

Likewise, there is little evidence that citizen participation in state supreme court elections has declined since the 1980s or even in the most recent election cycles, patterns that do not comport well with the voter demobilization hypothesis. This point is critical. A diminution of citizen participation in the form of rising roll-off rates would be an excellent indicator of one of the most serious consequences of televised attack advertising hypothesized in the political science literature. However, there are no observable behavioral manifestations of a disaffected electorate in recent state supreme court elections, even with the emergence of television campaigns and sharp attacks.

Remarkably, in some significant ways, partisan state supreme court elections have become *less competitive* in the most recent election cycles. As the tests in Chapter 2 for differences between the pre-*White* and post-*White* periods indicate, the only statistically discernable changes in partisan elections in challenger emergence, incumbent vote shares, defeats, and ballot roll-off are *opposite* to those predicted by most pundits. Electoral defeats have declined while vote shares have increased in partisan elections in the post-*White* period. Stated differently, on two key dimensions, state supreme court elections have become more electorally secure for incumbents and more interesting to voters when partisan ballots are used to select judges.

In nonpartisan elections, there are no statistically significant changes in contestation, defeats, vote shares, and ballot roll-off between the pre-*White* and post-*White* periods, as indicated in Chapter 2. In fact, none of the post-*White* variables is significant in nonpartisan elections.

These various findings are consistent with other recent studies examining temporal trends in state supreme court elections. In the most comprehensive examinations covering state supreme court races from 1946 though 2012, Kritzer (2011, forthcoming) shows that patterns of competition have been relatively stable during the entire post–World War II period, with the exception of the partisan realignment of the South starting in the 1980s. Similarly, Bonneau, M. G. Hall, and Streb (2011) did not detect significant changes in the basic features of state supreme court elections in the period just after the *White* decision.

At least part of the explanation for the lack of the impact of *White*, apart from the fact that many failed to recognize the traditionally competitive nature of these races, is that pundits almost certainly underestimated the amount of partisan-based and issue-based campaign speech already occurring at the time of the Supreme Court's decision. In 2002, eight states used partisan elections to select or retain supreme court justices, which means that partisanship was easily known to voters in these states. The U.S. Supreme Court also mentioned in *White* (536 *U.S.* 765, 786) that five states (Alabama, Idaho, Michigan, North Carolina, and Oregon) had virtually no candidate speech restrictions at the time of the decision. Four of these five states (Idaho, Michigan, North Carolina, and Oregon) used nonpartisan elections.[1]

From the perspective of the costs of campaigns for the candidates, there are no systematic differences in total candidate spending between the pre-*White* and post-*White* periods in either nonpartisan or partisan elections. These findings comport well with those reported by Kritzer (forthcoming), who shows that changes in campaign spending in state supreme court elections parallel trends in other elections starting in the 1980s, including notable increases in the 1990s. Bonneau (2007) and Bonneau and M. G. Hall (2009) find similar patterns of increased spending in the 1990s.

Thus, the interjection of outside money into state supreme court elections has not translated into any radical changes in campaign spending by the candidates or observable shifts in various forms of electoral competition or citizen participation in these races. This is not to say that scholars and other political observers should not be concerned about the high costs of campaigns, unrestrained spending independent of the candidates, or other possible adverse effects of campaign politics than those tested in this project. However, the very good news is that any financial involvement in state supreme court elections by moneyed activists has yet to alter some of the most fundamental and politically significant features of these races.

Regarding the states, average rates of contestation, the vote shares of challengers, unsafe seats, and defeat rates vary considerably. These various measures of electoral insecurity individually and when combined into an index illustrate the wide range of electoral experiences across the American states, including the intriguing finding that nonpartisan and partisan elections fall along the full range of the competition continuum. From a temporal perspective, the electoral security index shows a change in the relative rankings of states over time but a net change of virtually none. Overall, nine states have become more electorally secure since 2000, nine have become less, and two have remained the same. These fascinating patterns merit additional systematic exploration and explanation.

State Supreme Court Election Campaigns

There is limited evidence (K. Hall 1984, 2005) to suggest that heated campaigns, replete with nasty attacks and issue-based dialogue, are not a modern invention. At least some state supreme court campaigns going back to the late nineteenth and early twentieth centuries resemble contemporary advertising campaigns, though quite obviously not conducted over television airwaves. Studies of state supreme court elections in the 1970s and 1980s (Hojnacki and Baum 1992; Schotland 1985) also describe intense televised campaigns that were issue focused and disparaging of opponents. Nonetheless, it is not clear what state supreme court campaigns were like across the nation in earlier eras or exactly when television emerged as a vital tool for seeking the state court bench.

Fortunately, extensive information is now available about campaign advertising beginning with the 2002 elections, and Chapter 3 uses these data to paint a detailed portrait of these campaigns through 2008. This exploration has provided some interesting insights into the nature of these campaigns, including notable differences between nonpartisan and partisan elections and variations across the states.

One of the most unexpected findings is that television advertising, although the norm in contested state supreme court elections, still is not used in a sizable proportion of these races. In 2008, which had the highest proportion of contested races with televised campaigns, 27.6 percent did not involve candidates, political parties, or interest groups taking to the airwaves. Moreover, most state supreme court elections do not draw attack advertising. During the four election cycles being examined, only 22.7 percent of all contested elections involved attacks of any sort, either against the incumbent or the challenger (with 20.7 percent in 2008). Regarding differences between contested nonpartisan and partisan elections, nonpartisan elections on a race-by-race basis are more likely to involve televised campaigns and attack advertising than partisan elections, but partisan elections with incumbents draw higher volumes of airings, including negativity, when television is used as a campaign strategy.

But perhaps the most intriguing trends relate to the involvement of organized interests, including single-issue groups and other financial high rollers, in the process of selecting and retaining state supreme court justices. Indeed, legal scholars and advocacy groups express particular concern about the intrusion of outside interests into judicial elections, and many consider these groups to be largely responsible for the gutter politics of campaign negativity and other forms of controversial discourse that in their view debase the judicial selection process.

In nonpartisan elections, these concerns are especially well founded. Although organized interests certainly sponsor attack advertising and issue-based appeals in contested partisan incumbent–challenger races and in open-seat elections, their biggest efforts on these fronts have been in nonpartisan elections in which justices are seeking reelection. Overall, interest groups sponsor larger shares of attack airings and broadcast larger proportions of issue appeals in nonpartisan elections than other major political actors, including the candidates. This may reflect the practical reality that attacks against any state's partisan majority are less effective when partisan labels are on the ballot or when there are no incumbents to criticize in open-seat races. Regardless, those concerned with the pernicious effects of organized interests and other big-money players in state supreme court elections should look carefully at nonpartisan elections.

Similarly, total interest group spending on televised advertising has increased substantially in contested nonpartisan elections with incumbents since 2002. Overall, total spending on airtime by outside interests tripled in nonpartisan elections over the four election cycles (2002–2008) evaluated in this project. These patterns are not evidenced in contested partisan elections with incumbents. Overall, spending on television advertising by interest groups has been substantially lower in partisan elections than nonpartisan elections, and there is a pronounced downward trend in partisan elections. As with attack airings and issue-based appeals, nonpartisan elections are the primary target for interest group involvement in the form of expenditures on television advertising in state supreme court elections.

The Incumbency Advantage

Studies of attack advertising in a variety of the nation's most visible elections have consistently shown that these controversial messages are not very effective in convincing voters to prefer or oppose particular candidates, and in this manner campaign negativity does not appear to pose a particular threat to incumbents. Contested partisan state supreme court elections from 2002 through 2008 reflect these same patterns. Attack airings directed at justices seeking reelection in partisan elections do not diminish their vote shares, other things being equal.

Nonpartisan state supreme court elections are another matter. As this project has illustrated, attack advertising takes a toll only on justices seeking reelection in nonpartisan elections. This is an especially fascinating finding because nonpartisan elections were explicitly designed to thwart the pervasion of politics into the judicial selection process.

Even so, it is important to recognize that campaign negativity is but one factor that helps to determine how well justices perform with voters. Although excessive negativity might tip election outcomes in extreme circumstances, attack advertising is only part of a complex process of winning or losing votes. By outspending their challengers, incumbents in nonpartisan elections can shield themselves from the injurious effects of televised attacks. Promote airings also bolster the electoral performance of incumbents in both nonpartisan and partisan elections.

Readers who place less value on the incumbency advantage will not find the ability of attack advertising to lower the vote shares of incumbents to be particularly distributing. In fact, many readers are likely to concede that not all incumbents are equally deserving of enthusiastic popular support and that, in reality, some incumbents deserve to lose. The advocacy literature, however, places a premium on the incumbency advantage. Electoral defeats frequently are used to illustrate the ills of judicial elections and to seek support for institutional alternatives.

Decisions of the states to opt for nonpartisan or partisan ballots are significant, but this project also has shown that decisions about how to structure state judiciaries also are crucial. State supreme court professionalization, which reflects the salaries and staff of state supreme courts and the extent to which high-volume routine appeals are relegated to intermediate appellate courts, strongly shapes the incumbency advantage. As extant research suggests (M. G. Hall 2014b), professionalization improves the supreme court's ability to attract quality members, decide cases more efficiency and effectively, and use dockets strategically to avoid some controversial cases and to control the timing of sensitive decisions that cannot be dodged. These benefits, in turn, reduce the effectiveness of challengers.

In this regard, professionalizing state supreme courts may provide an effective means for partially reconciling the interests of the judicial reform movement with the practice of electing judges. States can offset highly contentious electoral climates by increasing the salaries and staff of state supreme courts and removing the burdens of mandatory appeals from their dockets.

These tools to improve the status and function of state judiciaries have been widely supported in both the reform and legal communities and are not nearly as controversial as proposals to change methods of judicial selection.

From a different perspective, this study documents that, even in an era of unprecedented television advertising, big spending, and new rules of the game for candidates in some states, electorates continue to prefer challengers who have successfully attained judicial office to challengers who would be novices as judges. Indeed, this preference for quality challengers represents in significant ways a discerning choice to favor candidates for the state high court bench who have the professional experience appropriate for the job. Although this finding also reflects the name recognition and campaign experience that elected officials obtain from seeking and winning office, the electoral performance of quality challengers is inconsistent with any notion that voters are incapable of responding to candidate qualifications after exposure to the new politics of judicial elections. However, these results are entirely consistent with previous studies investigating the impact of quality challengers on the election returns (e.g., Bonneau and Cann 2011; Bonneau and M. G. Hall 2009; M. G. Hall 2007b, 2014b; M. G. Hall and Bonneau 2006, 2008).

In the same manner, voters draw meaningful distinctions among incumbents in systematic ways. Justices seeking reelection perform less well when they already hold unsafe seats or are newly appointed, as other studies have shown (e.g., Bonneau and Cann 2011; Bonneau and M. G. Hall 2009; M. G. Hall and Bonneau 2006, 2013). In other words, incumbents receive less electoral support when they were never selected by voters in the first place or reached the bench by narrow margins. As with quality challengers, state electorates still differentiate among incumbents while being bombarded with pejorative messages and costly campaigns in many races.

On balance, the various results in this project about televised attack advertising and the electoral performance of incumbents are consistent with well-established propositions about other American elections. Reduced to the most basic element, negative ads are not particularly successful in swaying voters about their choices of candidates because these choices are determined primarily by partisanship (e.g., Lewis-Beck et al. 2008). Short-lived events like attack ads, no matter how much mudslinging or name calling is involved, do not supplant partisanship for most voters in the United States. As a related matter, because information derived from campaigns is filtered through partisan predispositions, campaign advertising tends to reinforce rather than alter partisan-based candidate preferences (e.g., Ansolabehere and Iyengar 1995). Finally, any effects of televised advertising that do occur "dissipate rapidly" (Gerber et al. 2011: 135).

In nonpartisan elections, the ability of individual voters to connect the candidates to their own partisan preferences merely by looking at the ballot is absent. In this scenario, other information becomes critical. Televised attack advertising and other campaign messages may constitute most of what is available about the candidates and thus have greater power to shape the electoral fates of incumbents and challengers in nonpartisan elections.

Mobilizing the Electorate

This project detected no evidence whatsoever that televised attack advertising dampens citizen participation in state supreme court elections. In partisan elections, attack advertising has no measurable impact on the propensity of state electorates to vote, findings that are consistent with numerous studies of presidential, congressional, and gubernatorial elections (e.g., Geer 2006; Krasno and Green 2008; Lau, Sigelman, and Rovner 2007). Alternatively, televised attack advertising *mobilizes* voters in nonpartisan elections. These results also fit well with the larger body of political science scholarship (e.g., Finkel and Geer 1998; Goldstein and Freedman 2002) showing the beneficial effects of campaign negativity in some elections.[2]

Krasno et al. (2008: 267) effectively summarize the overall body of work on the demobilization hypothesis by observing that

> . . . there is one clear conclusion to be drawn about political advertising and turnout: Advertising can and sometimes does have a positive effect on voter turnout, but by no means is that effect large, universal, or consistent across election years. On the other hand, there is very little evidence that advertising, whatever its other effects, has any negative effect on voter participation in America.

This study offers a significant addendum: The mobilizing effects of caustic attacks are enhanced in nonpartisan elections, at least in state supreme court elections. Additional work is needed to assess the generalizability of this proposition for other nonpartisan contests across the nation.

From the perspective of citizen participation, televised attack advertising has the capacity to mobilize voters in some elections by enriching the information environment, especially through issue-based appeals and critiques of performance in office that by definition are excluded in positive appeals (e.g., Geer 2006; Mayer 1996; West 2010). Negativity also heightens the degree to which citizens become engaged and invested in election outcomes and strengthens the ties between voters and their party's nominees (e.g., Finkel and Geer 1998). All of these effects should stimulate, not impair, voting in American elections.

Chapter 3 confirms that attack ads in state supreme court elections are much more likely than other types of campaign messages to discuss issues. If issue appeals are more effective in educating and mobilizing voters, attack advertising in state supreme court elections seems to hold promise for advancing informed and active electorates.

More broadly, voters in state supreme court elections respond to campaign stimuli in exactly the opposite manner posited by normative legal theory and critics of contestable judicial elections. In fact, aggressive advertising, expensive campaigns, and partisan ballots are essential keys to an active and engaged electorate. Especially notable are the differences in ballot roll-off between partisan and nonpartisan elections, as also evidenced in previous research (e.g., Bonneau and M. G. Hall 2009; Dubois 1980; M. G. Hall 2007b; M. G. Hall and Bonneau 2008, 2013).[3]

The professionalization of state supreme courts is another significant factor in state supreme court elections. Professionalization enhances the incumbency advantage but increases ballot roll-off. What explains these seemingly enigmatic results? As studies (Berry, Berkman, and Schneiderman 2000; Hogan 2004) of state legislatures have shown, professionalization "promotes institutionalization by establishing boundaries that shield members from external shocks" (Carey, Niemi, and Powell 2000: 859). By decreasing the effectiveness of challengers and improving the incumbency advantage, professionalization makes elections less interesting to voters and reduces the need for careful monitoring. In other words, professionalization reduces the civic responsibilities of state electorates.

Are Empirical Studies of Elections before the Twenty-First Century Time Bound?

One of the most sweeping condemnations in the judicial advocacy literature was directed at empirical scholarship rather than judicial elections. In reviewing Bonneau and M. G. Hall's (2009) book on state supreme court elections, Brandenburg and Caufield (2009: 80) argued that scientific studies before the pivotal year of 2000 are relics of "a bygone era." Brandenburg and Caufield described a perfect storm of campaign money, liberalized campaign speech codes, televised attack advertising, and other characteristics of highly competitive elections emerging in state supreme court elections beginning around the 2000 election cycle that render as time bound any empirical findings predating these trends.

Brandenburg and Caufield's (2009) assertion merits serious attention because this criticism applies to the vast majority of empirical work on state supreme court elections conducted to date by political scientists. Remarkably, one of the most fascinating aspects of this project is the striking congruence of the various empirical results generated herein with studies of state supreme court elections from earlier decades. Indeed, this new work and the studies of elections held decades earlier tell virtually the same story. State electorates make candidate-based choices in state supreme court elections by preferring quality challengers to their inexperienced counterparts (e.g., Bonneau and Cann 2011; Bonneau and M. G. Hall 2009; M. G. Hall and Bonneau 2006, 2013; M. G. Hall 2014b). State electorates draw interesting distinctions among various types of incumbents, especially by disfavoring marginal justices or those who were appointed and have yet to receive voter approval in the first place (e.g., Bonneau 2007; Bonneau and M. G. Hall 2009; M. G. Hall 2014b; M. G. Hall and Bonneau 2006). State electorates are not obdurately disinterested in judicial elections (e.g., Baum and Klein 2007; Bonneau and M. G. Hall 2009; M. G. Hall 2007b; M. G. Hall and Bonneau 2008, 2013; Hojnacki and Baum 1992; Klein and Baum 2001). The most aggressive, contentious, and high-priced campaigns enhance rather than diminish voter participation (Baum and Klein 2007; M. G. Hall 2007b; M. G. Hall and Bonneau 2008, 2013). And nonpartisan elections significantly shrink active supreme court electorates (e.g., Bonneau and M. G. Hall 2009; Dubois 1980; M. G. Hall and Bonneau 2008, 2013). This study adds to these findings by showing that television advertising has pernicious consequences for incumbents only in nonpartisan elections but at the same time has beneficial effects on citizen engagement in these same races. The impressive congruence of these results with those in previous studies demonstrates the speciousness of Brandenburg and Caufield's (2009) imprudent claim.

The Advantages of Comparative State Political Science Scholarship

The results of this project are a powerful testament to the value of theoretically driven comparative state research for exploring competing theoretical frameworks and for testing vital propositions about the impact of context in American politics. In this study, state supreme court elections have provided an outstanding analytical opportunity to evaluate how institutional arrangements shape the impact of campaigns (including televised attack advertising) on the election returns and mass electoral behavior, two of the discipline's most enduring concerns. Variations across the states in the use of partisan and nonpartisan ballots, as well as the fact that judicial elections are low-salience, low-information events relative to the elections typically studied by political scientists, have provided the perfect laboratory for expanding the boundaries of scientific knowledge.

Within the discipline of political science, scholars reasonably might surmise that if support for the demobilization hypothesis would be found anywhere, it would be found with institutions shielded by the heavy weight of the purple curtain. Nevertheless, even in institutions steeped in normative expectations of apolitical decision makers and staffed using nonpartisan elections in some states, negative advertising does not have the damaging effects on citizen mobilization initially predicted or widely feared.

This is not to suggest that attack advertising and other forms of intense campaigning cannot have other adverse consequences. This project merely shows that on two of the most important dimensions raised in the debate about televised negativity, the harms are not as acute as initially predicted. These findings are a welcome relief indeed and should help to alleviate at least some of the fears about televised campaign negativity in judicial elections.

An interesting aspect of this project is the demonstration that studies of judicial elections can be useful for informing our understanding of legislative and executive elections and enhancing opportunities for crafting general theories of voter choice, citizen mobilization, and democratic representation that better delineate the impact of institutions and other contextual contingencies in American politics. Indeed, these findings add to a rapidly developing body of evidence showing remarkable similarities between state supreme court elections and elections to other important offices in the United States.

Previous work has demonstrated, among other things, that supreme court elections (partisan and nonpartisan) resemble legislative and executive elections in the strategies of challengers (Bonneau and M. G. Hall 2003; M. G. Hall and Bonneau 2006, 2008), strategic retirements by electorally vulnerable incumbents (M. G. Hall 2001b), the preference for quality challengers (e.g., Bonneau and Cann 2011; Bonneau and M. G. Hall 2009; M. G. Hall 2014b; M. G. Hall and Bonneau 2006), and citizen mobilization (e.g., M. G. Hall 2007b; M. G. Hall and Bonneau 2006, 2013; Hojnacki and Baum 1992; Klein and Baum 2001). Specifically on the issue of mobilization, many of the same factors that increase citizen participation in presidential, congressional, and gubernatorial elections also influence the willingness of citizens to vote in lower ballot races like state supreme courts, despite measurement differences in the key concept (i.e., voter turnout versus ballot roll-off) between nonjudicial and judicial elections.

Scientific accounts of elections to representative institutions also are highly relevant to judicial elections and should serve as a valuable theoretical and methodological guide for scientific analysis. Obviously much remains to be explained about state supreme court elections, and a great deal of effort will be needed to fill in the very large blanks in extant knowledge.

Overall, this project serves as an excellent example of the relevance of theoretically driven political science research to real-world problems. Although political science has been criticized for being divorced from practical reality, this pejorative stereotype is far from accurate. This project reminds us in a straightforward manner that anecdotal evidence and other observational accounts from pundits and other political observers often do not provide the accurate and unbiased information needed to make some of the nation's most fundamental and critically important policy decisions. In the case of the judicial selection controversy, political science scholarship will help to replace conjecture and unsubstantiated claims with scientifically validated facts. These works also will elevate the tone of the discussion to a rational dialogue over the current crisis-centered frame wracked with stridency.

There are, and will continue to be, reasonable worries about the harsh negativity in televised campaigns and other aspects of the practice of electing judges, including issues related to campaign contributions and unregulated money in these races. These and other unanswered questions merit careful thought and systematic empirical examination. Generally speaking, these are concerns that many Americans share about contemporary elections, concerns that should become part of the larger dialogue about democratic politics in the United States.

Likewise, many compelling questions remain about the potentially undesirable effects of the Missouri Plan and various types of appointment schemes. Among the most worrisome and monumental concerns meriting systematic examination are the closed-door and elitist nature of commission-based appointments, renewable terms that impair judicial review when judges must seek reappointment from the other branches of government, and the costs to legitimacy when voters play little or no role in selecting and retaining state court judges who necessarily engage in judicial policy making.

But in all of these matters, evidence derived from rigorous scientific analysis should inform any public and academic discourse and certainly should guide any policy choices by the states. There is much to be learned but, as this project illustrates, these inquiries are theoretically rich, methodologically complex, and eminently worthwhile.

REFERENCE MATTER

Notes

Chapter 1

1. There are exceptions among scholars in the legal community who have challenged untested assumptions about the harmful effects of judicial elections. An excellent example is Dimino (2005: 268), who famously quipped that "democracy may indeed be the worst method of choosing judges . . . except for all the other ones."

2. The recommendations in the American Bar Association Commission on the 21st Century Judiciary's report *Justice in Jeopardy* (2003) were adopted by the ABA House of Delegates in August 2003 and are fully delineated in Appendix A of the report. *Justice in Jeopardy* (2003) can be retrieved at www.americanbar.org/content/dam/aba/migrated/judind/jeopardy/pdf/report.authcheckdam.pdf, last visited on June 21, 2013.

3. As will be discussed in Chapter 2, state supreme court elections are conducted using three basic formats: partisan elections, nonpartisan elections, and retention elections. Partisan and nonpartisan elections both permit challengers. However, nonpartisan elections remove partisan labels from general election ballots and typically use nomination procedures that are not centered on political parties. Retention elections preclude challengers and partisan labels and ask simply whether an incumbent justice should be retained for another term.

4. Specifically, the American Bar Association (2003) recommends that states replace all election schemes currently operating in the states with a commission-based gubernatorial appointment system in which tenure is guaranteed to a specified age. Interestingly, the American Bar Association Commission on the 21st Century Judiciary (2003: 71) explicitly rejects legislative confirmation, arguing that "the protracted and combative confirmation process in the federal system, coupled with the highly

politicized relationship between governors and legislators in many states, has led the Commission not to recommend such an approach." If adopted, this system would be unlike any other currently operating in the United States and certainly the least democratic (Bonneau and M. G. Hall 2009; M. G. Hall 2011).

5. Justice O'Connor's plan for judicial selection is available online at http://iaals .du.edu/images/wygwam/documents/publications/OConnor_Plan_talking_points .pdf, last visited on June 21, 2013. Essentially, Justice O'Connor is advocating the Missouri Plan, which is a commission-based gubernatorial appointment system combined with retention elections. The innovations in Justice O'Connor's plan seem to lie in the requirement that performance evaluations be available to voters in each election and that the deliberations of the nominating commission be public and include citizen input.

6. In 1998, the University of Wisconsin Advertising Project, under the direction of Kenneth Goldstein, began to assemble and code campaign advertising in the nation's most visible elections using storyboards and streaming video captured by the Campaign Media Analysis Group (CMAG) (http://wiscadproject.wisc.edu, last visited on June 21, 2013). Initially this information was collected and coded for presidential, congressional, and gubernatorial elections only. In 2000, the Brennan Center for Justice, working in conjunction with the Wisconsin Advertising Project and CMAG, expanded this enterprise to state supreme courts (Goldberg, Holman, and Sanchez 2001). According to Goldberg, Holman, and Sanchez (2001), the 2000 election cycle is the first for which advertising data were captured and coded for state supreme court elections.

7. *White* invalidated announce clauses in nine states (Caufield 2007). Penalties to enforce these restrictions were severe and included removal of judges from office and disbarment of attorneys seeking office (*Republican Party of Minnesota* v. *White* 2002).

8. A substantial body of work has evaluated the impact of electoral politics on judicial voting behavior (e.g., Brace and M. G. Hall 1995, 1997; M. G. Hall 1987, 1992, 1995, 2014a; M. G. Hall and Brace 1994, 1996), and some intriguing new work is beginning to emerge on the connection between campaign contributions and judicial decisions. However, this line of inquiry is in its infancy and poses significant methodological challenges in assigning causation, as scholars of Congress have long since found. Fundamentally, contributors tend to support public officials whose decisions comport well with the contributors' preferences and goals, which can result in strong statistical correlations between money and votes. However, these correlations are a far cry from evidence of a quid pro quo relationship between donors and officials, which is the central concern in this work. Stated differently, the serious endogeneity problem in these studies has not been solved.

9. As discussed in the following chapters, two sets of studies have emerged recently on the impact of campaign advertising in judicial elections. First, in a series of studies using individual-level survey data (Gibson 2008, 2009, 2012; Gibson et al.

2011), James L. Gibson has evaluated the proposition that issue-based discourse, attack advertising, and campaign contributions harm the legitimacy of state courts. Second, using aggregate elections data from 2002 through 2006, M. G. Hall (2014b; M. G. Hall and Bonneau 2013) has assessed whether attack advertising and other aspects of competitive elections influence the electoral performance of incumbents or citizen participation in these races. Notably, the evidence generated in these sets of studies is consistent. On balance, campaigning in judicial elections does not appear to have the harmful impacts initially posited by scientists and activists.

10. Almost uniformly, the legal community decries electoral defeats and uses each as an example of the degenerating climate for judges and impending danger to state judiciaries. Alternatively, political scientists typically have been concerned about the high levels of electoral security for incumbents and in identifying the factors that systematically predict electoral competition and defeat.

11. Neoinstitutionalism weds assumptions of rationality with a focus on how the rules of the game created by institutions serve to structure both individual behavior and collective outcomes. Among other things, institutions shape goals and create incentives and disincentives for various forms political action and political choice. In the context of this study, a primary focus is how alternative election formats exert direct and conditional impacts on the propensity of the electorate to vote and support for incumbents seeking reelection. For a discussion of neoinstitutionalism and the behavior of state supreme court justices, see M. G. Hall and Brace (1999).

12. As will be discussed in Chapter 2, sixteen states currently use the Missouri Plan (retention elections), seven states use partisan elections, and fifteen states use nonpartisan elections (Council of State Governments 1960–2012). The remaining twelve states select their judges through gubernatorial (ten states) or legislative appointment (two states).

13. Dubois (1980: 36) cites nonvoting as "the leading indicator" that voters are "unwilling and incapable of holding its judiciary accountable through elections."

14. As will be discussed in Chapter 2 and Chapter 3, caution is essential in discussing historical trends in state supreme court elections given the paucity of scholarly attention to this subject. For instance, Kermit Hall (1984: 361) notes that appellate court elections from 1880 through 1910 produced "a level of public interest unmatched before or after" as judges "wrestled with the legal impact of industrialization and urbanization of public life." This contradicts the widely held assumption that state supreme court elections have only recently become visible and contentious. Much more scientific research is needed on this relatively uncharted topic.

15. It is imperative to observe that in no way does this project claim to provide an empirical test of the efficacy of judicial elections, nor do I offer any normative prescriptions about the desirability or undesirability of the practice. In fact, there probably are as many findings in this book that can be used to condemn judicial elections as support them. Instead, this project adds to the rapidly growing body of empirical evidence about the nature of judicial elections that collectively can be weighed to

assess the benefits and pitfalls of any selection scheme and thus counterbalance the tendencies of some to jump to conclusions based on narrow arguments, unsubstantiated claims, and myopic observations of seeming problems or projected fears.

16. The jurisdiction of the federal courts is restricted to cases involving federal law or the United States as a party and to high-dollar disputes involving citizens of different states suing each other under state law (i.e., diversity of citizenship cases). The average citizen is not likely to be party to these types of disputes except bankruptcy, which remains exclusively within the domain of the federal courts.

17. An excellent and well-known example is the political turmoil surrounding the Florida Supreme Court's decision in *Bush* v. *Schiavo* (2004), the Florida right-to-die case in which the state legislature and governor directly attempted to contravene judicial rulings and were struck down in their efforts by the Florida Supreme Court. This case, which played out before the nation and attracted media attention from around the world, involved the fate of Terri Schiavo, a married woman in a persistent vegetative state who became the focus of a bitter dispute between her husband and her parents over the matter of whether to continue artificial life support. After a series of judicial rulings granting guardianship to the husband and supporting his decision to withdraw nutrition and hydration over the vigorous objections of Mrs. Schiavo's parents, the Florida legislature passed special legislation entitled "Terri's Law," which authorized Governor Jeb Bush to order the reinstatement of nutrition and hydration to sustain Mrs. Shiavo's life. Although the Florida trial courts handled the lion's share of work in this matter, the Florida Supreme Court's decision invalidating Terri's Law signaled the Court's unwillingness to acquiesce to popular political demands or to allow the other branches of government to circumvent the judiciary.

18. These statistics from the 2011 term of the U.S. Supreme Court are reported on the Court's webpage at www.supremecourt.gov/opinions/slipopinions.aspx?Term=11, last visited on June 21, 2013.

19. North Dakota technically has an intermediate appellate court, but the docket is assigned exclusively by the North Dakota Supreme Court. The intermediate appellate court also has no permanent judges but sits instead in temporary panels of retired and active judges. Generally, this court has had a very light caseload (see www .Judgepedia.org/index.php/North_Dakota_Court_of_Appeals, last visited on August 27, 2013). Of the ten states without a formal intermediate appellate court, five use some form of elections to select supreme court justices. South Dakota and Wyoming use the Missouri Plan, Nevada uses nonpartisan elections, West Virginia uses partisan elections, and Montana uses nonpartisan elections when incumbents are challenged and retention elections when incumbents are unopposed.

20. Other less dramatic changes also have increased the power of state supreme courts, including state legislative decisions to narrow the range of mandatory appeals.

21. Patterson and McClure's (1976) seminal study of the 1972 presidential election was among the first systematic efforts to study television news and campaign advertising. This study generated considerable scholarly debate by suggesting that broadcast news tends to focus on the hoopla surrounding presidential elections rather than is-

sues and thus is not very informative. On the other hand, Patterson and McClure (1976) conclude that campaign advertisements effectively educate and inform the public.

22. The Honorable Harold See (2007), Justice of the Supreme Court of Alabama, reminds us that attacks are not limited to judicial elections. Justice See was the subject of a televised attack in 1996 depicting him as a skunk when challenging incumbent Kenneth Ingram for a seat on the state high court. As Justice See (2007: 95) observes:

> The principal difference between appointment and election is that in an appointment process some of the ugliest attacks will take place behind closed doors and even the candidate may never be aware of them; the attacks need only reach the key decision makers. In an elective process, the voters are the key decision makers; therefore, attacks must be public if they are to have their desired effect. Thus, the advantage of an elective process is that the candidate knows of the attack and has the opportunity to address it and to correct false information.

23. Gibson (2012) presents some provocative new evidence about the expectations of citizens about judicial campaigns. Using a national survey conducted in 2008, Gibson shows that 60 percent of the survey respondents believed that judicial candidates should be allowed to attack their opponents' views on public policy questions, and 86 percent thought that judicial candidates should make their policy positions known to voters. As Gibson (2012: 12) surmises, "Policy talk by judicial candidates seems to be *expected* by most Americans, not *rejected*." These fascinating statistics are consistent with the long-standing preference of voters in some states for partisan elections over other forms of judicial selection.

24. Justice Ginsburg's dissent in the *White* (2002: 806) decision argues forcefully that state governments have a compelling interest to treat judicial elections differently from elections for other offices:

> Legislative and elective officials serve in representative capacities. They are agents of the people; their primary function is to advance the interests of their constituencies . . . Judges, however, are not political actors. They do not sit as representatives of particular persons, communities, or parties; they serve no faction or constituency . . . Thus, the rationale underlying unconstrained speech in elections for political office—that representative government depends on the public's ability to choose agents who will act at its behest—does not carry over to campaigns for the bench.

25. At the same time, the Seventh Circuit in *Siefert* v. *Alexander* (2010) upheld the right of judicial candidates to join political parties and receive their endorsements. In the words of the Court, "The partisan affiliation ban acts to prohibit [Judge Siefert's] speech on both his political views and his qualifications for office . . . the state does not have a compelling interest in preventing candidates from announcing their views on legal or political issues, let alone prohibiting them from announcing their views by proxy" (2010: 981–982). The U.S. Supreme Court denied certiorari in this case.

26. A controversial reference to reversal rates was aired by incumbent Nancy Becker in her bid against challenger Judge Nancy Saitta to retain her seat on the Nevada Supreme Court in 2006. This ad, labeled "STSUPCT/NV Becker Saitta

Denouncement 15 2" by CMAG, stated the following: "Nancy Saitta's record as a judge has been less than supreme. One out of every three of Saitta's rulings has been over-turned by the Supreme Court, among the most reversals of all District Court Judges. Nancy Saitta, unfit for our state's highest court." The Brennan Center for Justice prop-erly classified this ad as an attack ad but also as having the theme of "controversial decisions," or an issue-based ad. In response, Judge Saitta ran an ad claiming that Justice Becker's claims were based on a student research paper and that "the Nevada Supreme Court declared that study wrong" ("STSUPCT/NV Saitta Vote the Truth"). Justice Becker lost the election.

27. The opening remarks of Chief Justice Roberts (on September 12, 2005) dur-ing his Senate nomination hearing are available on CNN.com at www.cnn.com/2005/ POLITICS/09/12/roberts.statement/, last visited on July 21, 2013.

28. Beginning with the legal realists and pathbreaking scholars like C. Herman Pritchett and Glendon Schubert, political scientists have challenged the validity of normative accounts of judging as closely bound by law. In studies of the U.S. Supreme Court, several generations of scholars have established the primacy of the justices' preferences in voting. Although critics assert that the arguments are overdrawn, evi-dence is overwhelming in the nation's highest court that "private attitudes . . . become public law" (Pritchett 1941: 890) to a significant extent. Studies of other federal and state courts also have documented the impact of preferences, as well as the political and legal context, on judicial choice.

29. Noting the long-standing opposition of the American Bar Association to con-testable judicial elections and the ABA's role in first promulgating model codes regu-lating judicial campaign conduct, the U.S. Supreme Court observed in *White* (2002: 788) that "the First Amendment does not permit [the ABA] to achieve its goal by leav-ing the principle of elections in place while preventing candidates from discussing what the elections are about." The Court goes so far in *White* as to conclude that the purpose of announce clauses is "the undermining of judicial elections" (2002: 782).

30. This is not an argument that recognizing that judges have discretion neces-sarily results in support for electing judges. Political beliefs about which selection sys-tems are preferable are inherently normative, and political scientists disagree on this issue. My point is that the theories used by the legal community are irreconcilable with social science theories and evidence about how appellate court judges actually decide cases.

31. All of the analyses in this project include the Texas Supreme Court, which has civil jurisdiction, and the Texas Court of Criminal Appeals, which has criminal jurisdiction. Both institutions are state courts of last resort.

32. The 2002, 2004, 2006, and 2008 data on airings, sponsors, cost, tone, and themes in state supreme court ads are reported in, respectively, Goldberg and Sanchez (2003), Goldberg et al. (2005), the Brennan Center webpage (www.BrennanCenter .org), and Sample et al. (2010).

33. Specifically, traditional advertisements fall into the traits category. Advertise-ments focused on family/conservative values or the role of judges fit into the values

category. Finally, ads involving civil justice, criminal justice, special interest influence, criticism for decisions, or civil rights fall into the issues category.

34. Goldberg, Holman, and Sanchez (2001) provide some information about televised advertising in the 2000 state supreme court races but do not include any details about the tone of each ad or report the storyboards from which tone can be coded. The absence of the storyboards also means that it is not possible to code the types of substantive appeals beyond the few categories described in the report. Thus, supreme court races in the 2000 election cycle cannot be included in this analysis due to missing data on key variables. Overall, there were thirteen elections in four states (Alabama, Michigan, Mississippi, and Ohio) with televised campaigns in 2000, of fifty-two total races (25 percent) and forty-two contested seats (31 percent). Although these rates are lower than in subsequent years (as shown in Chapter 3), these figures should be interpreted cautiously. In 2000, CMAG captured televised advertising in the nation's seventy-five largest media markets (Goldberg and Sanchez 2003), compared with the nation's 100 largest media markets in subsequent years. Thus, any changes between 2000 and later election cycles may relate to differences in methodology rather than real changes in state supreme court campaign advertising.

Chapter 2

1. In the words of Schotland (1985: 72), "It may well be that no subject in American law has provoked more articles, more speeches and meetings, more hearings and struggles in legislatures and for constitutional revision, than judicial elections."

2. Given the instrumental nature of political action (no matter how altruistically the goals of many advocacy organizations are stated) and the willingness to argue positions that may lack empirical support or use facts that do not meet standards of scientific validity and reliability (e.g., anecdotes, public opinion polls with poor question wording and sampling strategies, selective interpretation of evidence, and even ad hominem attacks on the scientists themselves), academic work is ignored, dismissed, or even caricatured outside the profession by some of the most active political opponents of judicial elections. For an excellent example of this problem, see Brandenburg and Caufield's (2009) essay reviewing Bonneau and M. G. Hall's (2009) *In Defense of Judicial Elections.* An ironic aspect of this essay is its title and theme, "Ardent Advocates." Bert Brandenburg is Executive Director of the Justice at Stake Campaign and Rachael Caufield is a research fellow with the American Judicature Society. Both organizations are advocacy groups that have been zealous in their condemnation of partisan judicial elections. Even so, Brandenburg and Caufield sharply criticize Bonneau and M. G. Hall (2009) for being "ardent advocates" when presenting empirical results and inferences that contradict the political positions of their employers. The review also accuses Bonneau and M. G. Hall of various forms of methodological incompetence, despite the fact that most of the work in the book was first published in top-tier peer-reviewed journals of political science. In fact, in a recent essay in *Judicature,* renowned

political scientist and law professor Lee Epstein (2013: 219) noted that the work "meets all the standards we use to assess the integrity of empirical work."

3. There are numerous other explanations for the wide gap that persists between political scientists and the legal community on the issue of judicial selection. One significant dimension of the problem is the absence of a common technical language or set of shared theoretical foundations that would promote effective intellectual exchanges. In this regard, despite the best intentions, political scientists and legal scholars and practitioners are likely to talk past each other.

4. There are exceptions to this generalization. For an excellent example, see Choi, Gulati, and Posner (2010).

5. Recent evidence, derived from an analysis of state supreme court opinions, shows that elected supreme court justices perform as well on balance as justices selected by other methods (Choi, Gulati, and Posner 2010). Regarding their decisions, justices chosen in partisan elections are the most independent of all when independence is measured as voting less often with partisan colleagues, an intriguing and highly counterintuitive finding (Choi, Gulati, and Posner 2010).

6. Multivariate analysis (e.g., Bonneau and M. G. Hall 2009) shows that nonpartisan elections are more expensive than partisan elections when other factors influencing expenditures are taken into account. These factors include the size of the electorate, whether the seat is open or involves an incumbent, whether the incumbent has a strong or weak challenger, and whether the incumbent is a seasoned campaigner or is seeking voter approval for the first time. If these various traits were immutable to partisan or nonpartisan elections, there would be no need to control for their effects. However, because these factors vary considerably, a more robust approach is necessary for valid inference. In other words, simply adding columns of numbers across all races in all states for partisan and nonpartisan elections is not sufficient for making sound inferences about differences in campaign costs.

7. Schotland (1985: 81) observed almost thirty years ago that "the Missouri Plan for reforming judicial selection has been debunked because the selection process is not only 'elitist' but has drawn so narrow a group, at least until recently, as to seem more like a private club." Schotland (1985: 81) notes that the Missouri Plan continues to be defended "because the alternatives are declared worse."

8. Some evidence suggests that judicial performance evaluations, which are widely supported by reform advocates for all elections but particularly with the Missouri Plan, may be tainted by implicit gender and racial bias (Gill, Lazos, and Waters 2011; Gill forthcoming). Specifically, in some surveys, women and minority judges consistently score lower than their colleagues even after objective measures of performance are taken into account in the statistical models evaluating the surveys.

9. This position appears to assume that lawyers have significant knowledge of, or the ready ability to acquire significant information about, the behavior of individual judges or candidates for judgeships, including their legal philosophies and the extent to which their decisions comport with the rule of law.

10. In 2009, Bolivia adopted popular elections as the means to select the national courts (Driscoll and Nelson 2013). Japan and Switzerland also elect judges (Kritzer forthcoming). In Japan, judges of the highest court are subject to retention elections, and in Switzerland trial court judges at the subnational level are directly elected.

11. The United Kingdom, a nation many Americans view as most politically similar to the United States, exemplifies the vast differences that are present in how courts are organized and judicial power accorded in other constitutional democracies. The United Kingdom is a unitary parliamentary system (no state governments and no separation of powers). Until 2009, the highest court was the Appellate Committee of the House of Lords. The House of Lords is the second chamber of Parliament, which with the House of Commons constitutes the legislature. In 2009, a new Supreme Court was established by moving the Appellate Committee to a new building while prohibiting members from sitting or voting in the House of Lords during their Supreme Court service. Even with these structural changes, Parliamentary supremacy prevails. No court in the United Kingdom has the power of judicial review. Acts of Parliament always supersede judicial interpretations, including interpretations of fundamental constitutional rights and liberties.

12. In fact, scholars have either recognized the futility of continuing to push for the Missouri Plan (e.g., Geyh 2003) or are pointing out the failings of this approach for insulating courts from expensive elections, attack advertising, interest group involvement, and other aspects of elections generally (e.g., Tarr 2009).

13. Since 1996, the choices of the South Carolina General Assembly have been limited to the recommendations of a judicial nominations committee.

14. For example, supreme court justices in Connecticut are screened by a judicial selection commission, nominated by the governor, and approved by the state legislature. For each subsequent eight-year term, incumbents must be renominated and reappointed in the same manner. Delaware is similar except that reappointments are confirmed by the state senate. Finally, in New Jersey justices must be reconsidered only once after their initial appointment. On successful renewal, justices serve to age seventy.

15. These data are taken from the webpage of the American Judicature Society's Judicial Selection in the States, retrieved on July 4, 2013, from www.judicialselection .us.

16. Other, less dramatic changes also occurred during this period. For example, Louisiana adopted a blanket primary system in 1976. Likewise, Connecticut and Delaware revised their gubernatorial appointment systems to restrict the choices of the governor to nominees identified by a selection commission.

17. If we include the less dramatic changes in Illinois, Pennsylvania, and New Mexico, the total number of states revising their selection plans for their highest courts increases by one in each of the 1960s, 1970s, and 1980s.

18. No state has opted for an appointment-based plan after using elections since New York's switch in 1978 for the state high court.

19. Abramson, Aldrich, and Rohde (2012) report defeat rates for 1954–1974.

20. M. G. Hall (2001a) lists the states using judicial elections in the 1980s and the specific format in each state. The 60 percent figure for contestable elections represents twelve of the twenty states using partisan or nonpartisan supreme court elections in the 1980s. California, a retention election state, is not included in the numerator. Of course, these are state-level statistics that may not accurately reflect race-level patterns.

21. Schotland (2002: 8) sharply criticized the *White* majority by writing that "the Supreme Court's decision . . . shows how unrealistic five justices can be about what happens in election campaigns, and also—ironically—about how much judges differ from legislators and others who run for office."

22. Schotland predicted that the effects of the *White* decision would extend beyond state judicial elections to U.S. Senate confirmation hearings for federal judicial nominees. In his words (Schotland 2002: 10), "*White* will figure, perhaps substantially, in the next U.S. Senate confirmation hearing of any nominee for a federal judgeship who holds back in answering senators' questions." There is no systematic evidence supporting the accuracy of this assertion, including the U.S. Supreme Court confirmation hearings since *White* for Justices Alito, Sotomayor, and Kagan.

23. The specific number of incumbents seeking reelection in nonpartisan elections in each of the sixteen election cycles from 1980 through 2010 is as follows: 23, 20, 19, 24, 15, 24, 22, 17, 23, 18, 28, 18, 26, 27, 29, and 21. The total number of incumbents seeking reelection in nonpartisan elections from 1980 through 2010 is 354. In partisan elections, the number of incumbents seeking reelection in each year is 19, 24, 16, 18, 19, 18, 20, 11, 11, 12, 11, 11, 10, 12, 10, and 10. The total for the series is 232.

24. Defeat rates in nonpartisan elections returned to average levels in 2012, falling again below the 10 percent mark. In 2012, twenty-four incumbents sought reelection in nonpartisan elections, and only two (both in Ohio) were defeated, for an overall rate of 8.3 percent.

25. Because contestation rates and vote shares in open-seat races vary little over time and across election systems other than as indicated, I have not shown detailed figures for these races.

26. In nonpartisan elections, rates of contestation (as percentages) for open seats from 1980 through 2010 by election cycle for eighty-two races are 100, 75, 100, 75, 100, 100, 100, 85.7, 100, 66.7, 100, 75, 87.5, 87.5, 100, and 100. For partisan open seats, rates (as percentages) by election cycle for 105 elections are 100, 87.5, 100, 100, 100, 72.7, 100, 100, 81.8, 100, 100, 100, 100, 100, 100, and 100.

27. The only loss in Ohio was in the chief justice race in 2010, in which newly appointed Democrat Eric Brown was seeking his first win on the state high court but was challenged and defeated by Republican incumbent Maureen O'Connor. Thus, because two incumbents were running, an incumbent defeat of some sort was inevitable in the chief justice race. However, even if Justice O'Connor had lost against Justice Brown, she would not have lost her seat on the court. She was reelected for a full term in 2008 and sought the chief justiceship while holding another place on the court.

28. The elections in Illinois had incumbents because three justices were appointed to fill unexpired terms and thus still faced their first elections to the state high court. Pennsylvania is not shown in the table because all of the races in this state were for open seats.

29. For state supreme court elections held contemporaneously with the national election cycle, the number of nonpartisan elections in each of the sixteen election cycles from 1980 through 2010 is as follows: 20, 13, 15, 19, 13, 15, 22, 14, 21, 17, 28, 10, 26, 17, 24, and 14. The total of nonpartisan elections from 1980 through 2010 for which ballot roll-off can be calculated is 288. In partisan elections, the number of these races in each year is 14, 14, 14, 18, 16, 18, 23, 10, 14, 14, 15, 13, 12, 12, 12, and 10. The total for the series is 229.

30. Bonneau, M. G. Hall, and Streb (2011) examined state supreme court elections from 1996 through 2008 and a subset of intermediate appellate court elections to test for any significant changes in the fundamental features of these contests after the *White* decision. Overall, the study failed to detect any significant shifts in the key features of supreme court or intermediate appellate court elections. I have reported some of these results in Table 2-3 and have replicated some of the analysis in this chapter. I very much appreciate and acknowledge the contributions of Chris Bonneau and Matt Streb to this enterprise.

31. Another significant advantage of classifying the election cycles of 1994, 1996, 1998, and 2000 as pre-*White*, and the elections in 2004, 2006, 2008, and 2010 as post-*White*, is that this method results in two presidential election cycles and two midterm election cycles in each of the pre- and post-*White* periods.

32. I am grateful to Chris Bonneau for generously sharing his campaign finance data. The candidate spending figures reported in this chapter and used in the empirical tests are largely the product of Chris's efforts.

Chapter 3

1. This advertisement was aired in the 2006 Georgia Supreme Court race between Mike Wiggins and Carol Hunstein. CMAG entitled the ad "ST SUPCT/GA Hunstein Wiggins Wrong."

2. In this election, Justice Hunstein faced the first opponent of her high court career, after fourteen years of service. Three other Georgia Supreme Court justices were up for reelection without challengers. In a video posted on YouTube (available at www.youtube.com/watch?v=FyCgkhkjxQY), Justice Hunstein claims that Mr. Wiggins was an insurance company and business community shill who falsely painted her as soft on crime. She also describes the ad as "devastating for him" and notes that the ad won an award for the most effective down-ballot ad in the United States during that year. Mr. Wiggins denied the charges in Justice Hunstein's ad. I have not been able to find any definitive evidence of whether the charges in the ad are true or false, but the

allegations appear to be grounded in actual proceedings. In his defense, Mr. Wiggins agued that the proceedings were grossly misinterpreted (Bell 2006).

3. CMAG labeled this ad "ST SUPCT/WV Ketchum Ketchup Guy."

4. CMAG labeled this ad "ST SUPCT/MS Kitchens Out of My Kitchen."

5. CMAG labeled this ad "ST SUPCT/WV Bastress Warped Justice." Challenger Menus Ketchum ran a similar ad entitled "ST SUPCT/WV Ketchum Take a Hike."

6. In a study of the Ohio Supreme Court elections from 1986 through 2006, Rock and Baum (2010) show that higher levels of spending and media coverage in these nonpartisan elections increased partisan voting. Thus, information derived from high-intensity campaigns in nonpartisan elections helps voters to select candidates more compatible with their own partisan preferences, as would be the case in partisan elections. The results of this study comport well with studies documenting that campaign advertising tends to reinforce extant partisan proclivities (e.g., Ansolabehere and Iyengar 1995).

7. As these studies (K. Hall 1984, 2005) explain, California and Ohio were more competitive than Tennessee and Texas largely because of differences in interpartisan competition. California and Ohio were vigorous, two-party states, while Tennessee and Texas were strongly supportive of the Democratic Party.

8. Kermit Hall (1984: 346) writes that "these four states are meant to be broadly representative of the national experience with election of appellate court judges during the period from 1850 to 1920." Given the broad diversity of the states, this is a bold assertion that merits scientific investigation.

9. These high participation rates were not affected by the introduction of the Australian ballot in place of the party-strip system (K. Hall 1984). With party-strip ballots, separate color-coded lists of all of the candidates for each party were provided to voters, and voters generally had to choose all or none of a party's candidates. In some states, voters were allowed to strike through the names of candidates and write in other names. The Australian ballot, first introduced in the United States in 1888, actually makes it easier not to vote in judicial elections and other down-ballot races. Australian ballots list all of the candidates' names on a single uniform ballot, and voters can divide their votes between parties or just skip races altogether. Also, balloting is done in private rather than handing over easily identifiable color-coded ticket strips to vote counters.

10. Kermit Hall (1984) shows that voter turnout and ballot roll-off during the 1850–1920 period were influenced by the same factors driving citizen participation today. Among the many forces contributing to voter interest then and now are competitive elections, vigorous two-party competition, the timing of elections (at the time of the national election cycle, or not), and partisan versus nonpartisan ballots.

11. A succinct description of these events is available online at http://en.wikipedia.org/wiki/Duncan_Brown_Cooper, last visited on August 2, 2013.

12. The sources of campaign information listed in the survey were voters' pamphlets, mailings from candidates, television ads, newspaper editorials, discussions with family and friends, newspaper ads, lawn signs and billboards, door-to-door con-

tacts with candidates, recommendations of law enforcement, radio ads, recommendations from attorneys, bar polls, endorsements by special groups, voters' meetings with candidates, and small neighborhood meetings (Schotland 1985).

13. Information about the Texas Supreme Court elections was provided by Chief Justice Phillips in an e-mail to Anthony Champagne, who with the Chief Justice's permission shared the information with Herbert Kritzer, who then with permission forwarded the message to me. The correspondence between the Chief Justice and Professor Champagne took place on May 15, 2013. I am grateful to Chief Justice Phillips, Tony Champagne, and Bert Kritzer for generously including me in the discussion.

14. The 2002, 2004, 2006, and 2008 data on airings, sponsors, cost, tone, and themes are reported in, respectively, Goldberg and Sanchez (2003), Goldberg et al. (2005), the Brennan Center webpage (www.BrennanCenter.org), and Sample et al. (2010). Additional information about the 2006 elections is found in Sample, Jones, and Weiss (2007).

15. In this work, I have accepted the coding of the Brennan Center, making only minor corrections when clearly necessitated. For example, an advertisement included by the Brennan Center in the 2008 West Virginia races was actually an ad for the state attorney general election. (The 2008 West Virginia ad was entitled "WVCOC McGraw Enough.") Thus, I removed this ad and corrected all of the airings and costs totals. In other examples, a few of the ads were coded twice. Overall, these corrections were minimal and are to be expected in any large-scale data enterprise.

16. Chapter 4 and Chapter 5 discuss the fact that a small handful of elections in Texas involved only minor-party challengers in the general elections. When these nine races are discounted as uncontested, the patterns in Figure 3-1 do not change substantially. Rates of televised attacks in 2002, 2004, 2006, and 2008 are, respectively, 42.9 percent, 72.2 percent, 77.4 percent, and 75.0 percent. Even without these races, there is no overall increase in the propensity to advertise beyond the big increase from 2002 to 2004, and one of every four contested elections still failed to draw televised ads from any of the typical sponsors, including interest groups.

17. Even in the 2006 elections, which is the election cycle being discussed by Sample, Jones, and Weiss (2007), only 43.5 percent of all state supreme court elections involved television advertising, and only 60 percent of all contested races had television ads. The 2007 report exaggerates the extent of television advertising by discussing states rather than individual seats. Specifically, Sample, Jones, and Weiss (2007: 1) report that ten of eleven states (91 percent) in 2006 had televised supreme court campaigns, a figure significantly higher than the 60 percent figure for individual races but more consistent with their description of televised campaigning as "almost invariably" used in state supreme court elections.

18. Another limitation is that the 2002 storyboards are not available for additional content analysis. However, the information reported about these ads (especially their titles and sponsors) makes it simple to categorize them by the types of appeals to voters.

19. When airings are used rather than ads as the basis for the analysis, the results look remarkably similar.

20. Bivariate correlations support the same story. Bivariate correlations between attack ads and the appeals categories of traits, values, and issues are, respectively, –0.4272, –0.1631, and 0.4019. Bivariate correlations between contrast ads and traits, values, and issues are, respectively, –0.0423, –0.1101, and 0.1135. Finally, bivariate correlations between promote ads and traits, values and issues are, respectively, 0.3956, 0.2155, and –0.4228.

21. As explained in the plurality opinion written by Chief Justice Roberts, the Federal Election Campaign Act as amended in 2002 set aggregate caps of $48,600 on donations by individuals to federal candidates and $74,600 to other political committees (party and political action committees) during the 2013–2014 election cycle. The Supreme Court invalidated these restrictions but left in place maximum limits on contributions to any particular candidate or committee.

22. There is not enough information available to include the three 2007 elections in Pennsylvania and Wisconsin in these figures.

23. There is not enough information available to include the three 2007 elections in Pennsylvania and Wisconsin in these figures.

24. Reclassifying Michigan and Ohio as hybrid states rather than nonpartisan states does not negate the sharp increase in interest group spending on airtime in nonpartisan elections from 2002 through 2008. Total spending in incumbent–challenger nonpartisan elections excluding Michigan and Ohio was $263,820 in 2002, $159,680 in 2004, $2,689,286 in 2006, and $4,238,172 in 2008.

25. Some of the subtitles of the *New Politics of Judicial Elections* series illustrate well the crisis-based framing of these reports: "How 2000 Was a Watershed Year for Big Money, Special Interest Pressure, and TV Advertising in State Supreme Court Campaigns," "How the Threat to Fair and Impartial Courts Spread to More States in 2002," "How Special Interest Pressure on Our Courts Has Reached a 'Tipping Point,'" and "How 2006 Was the Most Threatening Year Yet to the Fairness and Impartiality of Our Courts."

Chapter 4

1. In an essay on the impact of attack advertising in judicial elections, Iyengar (2001/2002: 699) speculates that "after seeing judicial candidates and their surrogates hurling charges and countercharges at each other, the public will probably think less of the candidates, the selection process, and the judiciary."

2. Brooks and Geer (2007) were examining incivility as an extreme form of campaign negativity. Brooks and Geer (2007: 1) defined incivility as "attacks that go beyond facts and differences, and move instead towards name-calling, contempt, and derision of the opposition." Even from this perspective, Brooks and Geer (2007) failed

to find evidence of any harmful effects of negativity on the political interest of citizens or their likelihood of voting.

3. Lau, Sigelman, and Rovner (2007: 1183) argue that "there is an overriding lack of evidence that negative campaigning itself works as it is supposed to," even though attacks are widely perceived to be advantageous to the attacker. As Lau, Sigelman, and Rovner (2007: 1185) speculate, "Although attacks probably do undermine evaluations of the candidates they target, they usually bring evaluations of the attackers down even more, and the net effect on vote choice is nil."

4. This chapter builds on my previous work (M. G. Hall 2014b), examining the impact of advertising tone on the incumbency advantage in state supreme court elections. However, M. G. Hall (2014b) analyzed elections from 2002 through 2006 only and did not provide the range of robustness checks included in this chapter.

5. The same charge could reasonably be leveled against some aspects of the Goldberg et al. (2005) *New Politics* report. As an example of a "disturbing" attack ad, Goldberg et al. (2005: 11) cite a soft-on-crime attack ad aired by challenger Brent Benjamin against incumbent Warren McGraw in a 2004 West Virginia Supreme Court race. According to Goldberg et al. (2005: 11), an opening discussion of a person who "sexually molested multiple West Virginia children" was "structured to mislead voters into thinking that the judicial candidate himself had committed the crime." Goldberg et al. (2005: 11) go on to report that "halfway though the ad" this impression was corrected. The ad actually showed and said the following:

> Announcer [with a dark silhouette on the screen, brightening to a photo of an adult and then another silhouette of a child]: "According to the prosecutor, he sexually molested multiple West Virginia children. One only four years old. For this terrible crime, Tony Harbaugh was sentenced to serve 15 to 35 years. But just three years later, a shocking turn of events. Liberal Judge Warren McGraw [the screen at this point shows Judge Warren McGraw's name and photo for the first time] cast the deciding vote to set this reprehensible criminal free."

After viewing this ad, it is difficult to imagine that a reasonable person would have confused Tony Harbaugh with Judge McGraw or would have known that the ad was about Judge McGraw until his name and photo were displayed.

6. Gibson (2012) shows that campaign contributions have an adverse effect on judicial legitimacy, much more so than do policy pronouncements or attack ads. Even so, the net effects of judicial elections on institutional legitimacy are positive.

7. Schaffner and Diascro (2007) have shown that local newspaper coverage of state supreme court elections is considerably higher when races are competitive.

8. For the handful of multimember races ($n = 7$), vote shares were adjusted using the procedure routinely practiced in judicial elections studies (e.g., M. G. Hall 2001a, 2007a; M. G. Hall and Bonneau 2006) and classic studies of state politics (e.g., Jewell 1982; Tucker 1986; Tucker and Weber 1987). As Jewell (1982) explains, each incumbent's vote is divided by the total votes cast in the race and then is multiplied by the total number of seats being filled. With these data, this method simply requires

multiplying each incumbent's percentage by two because all multimember races involved two seats only. This process has been shown to produce vote shares closely equivalent to those for candidates in single-member districts. As a robustness check, however, I used an alternative method. Specifically, I first calculated the sum of the votes cast for challengers, excluding the votes for either incumbent. I then calculated each incumbent's vote share by dividing each incumbent's vote by the sum of that incumbent's vote plus half of all challenger votes (divided by two to reflect the number of seats). This procedure produces very similar results to the method recommended by Jewell (1982). Average incumbent vote in multimember elections using Jewell's method is 65.96 percent, compared with 65.88 percent using the alternative. Importantly, this alternative measure when substituted in the models does not affect the substantive inferences in this chapter. Dropping the multimember races matters little either, nor does adding a control variable for these races. As a final matter, because the focus in these models is on the electoral performance of the incumbent relative to all other candidates and not his or her share of the two-party vote, methods designed to measure the two-party vote in multimember elections are not appropriate for this inquiry.

9. During this period, all races in Pennsylvania and Wisconsin were for open seats, and the seats in North Dakota were not contested.

10. Peters (2009) and Bonneau and Cann (2011) have shown that various rules governing the conduct of elections, including state codes of judicial conduct and campaign finance restrictions, strongly disfavor challengers relative to incumbents.

11. Michigan and Ohio use partisan nomination processes (party conventions and partisan primaries, respectively) but do not list the candidates' partisan affiliations in the general election. Given the focus in this project on formal institutional arrangements and information readily available to voters, these states appropriately are classified as nonpartisan, as is standard practice in judicial election studies (e.g., Bonneau 2007; Bonneau and Cann 2011; M. G. Hall 2001a; M. G. Hall and Bonneau 2006). The interest here is not in nebulous concerns about how partisan or political any particular race might be but rather focuses systematically across states on what voters learn from the ballot. In Michigan and Ohio, all of these races were decided in the general elections in which the candidates' partisan designations were not provided.

12. The Campaign Media Analysis Group was not established until 1998, and it is not at all clear how much television advertising took place in state supreme court elections prior to CMAG's systematic collection of these data starting in 2000.

13. Because of the high levels of contestation in partisan elections during this time period, two-stage selection models that would estimate whether incumbents are challenged as the first stage of a statistical analysis are not appropriate for these data, just as these models are not used for the same reason in studies of congressional elections.

14. The 2002, 2004, 2006, and 2008 advertising data on airings, tone, and sponsors are from, respectively, Goldberg and Sanchez (2003), Goldberg et al. (2005), the Brennan Center webpage (retrieved on June 19, 2007, from www.BrennanCenter.org), and Sample et al. (2010).

15. Because the natural logarithm of zero is undefined, I follow the standard practice of transforming $x = 0$ using a constant number. Specifically, in the models I use $\ln(x + .1)$ as the functional form for the advertising variables with zero values.

16. Ideally the models would include spending independent of the candidates by political parties, organized interests, and other individuals and groups who pay considerable sums to promote or oppose candidates. However, these figures are not reported or assembled in any consistent way across states and thus are not available in reliable form for many elections.

17. Measuring spending separately for incumbents and challengers increases the potential for multicollinearity. However, none of the variance inflation factor (VIF) statistics for the models indicates the need for concern, although even mild collinearity may slightly alter some of the coefficients. Average VIF for Model 1 in Table 4-2 is 1.92 with a range of 1.13 to 2.84, and average VIF for Model 2 is 2.08 with a range of 1.24 to 2.84. In Model 1, the VIF for spending differences is 1.34, and in Model 2 the VIFs for incumbent spending and challenger spending are, respectively, 2.81 and 2.64. Moreover, estimating the models in Table 4-2 without the spending variables does not change the substantive inferences about the impact of attack airings targeting incumbents but does decrease the predictive power of the models.

18. M. G. Hall and Bonneau (2006) also show that the *type* of judicial experience matters to voters in state supreme court elections when choosing among challengers. Specifically, the electorate appears to differentiate between trial court and appellate court experience. In states without intermediate appellate courts, the effectiveness of challengers from the trial courts is much higher than in states with appellate courts. In states with intermediate appellate courts, challengers from the trial courts still are preferred to challengers with a complete lack of judicial experience, but challengers with appellate service are especially effective in reducing the vote shares of incumbents. Unfortunately, there is not enough variation in these data to allow for a more refined test of the quality challenger hypothesis.

19. The terms *professionalism* and *professionalization* are used interchangeably in the scholarly literature.

20. The bivariate correlation between professionalization and selection system is 0.15.

21. The Squire index is based on data from 2004 through 2006 and thus is a very good fit for this analysis.

22. Multiple interaction terms that fail to reach statistical significance can distort empirical models and threaten valid inference. For example, promote ads for incumbents are significant in the models in Tables 4-2, 4-4, and 4-5 but not in the models in Table 4-3. Even so, the inferences about attack ads targeting incumbents are consistent in all of the models, including Table 4-3.

23. The interaction term also improves the predictive power of the models in Table 4-2, by 4.4 percent in Model 1 and 5.5 percent in Model 2.

24. For additional evidence that this result is not a statistical artifact, I ran a bivariate t-test. Average incumbent vote in nonpartisan races with no attack ads is

60.4 percent but is 49.0 percent in nonpartisan races with attack ads. This difference is statistically significant. Similarly, when models are estimated for nonpartisan elections only, the coefficient for *Attack Airings against Incumbent* is negative and statistically significant.

25. For example, in a 2008 race for the Louisiana Supreme Court, incumbent Catherine ("Kitty") Kimball (D) was seeking her third electoral victory, against challenger Jefferson Hughes (R). Justice Kimball was the first woman elected to a Louisiana District Court, the first woman elected to the Louisiana Supreme Court, and the first woman to become chief justice. She won an open seat on the Louisiana Supreme Court against numerous contenders in 1992, was unopposed for reelection in 1998, and defeated her Republican challenger with 64.7 percent of the vote in a blanket primary in 2008, thus precluding the need for a general election in this race.

26. Predicted values of vote shares were estimated using CLARIFY (Tomz, Wittenberg, and King 2003). In Figure 4.1, "max ad" and "max ad, means prof" are the same but are shown twice for visual continuity.

27. As with the models in Table 4-2, the only statistically significant interaction among the campaign advertising variables in Table 4-4 is with attack advertising.

28. As an alternative approach to the third-party challenger races, I dropped these nine cases and reran the models in Table 4-2. Dropping these cases, generally on the grounds that they are not contested elections in the practical sense, does not change any of the inferences about attack advertising in state supreme court elections.

29. Specifically, Brandenberg and Caufield (2009: 80) opine that the statistical results reported in Bonneau and M. G. Hall (2009) would be "more credible if they hadn't tilted the scales by lumping Michigan and Ohio into the nonpartisan category" and that doing so results in a "conflation of apples and oranges."

30. Wheat and Hurwitz (2013) provide an interesting history of the evolution of the selection system in Michigan, which they describe as a hybrid system. Their categorization is consistent with the robustness checks in this project.

31. Arguments about differences between Michigan and some but not all other nonpartisan election states may have had some basis before the U.S. Supreme Court's decision in *Republican Party of Minnesota* v. *White* (2002). Prior to *White*, a wide range of campaign speech, including revealing partisan attachments or receiving partisan endorsements, was prohibited in some states. However, as Caufield (2007) reports, *White* invalidated announce clauses in only nine states, and the Supreme Court mentioned in *White* (536 *U.S.* 765, 786) that five states (Alabama, Idaho, Michigan, North Carolina, and Oregon—but not Ohio—had virtually no candidate speech restrictions at the time of the decision. Four of these five states (Idaho, Michigan, North Carolina, and Oregon) held nonpartisan supreme court elections. Now in the post-*White* era, because all candidates have greater freedom to discuss their partisanship and issue positions with voters, any differences between states with previously restrictive codes and Michigan (and possibly Idaho, North Carolina, and Oregon) should have dissipated. Even so, from the perspective of the average citizen, there still should

be distinct differences between voting with partisan labels on ballots and voting without this vitally important heuristic.

32. This point seems especially compelling with Michigan. Candidates are nominated at party conventions (or by a requisite number of signatures), which means that the state electorate never at any point in the election process sees a ballot with partisan labels attached to the candidates' names.

33. Interestingly, Caufield (2007) classifies Michigan and Ohio differently with regard to their statutory responses to the *White* decision and subsequent analysis of the impact of these rules on state supreme court election campaigns. Caufield argues that Michigan has taken a broad interpretation of *White* while Ohio has taken a narrow view. Thus, in her statistical analysis, Caufield places these two states in separate categories. Her analysis points to significant differences between Michigan and Ohio in both the legal environment structuring the conduct of campaigns and in the impact of these rules on the tone and issue content of campaign advertising in the aftermath of *White*.

34. Tests for advertising effects beyond those reported in Table 4-5 for hybrid elections are not possible because there are not enough of the other types of campaign ads in Michigan and Ohio to analyze. For instance, only one race involved attacks targeting challengers, and thus this effect cannot be modeled reliably.

35. Weak challengers can appear in nonpartisan elections as well, but without partisan labels it is difficult to identify these candidates systematically other than relying on the typical indicators (e.g., quality challenger, campaign spending) or resorting to unsound practices such as dropping cases producing sizable electoral margins. For example, in Georgia, Minnesota, and Mississippi, a few incumbents won with 70 percent of the vote in nonpartisan elections. Future research is needed to refine measures of electoral competition in state supreme court elections, for the states and for candidates.

36. Adding the variables *hybrid* and *hybrid × attack airings against incumbent* to Model 1 in Table 4-2 has little effect on the performance of the models. Values of R^2 without either variable, with *hybrid* only, and with *hybrid* and *hybrid × attack airings against incumbent* are, respectively, 0.7022, 0.7055, and 0.7078. These variables have little explanatory power.

37. Caution should be exercised when deriving normative conclusions from empirical findings of constituency influence in state supreme courts. The fact that democratic pressures penetrate courts logically can be construed as an affront to the rule of law and fundamental due process. Scholars reasonably might argue that appellate review should never be influenced by voter preferences or the justices' personal desire to retain office. Indeed, interpreting democratic responsiveness as evidence for ending the practice of electing judges altogether comports well with traditional theories of the judiciary in American politics. Remarkably, the opposite construction also is plausible. In cases lacking reversible error, electoral pressures may prevent justices from disregarding the law and imposing their own preferences that contradict the

proper findings of juries and lower court judges. In fact, most of the studies showing constituency responsiveness are studies of state supreme court death penalty cases, and the death penalty *is* law in the majority of American states. In sum, we cannot necessarily assume that public preferences subvert the rule of law or that judges' unchecked preferences are less dangerous than the threat of majority tyranny. Likewise, judicial independence has never been defined normatively as judges simply voting as they wish.

38. In American elections studies, quality challengers are usually defined as candidates with any previous experience in winning elections regardless of the specific office. Thus, defining quality challengers in state supreme court elections as challengers who are, or have been, judges is more stringent than the definition typically employed in studies of nonjudicial elections and biases the results against the hypothesis. Nonquality challengers in supreme court elections may have held other nonjudicial elective offices before running for supreme court and thus may have acquired both experience in running campaigns and name recognition with voters. Likewise, not all lower court judges were elected to their positions but may have been appointed to fill unexpired terms, which in some states can be quite long. In fact, seeking a seat on the high court bench may be the first judicial election campaign for some challengers though they already hold judgeships.

Chapter 5

1. As Hajnal and Trounstine (2005: 515) summarize, "Roughly half of eligible voters vote in national elections. At worst, fewer than 10% vote in local elections."

2. Perhaps equally provocative is the claim that demobilization is a calculated strategy in campaigns using attack advertising. As Ansolabehere and Iyengar (1995: 9) explain, "The real concern for Twenty-First Century democracy is not manipulation of naïve voters by sophisticated 'image-makers,' but the shrinking of the electorate by political strategists who are fully aware of the consequences of their actions." Ansolabehere and Iyengar (1995: 9) likewise refer to the demobilizing effects of attack ads as "a well-kept secret, and a tacit assumption among political consultants."

3. In the words of Ansolabehere and Iyengar (1995: 99):

The cost of political advertising . . . is not that people cast uniformed votes or that they are tricked into voting for someone with whom they disagree. Rather, political advertising—at least as it is currently practiced—is slowly eroding the participatory ethos in America. In election after election, citizens have registered their disgust with the negativity of contemporary political campaigns by tuning out and staying home.

4. In one of the first systematic studies of campaign advertising in state supreme court elections, M. G. Hall and Bonneau (2013) found that attack advertising substantially increased voter participation in contested races from 2002 through 2006. However, this study did not analyze the impact of promote or contrast ads separately and did not explore differences in campaign advertising between partisan and non-

partisan elections. Similarly, this study did not investigate the impact of state supreme court professionalism on ballot roll-off.

5. Lau, Sigelman, and Rovner (2007) list and summarize 111 studies of campaign negativity through mid-2006. These 111 studies consider a wide range of possible consequences of attack ads, including demobilization, candidate choice, and affect toward the target and the attacker.

6. Ansolabehere and Iyengar (1995) found that these effects were particularly strong among independents and those poorly informed about politics.

7. There are contrary findings in the scholarly literature (e.g., Kahn and Kenney 1999), but many of these findings have been questioned if not refuted (e.g., Jackson and Sides 2006; Lau, Sigelman, and Rovner 2007). However, some interesting individual-level evidence generated from presidential elections shows that timing may be critical. Krupnikov (2011: 808) suggests that the impact of attack advertising is "highly conditional," based on (1) a voter already selecting a preferred candidate, and (2) being exposed to attacks targeting the preferred candidate after this choice has been made.

8. In contrast to claims by Ansolabehere and Iyengar (1995), scholars also have failed to find any distinct effects of negativity on any particular groups within the electorate, including independents (e.g., Finkel and Geer 1998; Jackson and Carsey 2007; Jackson and Sides 2006).

9. In an article speculating about the impact of campaign negativity in judicial elections, Iyengar (2001/2002: 697) states that "the spread of negative campaigning in judicial races is likely to have adverse consequences for the court system. The motives of the judicial candidates will be cast into doubt, and public esteem for the judiciary will suffer . . . and the impartiality, independence, and professionalism of the judiciary will also be called into question."

10. At least to my knowledge, neither the American Bar Association nor any other advocacy group has expressed any concerns that aggressive or nasty campaigns will inhibit voter participation. However, a fundamental premise of the case against contestable elections is that campaigning dampens citizen support for judges and courts, including the feelings of trust and confidence believed to underlie judicial legitimacy. To political scientists, and as extensive research on executive and legislative elections documents, the most pronounced symptom of political distrust and disillusionment is voter demobilization. In fact, Ansolabehere et al.'s (1994; Ansolabehere and Iyengar 1995) primary explanation for why attack ads should suppress the vote is that negativity undercuts efficacy and trust. Thus, the logical extension of the reformers' argument about the injurious effects of elections on citizens' positive perceptions of courts is an expectation of voter demobilization, even if the reform community itself has not recognized this connection.

11. An extensive body of work has evaluated the causes and consequences of public support for the U.S. Supreme Court. However, because of obvious differences between the nation's highest court and state supreme courts, including fundamental differences in function and institutional design, studies of the U.S. Supreme Court may not be generalizable to the states. Cann and Yates (2008) and Gibson (2012) provide

detailed and thoughtful summaries of this research and the relevance of these studies to state courts.

12. The survey used by Benesh (2006) and Kelleher and Wolak (2007) included questions about "courts in your community," which were not defined. Thus, it is not clear to which courts these findings might apply.

13. Gibson (2012) offers a critique of the early studies using national surveys. Because these surveys were not designed to be representative when disaggregated to the state or selection system level, caution should be exercised when evaluating the robustness of the inferences in this body of research. Even so, the findings of Kelleher and Wolak (2007) and Cann and Yates (2008) are consistent with the findings in Gibson (2012).

14. Although Benesh (2006) argued that the public can be assumed to know the details of how judges are selected in their states, Gibson (2012) shows that most citizens are unaware of what type of ballots are used to select judges. Thus, from the perspective of microlevel theory, Gibson (2012) challenges Benesh's (2006) substantive finding that citizens are likely to think worse of judges chosen in partisan elections. More work is needed to reconcile the findings of these studies and advance our understanding of judicial legitimacy, including its causes and consequences.

15. Michigan and Ohio use partisan nomination processes but do not list the candidates' partisan affiliations in the general election. Given the focus in this project on formal institutional arrangements and information readily available to voters, these states appropriately are classified as nonpartisan, as is standard practice in judicial election studies (e.g., Bonneau 2007; Bonneau and Cann 2011; M. G. Hall 2001a, 2007a, 2007b; M. G. Hall and Bonneau 2006). The interest here is not in amorphous concerns about how partisan or political any particular state's supreme court elections might be but rather on what voters know merely by reading the ballot.

16. Although twenty-two states use partisan or nonpartisan elections to staff their high courts, only eighteen states are included in this analysis. Idaho had two contested races, but both were decided in primaries. Pennsylvania and Wisconsin hosted a total of three contested races, but all were held outside the national election cycle (in odd years). Finally, North Dakota had no contested races (of five total) during this period.

17. The 2002, 2004, 2006, and 2008 advertising data on airings, tone, and sponsors in state supreme court elections are from, respectively, Goldberg and Sanchez (2003), Goldberg et al. (2005), the Brennan Center webpage retrieved on June 19, 2007, from www.BrennanCenter.org), and Sample et al. (2010).

18. Consistent with common practice, two types of elections are excluded that preclude a calculation of roll-off: (1) elections held during the regular November election cycle but without a presidential, senatorial, or gubernatorial race on the ballot; and (2) elections held outside the national election cycle (in odd years or in months other than November). For these situations, scholars have yet to calculate normal turnout, and thus there is no baseline from which to gauge participation in judicial elections. More importantly, there are theoretical reasons to expect that the factors influencing citizen participation in that minority of supreme court elections not held

contemporaneously with major elections will differ significantly from the regular elections. Thus, pooling these observations is problematic, and simply looking at turn-out rather than roll-off does not address the problem. In total, fifteen of 111 contested nonpartisan and partisan elections, or 13.5 percent, are excluded by these criteria. The conclusions in this study should not be generalized to these races.

19. Ballot roll-off in multimember elections was calculated following conven-tional practice in judicial election studies (e.g., Dubois 1980; M. G. Hall 2007b). Spe-cifically, the total number of votes cast in each race was divided by the total number of seats in the electoral constituency. With these elections, this method simply requires dividing total votes cast by two, because all multimember races involved two seats per electoral constituency. The eight multimember races in the data set are from Michigan (a nonpartisan election state) and West Virginia (a partisan election state).

20. Ansolabehere and Iyengar (1995: 108) describe ballot roll-off as "an even more stringent test of the demobilization effects of negative campaigning."

21. Recall that all of the races being analyzed in this chapter were both contested and held contemporaneously with a presidential, gubernatorial, or senatorial election. On average, ballot roll-off is considerably higher in uncontested races. Also, voter par-ticipation is much lower in elections held outside the November national general elec-tion cycle, whether in the primaries or elections held in earlier months or odd versus even years.

22. The 2002 Mississippi Supreme Court race in which incumbent Chuck McRae was defeated drew more voters than the highest race on the ballot, a U.S. Senate race. This is the only negative value of ballot roll-off in the data set.

23. The models in this chapter are essentially mobilization models of political participation, or models in which "participation is a response to contextual cues and political opportunities structured by the individual's environment" (Leighley 1995: 188). Patterson and Caldeira (1983), Leighley (1995), and Jackson and Carsey (2007) provide excellent descriptions of mobilization models in political science.

24. Wattenberg, McAllister, and Salvanto (2000: 247) compare voting and ballot roll-off to taking an SAT test: "If people do not know enough to make an informed decision, they leave the question blank."

25. Because the natural logarithm of zero is undefined, I follow the standard prac-tice of transforming $x = 0$ using a constant number. Specifically, in the models I use $\ln(x + .1)$ as the functional form for the advertising variables with zero values.

26. Berry, Berkman, and Schneiderman (2000) also show, for example, that coat-tail effects in state legislative elections are greatest from presidential elections, fol-lowed by gubernatorial elections, and then senatorial races.

27. Benesh (2006) failed to find any connection between professionalization and citizen support for state courts at the individual level of analysis. Her argument was that citizens are unlikely to know how courts are organized and managed and thus are not influenced by these factors.

28. The Squire index is based on data from 2004 through 2006 and thus is a very good fit for this analysis.

29. The bivariate correlation between professionalization and selection system is 0.21.

30. Another institutional feature that might affect ballot roll-off in partisan elections is the option to cast a straight-ticket, or straight-party, vote, wherein voters select all candidates of a political party by casting one vote for the ticket instead of making individual choices in each race. Although only fifteen states now provide this option to voters (National Conference of State Legislatures 2012), all partisan election states except two in this analysis allow for straight-ticket voting, including in state supreme court elections. Only Illinois and Louisiana do not. Unfortunately, there are only three observations from these states from 2002 through 2008, thus precluding a reliable test of any hypotheses related to this option.

31. Challengers in some contested partisan elections in Texas were libertarian candidates who were not likely to detract significantly from incumbents' vote shares or excite voters. When these races are removed, the ballot roll-off rate in partisan elections is 6.6 percent rather than 10.3 percent. This adjusted rate is quite similar to the roll-off rates reported by M. G. Hall (2007b) for state races for attorney general (6.4 percent), secretary of state (6.2 percent), and treasurer (7.7 percent) from 1980 through 2000 in states electing supreme court justices in retention, nonpartisan, and partisan elections.

32. Even with campaign spending in the models, variance inflation factor statistics (VIF) do not indicate any issues with collinearity. In Model 2 in Table 5-2, average VIF is 1.94, and the highest VIF (which results from *spending per capita*) is 3.89. In Model 2 in Table 5-3, average VIF is 2.15, and the highest VIF (which also results from *spending per capita*) is 3.93. These numbers indicate the presence of mild collinearity but certainly raise no major concerns about model specification. Even so, many econometricians caution that multicollinearity is a likely possibility with interaction terms even when VIF statistics are reasonable.

33. Interestingly, the coefficients for contrast airings in both nonpartisan and partisan elections are negative in Table 5-2 and Table 5-3 when the interaction term is removed from the models. This makes sense given the small number of races with contrast airings in these data and the lack of a conditional relationship based on ballot type.

34. When attack airings and contrast airings are combined to form a single variable for negative advertising, the results (not shown) are entirely consistent with the models in Table 5-2 and Table 5-3 that estimate the effects of these messages separately. This is true regardless of whether campaign spending is included in the models. Negative campaigns reduce ballot roll-off in nonpartisan elections but have no discernable statistical impact in partisan elections.

35. Predicted values of ballot roll-off were estimated using CLARIFY (Tomz, Wittenberg, and King 2003).

36. As we would expect, estimates of predicted ballot roll-off using Model 1 in Table 5-2, which excludes per capita spending, are very similar to estimates of predicted roll-off when campaign spending is set at the mean value using Model 2 in Table 5-2.

In Model 1, when attack airings and contrast airings are at their minimum values (i.e., these messages did not air) in nonpartisan elections but all other variables are set at their means, estimated roll-off is 21.3 percent. However, predicted roll-off decreases to 10.2 percent when attack and contrast airings are increased to their maximum values.

37. The bivariate correlation between *district* and *per capita spending* is 0.48.

38. When the same practice is followed with partisan elections (not shown), the variable *attack airings* is not statistically significant in any of the models. Negative campaign advertising does not seem to influence the propensity to vote in these races. Likewise, the same results are obtained when *third-party challenger* is added as a control variable.

39. None of the Texas elections with libertarian challengers resulted in attack or contrast advertising. In fact, none of the campaigns for the twenty-six elections in Texas from 2002 through 2008 included attack advertising for or against any candidate, and only three elections involved contrast airings.

40. Dropping these nine elections in Texas from the analysis does not change the substantive inferences about attack airings.

41. From 2002 through 2008, incumbent vote shares were, on average, *higher* (i.e., less competitive) in Michigan and Ohio (60 percent) relative to other nonpartisan election states (57 percent). Similar patterns are evidenced with ballot roll-off. Average roll-off in state supreme court elections was 24.8 percent in the hybrid states but only 14.1 percent in nonpartisan states excluding Michigan and Ohio. This is unsurprising, especially in Michigan where the number of candidates in each race ranged from three to six, increasing the difficulty of candidate choice. In essence, Brandenberg and Caufield's (2009) assertion that Michigan and Ohio are more similar to partisan elections than nonpartisan elections is not supported for the elections analyzed in this project, at least with regard to ballot roll-off and the electoral performance of incumbents. Theoretically, this makes perfect sense given formal ballot provisions and the information available to voters when deciding whether to vote. Overall, the partisan ballot cue is considerably more powerful than any partisan information that may be available during the campaigns, whether because of partisan convention nominations (in Michigan), partisan primaries (in Ohio), or campaign messages and other information provided to voters in the post-*White* era.

42. Actually, that "voters are not fools" is an oft-cited quip from V. O. Key (1966: 7) in his final book *The Responsible Electorate*. Key argued that the choices of American voters are eminently rational, in contrast to prevailing theories suggesting otherwise.

Chapter 6

1. Gibson (2012) asserts that voters *prefer* issue-based campaigns, based in part on a 2008 national survey in which 86 percent of all respondents believed that judges should announce their policy positions. As Gibson (2012: 131) argues, "Citizens want to know the policy views of those who are candidates for state courts of last resort,

and they are pleased when provided this sort of information." Underlying this finding is that voters recognize the policy-making role of courts and are not disillusioned or alienated by it.

2. These findings about the absence of a demobilization effect in state supreme court elections comport well with recent studies using surveys to measure citizen attitudes. Gibson (2012) has shown that policy pronouncements, attack advertising, and accepting campaign contributions may have some unfavorable consequences for state court legitimacy, but these effects are eclipsed by the strongly legitimizing influence of the elections themselves. In other words, the net effects of electing judges even under some of the worst conditions are positive.

3. As Chapter 3 indicates, differences between contested nonpartisan and partisan elections with incumbents are, respectively: races with television campaigns (68.9 percent versus 41.0 percent), races with attack advertising (21.3 percent versus 15.4 percent), the proportion of attack airings sponsored by interest groups (67.9 percent versus 47.9 percent), and the proportion of issue appeals sponsored by interest groups (56.6 percent versus 29.9 percent).

References

Abramson, Paul R., John H. Aldrich, and David W. Rohde. 2012. *Change and Continuity in the 2008 and 2010 Elections*. Washington, DC: Congressional Quarterly Press.

Adamany, David, and Philip Dubois. 1976. "Electing State Judges." *Wisconsin Law Review* 3: 731–779.

American Bar Association Commission on the 21st Century Judiciary. 2003. *Justice in Jeopardy*. Chicago: American Bar Association.

American Judicature Society. *Judicial Selection in the States*. Retrieved on July 4, 2013, from www.judicialselection.us.

Ansolabehere, Stephen, and Shanto Iyengar. 1995. *Going Negative: How Political Advertisements Shrink and Polarize the Electorate*. New York: The Free Press.

Ansolabehere, Stephen, Shanto Iyengar, Adam Simon, and Nicholas Valentino. 1994. "Does Attack Advertising Demobilize the Electorate?" *American Political Science Review* 88 (December): 829–838.

Baum, Lawrence. 1987. "Explaining the Vote in Judicial Elections: The 1984 Ohio Supreme Court Elections." *Western Political Quarterly* 40 (June): 361–371.

Baum, Lawrence, and David Klein. 2007. "Voter Responses to High-Visibility Judicial Campaigns." In *Running for Judge: The Rising Political, Financial, and Legal Stakes of Judicial Elections*, Matthew J. Streb, ed. New York: New York University Press.

Bayne, William C. 2000. "Lynchard's Candidacy: Ads Putting Spice into Judicial Race: Hernando Attorney Challenging Cobb." *Commercial Appeal*, October 29, at DS1.

Bell, Bret. 2006. "Hunstein: 'Can They Buy a Judgeship?'" *Savannah Morning News*, October 23. Retrieved on July 24, 2013, from http://savannahnow.com/coastal-empire/2006-10-24/hunstein-can-they-buy-judgeship.

Benesh, Sara. 2006. "Understanding Public Confidence in American Courts." *Journal of Politics* 68 (August): 697–707.

Berry, William D., Michael B. Berkman, and Stuart Schneiderman. 2000. "Legislative Professionalism and Incumbent Reelection: The Development of Institutional Boundaries." *American Political Science Review* 94 (December): 859–874.

Bonneau, Chris W. 2004. "Patterns of Campaign Spending and Electoral Competition in State Supreme Court Elections." *Justice System Journal* 25 (1): 21–38.

———. 2005. "What Price Justice(s)? Campaign Spending in State Supreme Court Elections." *State Politics & Policy Quarterly* 5 (Summer): 107–125.

———. 2007. "Campaign Fundraising in State Supreme Court Elections." *Social Science Quarterly* 88 (March): 68–85.

Bonneau, Chris W., and Damon M. Cann. 2011. "Campaign Spending, Diminishing Marginal Returns, and Campaign Finance Restrictions in Judicial Elections." *Journal of Politics* 73 (October): 1267–1280.

Bonneau, Chris W., and Melinda Gann Hall. 2003. "Predicting Challengers in State Supreme Court Elections: Context and the Politics of Institutional Design." *Political Research Quarterly* 56 (September): 337–349.

———. 2009. *In Defense of Judicial Elections*. New York: Routledge.

Bonneau, Chris W., Melinda Gann Hall, and Matthew J. Streb. 2011. "*White* Noise: The Unrealized Effects of *Republican Party of Minnesota* v. *White* on Judicial Elections." *Justice System Journal* 32 (3): 247–268.

Bonneau, Chris W., and Heather Marie Rice. 2009. "Impartial Judges? Race, Institutional Context, and U.S. State Supreme Courts." *State Politics & Policy Quarterly* 9 (Winter): 381–403.

Bowler, Shaun, Todd Donovan, and Trudi Happ. 1992. "Ballot Propositions and Information Costs: Direct Democracy and the Fatigued Voter." *Western Political Quarterly* 45 (June): 559–568.

Brace, Paul, and Melinda Gann Hall. 1995. "Studying Courts Comparatively: The View from the American States." *Political Research Quarterly* 48 (March): 5–29.

———. 1997. "The Interplay of Preferences, Case Facts, Context, and Structure in the Politics of Judicial Choice." *Journal of Politics* 59 (November): 1206–1231.

———. 2001. "'Haves' Versus 'Have-Nots' in State Supreme Courts: Allocating Docket Space and Wins in Power Asymmetric Cases." *Law & Society Review* 35 (2): 393–417.

Brace, Paul, Melinda Gann Hall, and Laura Langer. 1999. "Judicial Choice and the Politics of Abortion: Institutions, Context, and the Autonomy of Courts." *Albany Law Review* 62 (4): 1265–1303.

Brace, Paul, Laura Langer, and Melinda Gann Hall. 2000. "Measuring the Preferences of State Supreme Court Judges." *Journal of Politics* 62 (May): 387–413.

Brandenburg, Bert, and Rachel Paine Caufield. 2009. "Ardent Advocates." *Judicature* 93 (September–October): 79–81.

Brandenburg, Bert, and Roy A. Schotland. 2008. "Justice in Peril: The Endangered Balance between Impartial Courts and Judicial Election Campaigns." *Georgetown Journal of Legal Ethics* 21 (Fall): 1229–1258.

Brennan Center for Justice. 2006. "Buying Time 2006." Retrieved on June 19, 2007, from www.brennancenter.org/analysis/buying-time-2006-1.

Brennan, William. 1966. "State Supreme Court Judges Versus United States Supreme Court Justices: A Change in Function and Perspective." *University of Florida Law Review* 29 (Fall): 225–237.

Brooks, Deborah J. 2006. "The Resilient Voter: Moving toward Closure in the Debate over Negative Campaigning and Turnout." *Journal of Politics* 68 (August): 684–696.

Brooks, Deborah, and John G. Geer. 2007. "Beyond Negativity: The Effects of Incivility on the Electorate." *American Journal of Political Science* 51 (January): 1–16.

Bullock, Charles S. III, and Richard E. Dunn. 1996. "Election Rolloff: A Test of Three Explanations." *Urban Affairs Review* 32 (September): 71–86.

Bush v. Schiavo. 2004. 885 *So.2d* 321.

Cann, Damon M., and Jeff Yates. 2008. "Homegrown Institutional Legitimacy: Assessing Citizens' Diffuse Support for State Courts." *American Politics Research* 36 (March): 297–329.

Caperton v. Massey Coal Company. 2009. 556 *U.S.* 868.

Carey, John M., Richard G. Niemi, and Lynda W. Powell. 2000. "Incumbency and the Probability of Reelection in State Legislative Elections." *Journal of Politics* 62 (August): 671–700.

Caufield, Rachel Paine. 2005. "In the Wake of *White*: How States are Responding to *Republican Party of Minnesota v. White* and How Judicial Elections are Changing." *Akron Law Review* 38 (3): 625–647.

———. 2007. "The Changing Tone of Judicial Election Campaigns as a Result of *White*." In *Running for Judge: The Rising Political, Financial, and Legal Stakes of Judicial Elections*, Matthew J. Streb, ed. New York: New York University Press.

Champagne, Anthony. 2002. "Televised Ads in Judicial Campaigns." *Indiana Law Review* 35 (3): 669–689.

Chen, Edwin. 1988. "Fund-Raising Ills: For Judges, the Stakes Are Rising." *Los Angeles Times*, March 4, Metro Desk Section, Home Edition.

Choi, Stephen J., G. Mitu Gulati, and Eric A. Posner. 2010. "'Professionals or Politicians': The Uncertain Empirical Case for an Elected Rather Than Appointed Judiciary." *Journal of Law, Economics, & Organization* 26 (August): 290–336.

Citizens United v. Federal Communications Commission. 2010. 558 *U.S.* 310.

Clinton, Joshua D., and John S. Lapinski. 2004. "'Targeted' Advertising and Voter Turnout: An Experimental Study of the 2000 Presidential Election." *Journal of Politics* 66 (February): 69–96.

Council of State Governments. 1960–2012. *Book of the States* (editions as listed). Lexington, KY: Council of State Governments.

Cover, Albert D., and David R. Mayhew. 1981. "Congressional Dynamics and the Decline of Competition in Congressional Elections." In *Congress Reconsidered*, Lawrence C. Dodd and Bruce I. Oppenheimer, eds. Washington, DC: Congressional Quarterly Press.

Dimino, Michael R. 2004. "Judicial Elections versus Merit Selection: The Futile Quest for a System of 'Merit' Selection." *Albany Law Review* 67 (3): 803–819.

———. 2005. "The Worst Way of Selecting Judges—Except All the Others That Have Been Tried." *Northern Kentucky Law Review* 32 (2): 267–304.

Driscoll, Amanda, and Michael J. Nelson. 2013. "The Political Origins of Judicial Elections: Evidence from the United States and Bolivia." *Judicature* 94 (January/February): 151–160.

Dubois, Philip L. 1980. *From Ballot to Bench: Judicial Elections and the Quest for Accountability*. Austin: University of Texas Press.

Epstein, Lee. 2013. "Electoral Benefits: The Assault on the Assaulters of Judicial Elections." *Judicature* 96 (March/April): 218–222.

Finkel, Steven E., and John Geer. 1998. "A Spot Check: Casting Doubt on the Demobilizing Effects of Attack Advertising." *American Journal of Political Science* 2 (April): 573–595.

Fitzpatrick, Brian T. 2009. "The Politics of Merit Selection." *Missouri Law Review* 74 (Summer): 675–709.

Francia, Peter L., and Paul S. Herrnson. 2004. "The Synergistic Effect of Campaign Effort and Election Reform on Voter Turnout in State Legislative Elections." *State Politics & Policy Quarterly* 4 (Spring): 74–93.

Fridkin, Kim L., and Patrick J. Kenney. 2011. "Variability in Citizens' Reactions to Different Types of Negative Campaigns." *American Journal of Political Science* 55 (April): 307–325.

Geer, John G. 2006. *In Defense of Negativity: Attack Ads in Presidential Campaigns*. Chicago: University of Chicago Press.

Gerber, Alan S., James G. Gimpel, Donald P. Green, and Daron R. Shaw. 2011. "How Large and Long-Lasting Are the Persuasive Effects of Televised Campaign Ads? Results from a Randomized Field Experiment." *American Political Science Review* 105 (February): 135–150.

Geyh, Charles Gardner. 2003. "Why Judicial Elections Stink." *Ohio State Law Journal* 64 (1): 43–79.

———. 2008. "Methods of Judicial Selection and Their Impact on Judicial Independence." *Daedalus* 137:4 (Fall): 86–102.

Gibson, James L. 2008. "Challenges to the Impartiality of State Supreme Courts: Legitimacy Theory and 'New Style' Judicial Campaigns." *American Political Science Review* 102 (February): 59–75.

———. 2009. "'New Style' Judicial Campaigns and the Legitimacy of State High Courts." *Journal of Politics* 71 (October): 1285–1304.

———. 2012. *Electing Judges: The Surprising Effects of Campaigning on Judicial Legitimacy*. Chicago: University of Chicago Press.

Gibson, James L., and Gregory A. Caldeira. 2011. "Has Legal Realism Damaged the Legitimacy of the U.S. Supreme Court?" *Law & Society Review* 45 (1): 195–219.

Gibson, James L., Jeffrey A. Gottfried, Michael X. Delli Carpini, and Kathleen Hall Jamieson. 2011. "The Effects of Judicial Campaign Activity on the Legitimacy of Courts: A Survey-Based Experiment." *Political Research Quarterly* 64 (3): 545–558.

Gill, Rebecca D. Forthcoming. "Implicit Gender Bias in Judicial Performance Evaluations." *Justice System Journal.*

Gill, Rebecca D., Sylvia R. Lazos, and Mallory M. Waters. 2011. "Are Judicial Performance Evaluations Fair to Women and Minorities? A Cautionary Tale from Clark County, Nevada." *Law & Society Review* 45 (3): 731–759.

Glick, Henry R., and Craig Emmert. 1987. "Selection Systems and Judicial Characteristics: The Recruitment of State Supreme Court Justices." *Judicature* 70 (December–January): 228–235.

Goldberg, Deborah, Craig Holman, and Samantha Sanchez. 2001. *The New Politics of Judicial Elections, 2000.* Washington, DC: Justice at Stake Campaign.

Goldberg, Deborah, Sarah Samis, Edwin Bender, and Rachel Weiss. 2005. *The New Politics of Judicial Elections, 2004.* Washington, DC: Justice at Stake Campaign.

Goldberg, Deborah, and Samantha Sanchez. 2003. *The New Politics of Judicial Elections, 2002.* Washington, DC: Justice at Stake Campaign.

Goldstein, Ken, and Paul Freedman. 2002. "Campaign Advertising and Voter Turnout: New Evidence for a Stimulation Effect." *Journal of Politics* 64 (August): 721–740.

Hajnal, Zoltan, and Jessica Trounstine. 2005. "Where Turnout Matters: The Consequences of Uneven Turnout in City Politics." *Journal of Politics* 67 (May): 515–535.

Hall, Kermit L. 1983. "The Judiciary on Trial: State Constitutional Reform and the Rise of an Elected Judiciary, 1846–1860." *The Historian* 45 (May): 337–354.

———. 1984. "Progressive Reform and the Decline of Democratic Accountability: The Popular Election of State Supreme Court Judges, 1850–1920." *American Bar Foundation Research Journal* 1984: 345–369.

———. 2005. "Judicial Independence and the Majoritarian Difficulty." In *Institutions of American Democracy: The Judicial Branch*, Kermit L. Hall and Kevin T. McGuire, eds. New York: Oxford University Press.

Hall, Melinda Gann. 1987. "Constituent Influence in State Supreme Courts: Conceptual Notes and a Case Study." *Journal of Politics* 49 (November): 1117–1124.

———. 1992. "Electoral Politics and Strategic Voting in State Supreme Courts." *Journal of Politics* 54 (May): 427–446.

———. 1995. "Justices as Representatives: Elections and Judicial Politics in the American States." *American Politics Quarterly* 23 (October): 485–503.

———. 1999. "State Judicial Politics: Rules, Structures, and the Political Game." In *American State and Local Politics*, Ronald E. Weber and Paul Brace, eds. New York: Chatham House.

———. 2001a. "State Supreme Courts in American Democracy: Probing the Myths of Judicial Reform." *American Political Science Review* 95 (June): 315–330.

———. 2001b. "Voluntary Retirements from State Supreme Courts: Assessing Democratic Pressures to Relinquish the Bench." *Journal of Politics* 63 (November): 1112–1140.

———. 2007a. "Competition as Accountability in State Supreme Court Elections." In *Running for Judge: The Rising Political, Financial, and Legal Stakes of Judicial Elections*, Matthew J. Streb, ed. New York: New York University Press.

———. 2007b. "Voting in State Supreme Court Elections: Competition and Context as Democratic Incentives." *Journal of Politics* 69 (November): 1147–1159.

———. 2011. "On the Cataclysm of Judicial Elections and Other Popular Antidemocratic Myths." In *What's Law Got to Do with It? What Judges Do, Why They Do It, and What's at Stake*, Charles Gardner Geyh, ed. Stanford, CA: Stanford University Press.

———. 2013. "State Courts: Politics and the Judicial Process." In *Politics in the American States*, Virginia Gray, Russell L. Hansen, and Thad Kousser, eds. Washington, DC: CQ Press.

———. 2014a. "Representation in State Supreme Courts: Evidence from the Terminal Term." *Political Research Quarterly* 67 (June): 335–346.

———. 2014b. "Televised Attacks and the Incumbency Advantage in State Supreme Courts." *Journal of Law, Economics, & Organization* 30 (March): 138–164.

Hall, Melinda Gann, and Chris W. Bonneau. 2006. "Does Quality Matter? Challengers in State Supreme Court Elections." *American Journal of Political Science* 50 (January): 20–33.

———. 2008. "Mobilizing Interest: The Effects of Money on Citizen Participation in State Supreme Court Elections." *American Journal of Political Science* 52 (July): 457–470.

———. 2013. "Attack Advertising, the *White* Decision, and Voter Participation in State Supreme Court Elections." *Political Research Quarterly* 66 (March): 115–126.

Hall, Melinda Gann, and Paul Brace. 1992. "Toward an Integrated Model of Judicial Voting Behavior." *American Politics Quarterly* 20 (April): 147–168.

———. 1994. "The Vicissitudes of Death by Decree: Forces Influencing Capital Punishment Decisionmaking in State Supreme Courts." *Social Science Quarterly* 75 (March): 136–151.

———. 1996. "Justices' Responses to Case Facts: An Interactive Model." *American Politics Quarterly* 24 (April): 237–261.

———. 1999. "State Supreme Courts and Their Environments: Avenues to General Theories of Judicial Choice." In *Supreme Court Decision-Making: New Institutionalist Approaches*, Cornell W. Clayton and Howard Gillman, eds. Chicago: University of Chicago Press.

Hall, William K., and Larry T. Aspin. 1987. "The Roll-Off Effect in Judicial Retention Elections." *Social Science Journal* 24 (4): 415–427.

Hanssen, F. Andrew. 2004. "Learning about Judicial Independence: Institutional Change in the State Courts." *Journal of Legal Studies* 33 (June): 431–473.

Herndon, James. 1962. "Appointments as a Means of Initial Accession to Elective State Courts of Last Resort." *North Dakota Law Review* 38 (January): 60–73.

Hill, Kim Quaile, and Jan E. Leighley. 1993. "Party Ideology, Organization, and Competitiveness as Mobilizing Forces in Gubernatorial Elections." *American Journal of Political Science* 37 (November): 1158–1178.

Hogan, Robert E. 1999. "Campaign and Contextual Influences on Voter Participation in State Legislative Elections." *American Politics Quarterly* 27 (October): 403–433.

———. 2004. "Challenger Emergence, Incumbent Success, and Electoral Accountability in State Legislative Elections." *Journal of Politics* 66 (November): 1283–1303.

Hojnacki, Marie, and Lawrence Baum. 1992. "'New Style' Judicial Campaigns and Voters: Economic Issues and Union Members in Ohio." *Western Political Quarterly* 45 (December): 921–948.

Holbrook, Thomas M., and Charles M. Tidmarch. 1991. "Sophomore Surge in State Legislative Elections, 1968–1986." *Legislative Studies Quarterly* 16 (February): 49–63.

Holbrook, Thomas M., and Emily Van Dunk. 1993. "Electoral Competition in the American States." *American Political Science Review* 87 (December): 955–962.

Hurwitz, Mark S., and Drew Noble Lanier. 2008. "Diversity in State and Federal Appellate Courts: Change and Continuity across Twenty Years." *Justice System Journal* 29 (1): 47–70.

Iyengar, Shanto. 2001/2002. "The Effects of Media-Based Campaigns on Candidate and Voter Behavior: Implications for Judicial Elections." *Indiana Law Review* 35 (3): 691–699.

Jackson, Robert A., and Thomas M. Carsey. 2007. "U.S. Senate Campaigns, Negative Advertising, and Voter Mobilization in the 1998 Midterm Election." *Electoral Studies* 26 (March): 180–195.

Jackson, Robert A., Jeffrey J. Mondak, and Robert Huckfeldt. 2009. "Examining the Possible Corrosive Impact of Negative Advertising on Citizens' Attitudes toward Politics." *Political Research Quarterly* 62 (March): 55–69.

Jackson, Robert A., and Jason C. Sides. 2006. "Revising the Influence of Campaign Tone on Turnout in Senate Elections." *Political Analysis* 14 (Spring): 206–218.

Jewell, Malcolm E. 1982. *Representation in State Legislatures.* Lexington: University Press of Kentucky.

Kahn, Kim Fridkin, and Patrick J. Kenney. 1999. "Do Negative Campaigns Mobilize or Suppress Turnout? Clarifying the Relationship between Negativity and Participation." *American Political Science Review* 93 (December): 877–890.

Kelleher, Christine A., and Jennifer Wolak. 2007. "Explaining Public Confidence in the Branches of State Government." *Political Research Quarterly* 60 (December): 707–721.

Key, V. O. Jr. 1966. *The Responsible Electorate.* Cambridge, MA: Harvard University Press.

Kim, Jae-On, John R. Petrocik, and Stephen E. Enokson. 1975. "Voter Turnout among the American States: Systemic and Individual Components." *American Political Science Review* 69 (March): 107–123.

Klein, David, and Lawrence Baum. 2001. "Ballot Information and Voting Decisions in Judicial Elections." *Political Research Quarterly* 54 (December): 709–728.

Krasno, Jonathan S., and Donald P. Green. 2008. "Do Televised Presidential Ads Increase Voter Turnout? Evidence from a Natural Experiment." *Journal of Politics* 70 (January): 245–261.

Kritzer, Herbert M. 2011. "Competitiveness in State Supreme Court Elections, 1946–2009." *Journal of Empirical Legal Studies* 8 (June): 237–259.

———. Forthcoming. *Justices on the Ballot: Continuity and Change in State Supreme Court Elections.* New York: Cambridge University Press.

Krupnikov, Yanna. 2011. "When Does Negativity Demobilize? Tracing the Conditional Effect of Negative Campaigning on Voter Turnout." *American Journal of Political Science* 55 (October): 796–812.

Langer, Laura. (2002). *Judicial Review in State Supreme Courts: A Comparative Study.* Albany: SUNY Press.

Lau, Richard R., and Gerald M. Pomper. 2001. "Negative Campaigning by U.S. Senate Candidates." *Party Politics* 7 (January): 69–87.

Lau, Richard R., Lee Sigelman, Caroline Heldman, and Paul Babbitt. 1999. "The Effects of Negative Political Advertisements: A Meta-Analytical Assessment." *American Political Science Review* 93 (December): 851–876.

Lau, Richard R., Lee Sigelman, and Ivy Brown Rovner. 2007. "The Effects of Negative Political Campaigns: A Meta-Analytic Reassessment." *Journal of Politics* 69 (November): 1176–1209.

Leighley, Jan E. 1995. "Attitudes, Opportunities, and Incentives: A Field Essay on Political Participation." *Political Research Quarterly* (March): 181–209.

Lewis-Beck, Michael S., William C. Jacoby, Helmut Norpoth, and Herbert F. Weisburg. 2008. *The American Voter Revisited.* Ann Arbor: University of Michigan Press.

Magleby, David B. 1984. *Direct Legislation: Voting on Ballot Propositions in the United States.* Baltimore: Johns Hopkins University Press.

Mayer, William G. 1996. "In Defense of Negative Campaigning." *Political Science Quarterly* 111 (Autumn): 437–455.

McCutcheon v. Federal Election Commission. 2014. 572 U.S. ___.

McKenzie, Mark Jonathan, and Michael A. Unger. 2011. "'New Style' Campaigning, Citizen Knowledge, and Sources of Legitimacy for State Courts: A Case Study in Texas." *Politics & Policy* 39 (October): 813–834.

Milton, Sande. 1983. "A Cross-Sectional Analysis of the Rolloff Vote." *Polity* 15 (Summer): 613–629.

National Center for State Courts. 2002. *Call to Action: Statement of the National Summit on Improving Judicial Selection.* Williamsburg, VA: National Center for State Courts.

National Conference of State Legislatures. 2012. "Straight-Ticket Voting." Retrieved on May 17, 2013, from www.ncsl.org/legislatures-elections/elections/straight-ticket-voting.aspx.

Nichols, Stephen M., and Gregory A. Strizek. 1995. "Electronic Voting Machines and Ballot Rolloff." *American Politics Quarterly* 23 (July): 300–318.

Niven, David. 2006. "A Field Experiment on the Effects of Negative Campaign Mail on Voter Turnout in a Municipal Election." *Political Research Quarterly* 59 (June): 203–210.

Patterson, Samuel C., and Gregory A. Caldeira. 1983. "Getting out the Vote: Participation in Gubernatorial Elections." *American Political Science Review* 77 (September): 675–689.

Patterson, Thomas E., and Robert D. McClure. 1976. *The Unseeing Eye: The Myth of Television Power in National Politics*. New York: Putnam Press.

Peters, C. Scott. 2009. "Canons of Ethics and Accountability in State Supreme Court Elections." *State Politics & Policy Quarterly* 9 (Spring): 24–55.

Poovey, Bill. 1996. "State Supreme Court Justice Likens GOP Opponent to a Skunk." Associated Press, October 9. Retrieved on July 28, 2013, from www.apnewsarchive.com/1996/State-Supreme-Court-Justice-Likens-GOP-Opponent-to-a-Skunk/id-9406514862e14f0c9fb7b7ea3fb8707d.

Pritchett, C. Herman. 1941. "Divisions of Opinion among Justices of the U.S. Supreme Court, 1939–1941." *American Political Science Review* 35 (October): 890–898.

Republican Party of Minnesota v. *White*. 2002. 536 *U.S.* 765.

Rock, Emily, and Lawrence Baum. 2010. "The Impact of High-Visibility Contests for U.S. State Court Judgeships: Partisan Voting in Nonpartisan Elections." *State Politics & Policy Quarterly* 10 (Winter): 368–396.

Rottman, David B., and Roy A. Schotland. 2001. "What Makes Judicial Elections Unique?" *Loyola of Los Angeles Law Review* 34 (June): 1369–1373.

Sample, James, Lauren Jones, and Rachel Weiss. 2007. *The New Politics of Judicial Elections, 2006*. Washington, DC: Justice at Stake Campaign.

Sample, James, Adam Skaggs, Jonathan Blitzer, and Linda Casey. 2010. *The New Politics of Judicial Elections, 2000–2009*. Washington, DC: Justice at Stake Campaign.

Savchak, Elisha Carol, and A. J. Barghothi. 2007. "The Influence of Appointment and Retention Constituencies: Testing Strategies of Judicial Decisionmaking." *State Politics & Policy Quarterly* 7 (Winter): 394–415.

Schaffner, Brian F., and Jennifer Segal Diascro. 2007. "Judicial Elections in the News." In *Running for Judge: The Rising Political, Financial, and Legal Stakes of Judicial Elections*, Matthew J. Streb, ed. New York: New York University Press.

Schaffner, Brian F., Matthew J. Streb, and Gerald Wright. 2001. "Teams without Uniforms: The Nonpartisan Ballot in State and Local Elections." *Political Research Quarterly* 54 (March): 7–30.

Schotland, Roy A. 1985. "Elective Judges' Campaign Financing: Are State Judges' Robes the Emperor's Clothes of American Democracy?" *Journal of Law and Politics* 2 (Spring): 57–167.

———. 2002. "Should Judges Be More Like Politicians?" *Court Review* 2002 (Spring): 8–11.

Schultz, David. 2006. "*Minnesota Republican Party* v. *White* and the Future of State Judicial Selection." *Albany Law Review* 69 (4): 985–1011.

See, Harold. 2007. "An Essay on Judicial Selection: A Brief History." In *Bench Press: The Collision of Courts, Politics, and the Media*, Keith J. Bybee, ed. Stanford, CA: Stanford University Press.

Siefert v. *Alexander.* 2009. *597 F. Supp.2d 860.*

Siefert v. *Alexander.* 2010. 608 *F.3d* 974 (7th Cir.).

Shugerman, Jed Handelsman. 2010. "Economic Crisis and the Rise of Judicial Elections and Judicial Review." *Harvard Law Review* 123 (March): 1063–1145.

———. 2012. *The People's Courts: Pursuing Judicial Independence in America.* Cambridge, MA: Harvard University Press.

Squire, Peverill. 2008. "Measuring the Professionalization of U.S. State Courts of Last Resort." *State Politics & Policy Quarterly* 8 (Spring): 223–238.

Squire, Peverill, and Eric R. A. N. Smith. 1988. "The Effect of Partisan Information on Voters in Nonpartisan Elections." *Journal of Politics* 50 (February): 169–179.

Streb, Matthew J., Brian Frederick, and Casey LaFrance. 2009. "Voter Rolloff in a Low Information Context: Evidence from Intermediate Appellate Courts." *American Politics Research* 37 (July): 644–669.

Tarr, G. Alan. 2006. "Creating and Debating Judicial Independence and Accountability." Paper presented at the annual meeting of the American Political Science Association, Philadelphia, PA, August 31–September 3.

———. 2007. "Politicizing the Process: The New Politics of State Judicial Selection." In *Bench Press: The Collision of Courts, Politics, and the Media*, Keith J. Bybee, ed. Stanford, CA: Stanford University Press.

———. 2009. "Do Retention Elections Work?" *Missouri Law Review* 74 (Summer): 605–633.

Tomz, Michael, Jason Wittenberg, and Gary King. 2003. "CLARIFY: Software for Interpreting and Presenting Statistical Results." Version 2.1. Cambridge, MA: Harvard University. Available at http://gking.harvard.edu/.

Tucker, Harvey J. 1986. "Contextual Models of Participation in U.S. State Legislative Elections." *Western Political Quarterly* 39 (March): 67–78.

Tucker, Harvey, and Ronald E. Weber. 1987. "State Legislative Election Outcomes: Contextual Effects and Legislative Performance Effects." *Legislative Studies Quarterly* 12 (November): 537–553.

Vanderleeuw, James M., and Richard L. Engstrom. 1987. "Race, Referendums, and Rolloff." *Journal of Politics* 49 (November): 1081–1092.

Ware, Stephen J. 2009. "The Missouri Plan in National Perspective." *Missouri Law Review* 74 (Summer): 751–775.

Wattenberg, Martin P., Ian McAllister, and Anthony Salvanto. 2000. "How Voting Is Like Taking an SAT Test: An Analysis of American Voter Rolloff." *American Politics Quarterly* 28 (April): 234–250.

West, Darrell M. 2010. *Air Wars: Television Advertising in Election Campaigns 1952–2008*. Washington, DC: CQ Press.

Wheat, Elizabeth, and Mark S. Hurwitz. 2013. "The Politics of Judicial Selection: The Case of the Michigan Supreme Court." *Judicature* 96 (January / February): 1–11.

Index

ABA. *See* American Bar Association
abortion, 39
Abramson, Paul R., 43, 46, 193n19
Adamany, David, 7
Alabama: ballot roll-off in, 139;
   campaign spending in, 44, 69–70;
   contestation rate in, 51, 52; defeat
   rate in, 51; electoral insecurity in,
   51, 52, 53; partisan judicial elections
   in, 37, 54; speech restrictions
   absent in, 171, 202n31; Supreme
   Court elections of 1994 and 1996,
   71, 189n22; televised campaign
   advertising in, 71, 91, 92, 189n22,
   191n34; term of office in, 37;
   unsafe seats in, 51; vote shares of
   challengers in, 51, 52
Alaska: Missouri Plan in, 37
Aldrich, John H., 43, 46, 193n19
Alito, Samuel, 84, 194n22
American Bar Association (ABA),
   205n10; on appointment of
   judges, 31; on attack ads, 102; on
   commission-based gubernatorial
   appointment, 185n4; Commission

on the 21st Century Judiciary, 11,
   25, 44, 80, 115, 185nn2,3; on judicial
   elections, 1–2, 3, 33, 73, 80, 99, 131,
   166, 185n4, 190n29; on Missouri
   Plan, 36–37; on voter competence,
   115
American Judicature Society, 37, 41,
   191n2, 193n15
anecdotal evidence, 7, 32, 35, 40, 180
Ansolabehere, Stephen: on attack
   ads, 4, 54, 96, 127–28, 135–36, 151,
   165, 204nn2,3, 205n10; on ballot
   roll-off, 138, 207n20; on campaign
   negativity, 6, 12, 96, 127–28, 129,
   132, 135–36, 161, 165, 168–69,
   205nn6,8; on educational value of
   TV ads, 13; on electoral outcomes
   and campaign advertising, 97; on
   partisan predispositions, 66, 176;
   on positive messages, 140; on U.S.
   Senate elections, 138; on voter
   turnout, 204nn2,3, 205nn6,10
appeals in campaign advertising. *See*
   issue appeals; traits appeals; values
   appeals

Stanford Studies in Law and Politics

Edited by Keith J. Bybee

G. Alan Tarr,
Without Fear or Favor: Judicial Independence and Judicial Accountability in the States
2012

Charles Gardner Geyh, editor,
What's Law Got to Do with It? What Judges Do, Why They Do It, and What's at Stake
2011

Keith J. Bybee, editor,
Bench Press: The Collision of Courts, Politics, and the Media
2007